The Taking of the Tongass:

Alaska's Rainforest

by

Bill Shoaf

W. R. Shof

First Edition

Running Wolf Press

Published by:
 Running Wolf Press
 Post Office Box 3011
 Sequim, WA 98382

First Printing 2000
10 9 8 7 6 5 4 3 2 1
Printed in the United States of America

Cover photos were provided by a very good friend.

Library of Congress Catalog Card No. 99-091561
ISBN 0-9676614-0-4

Additional copies of this and other Running Wolf Press books are available. For more information contact:
 runningwolf@olympus.net

CONTENTS

Dedicated to truth-tellers,
may the gods have mercy upon your soul;
to the Tongass National Forest;
and especially to my dogs/wolf.

Author's note:

This book is a work of fact. The characters, events, places, corporations, and agencies are real, based upon the author's recollections and documented evidence. Any resemblance to fictitious characters, events, corporations, or agencies is strictly coincidental and is unintentional.

Tongass National Forest

1

The Spirit of Jeremiah Johnson

(March 1998)

"Little boxes on the hillside,
Little boxes made of ticky-tacky,
Little boxes, little boxes, little boxes, All the same."
-- Malvina Reynolds

It's tricky business putting a human life into boxes. Psychotherapists charge hefty fees for compartmentalizing a client's psyche and life experiences, while undertakers are well paid for stuffing their customer's final earthly remains into a rather elaborate box.

I'm dead broke, so it's fortunate that my boxes are neither quite so Gestaltic nor permanent. My boxes are simply cardboard ... lidded ones when I can get them. Every aspect of my life is being put into a box, into one of four piles. There are the ones that are going to the dump, the ones to be sold at a garage sale, the ones making the trip Down South with me, and the ones that will be sold with my beloved fishing boat. Melancholy is unescapable as I consider whether this pathetic pile of rubble is all I can claim as a measure of my existence. It's not much. I wonder if less is more, and how society would have judged Thoreau's boxes as he packed to leave Walden Pond.

Equally depressing is the awareness this is an irrevocable step toward leaving what I had hoped would be my forever home on this remote island paradise in Southeast Alaska. I'm heading Down South, under the vague pretext of trying to recapture my soul and perhaps finding something to do with the remainder of my life.

As I sort through my belongings and pack them into boxes, I feel that I'm searching for some one specific item that was responsible for the incredible chain of events that led me into a running shootout with the federal government over the Tongass National Forest, the world's largest temperate rainforest. It seems vitally important to find whatever it was that drew me to Southeast Alaska in the first place, then shattered my dream by forcing me to leave. Maybe, by holding this thing in my hand, I'll finally be able to figure out exactly what happened up here. Through the years, I'm still clueless.

My gaze turns fondly to my old Stihl 045 chain saws. I bought one in 1976 and its mate in 1977. They ran faithfully until 1992, when they finally gave out within hours of each other, part way through a huge pile of beach logs I was cutting into firewood. Their mutual demise reminded me of an old man who simply lost the will to live after the passing of his longtime spouse. At one point in time, the United States Forest Service had promised me that I could use this matched set of saws to cut the symbolic first tree on the nation's largest timber sale, as my reward for a job well done. But that was not to be. While those saws certainly influenced some events in my life, there's no way I can hang the blame solely on them. No, they weren't responsible, they're just chain saws. They go in the garage sale pile. Maybe someone will want to tear them apart and rebuild them into a single, serviceable saw. I'd like that.

My lip involuntarily curls at the tall stacks of formidable-looking environmental impact statements on proposed National Forest System timber sales. Alongside them are equally impressive stacks of documents opposing these same sales: administrative appeals, litigation strategies, and legal briefs. I am guilty of having written some of the environmental documents, as well as some of the corresponding legal challenges. It was odd to sue my own timber sale, but things WERE odd here in Southeast Alaska. In a great whoosh, my passion ignites, but I don't know whether to weep or to punch someone. I've done my share of each. I shake my head and pile this stuff to go to the dump.

Fishing gear is everywhere. There are different sizes and shades of salmon gillnets, carefully folded into net bags, and ready to be drummed onto my boat's hydraulic reel. Miles and miles of groundline lie neatly coiled, along with thousands of circle hooks for fishing halibut. Precisely measured buoy lines for my shrimp pots are piled under the cedar tree. The rest of the paraphernalia includes mounds of multi-purpose inflatable buoys, hydraulic valves, gaffs, chains, blocks, and other what's-it items that no one but a fisherman would recognize. And my boat's in the harbor, awaiting sale, along with my associated fishing permits and licenses. It breaks my heart to let go of my dream to remain in Alaska as a fisherman, after the great fall I took as a forester. But I simply can't stay here anymore. No, my boat and fishing gear aren't responsible for the mess I'm in. Fishing didn't cause it.

Racing back and forth and leaping against the side walls of his kennel is Chacon, the timber wolf who lives with me. It's normal to refer to an animal as "my pet," but Chacon is no more mine than the ravens in the sky. We've been together since he was 4 weeks old, when he was the size of my hand. Now Chacon puts his paws on my shoulders and peers intently down at me, with blazing yellow eyes. Sometimes it seems he is using his stare to infuse me with some wondrous, vital substance, like a wolfy-version of CPR. While he is completely undomesticated, with no discernible urge to please me, we are very close. I refer to him as my "significant other," while he knows the same concept merely as "pack." He's going with me somehow, but I dread the struggle to move him from Alaska. It's all he's known and he won't leave willingly ... and a reticent 120-pound timber wolf can make the worst two-year-old child look downright complacent.

The boxes fill quickly, and I wonder if maybe I'm searching for something that simply doesn't exist. Maybe there isn't any single entity on which I can lay blame for the whole fiasco, but rather a collage of events that brewed the cosmic soup in which I landed. My left-brained, Teutonic mind doesn't let go easily of its need to establish order, and I can't resist the urge to at least figure out "why me?" I've always considered myself an average guy ... hardly the type to declare war against my government. What is there about my nature or background that caused me to go off the deep end, if that's what it was that I did. I decide to revisit in my mind the day I first decided to be a forester.

I guess it started back in Connecticut in 1975 at a drive-in movie showing "Jeremiah Johnson," starring Robert Redford. Yeah, that's a good place to start.

(June 1975)

"Jeremiah Johnson
Made his way into the mountains,
Bettin' on forgettin'
All the troubles that he knew."
-- "The Ballad of Jeremiah Johnson"

Friday nights back then would often find my wife, Diane, and me at the local drive-in. We'd load a cooler with beer and wine, throw together some snacks, and pile into our pickup truck. Riding in the back was our dog, Diablo (named after the Cisco Kid's horse), a savage, 110-pound cross between a Saint Bernard and a German shepherd. That night the three of us were going to see Robert Redford in "Jeremiah Johnson."

We lived in a tiny, rural cottage about 20 miles from Hartford, Connecticut. Diane was a kindergarten teacher, while I was reluctantly using my mathematics degree to market myself as a computer programmer with one of the local insurance behemoths. We were heavily into the "Mother Earth" lifestyle of low-impact self-reliance. We figured if we stayed the helm another 10 years, we could retire financially independent to our own farm in the Ozarks. Hell, we were banking the entirety of her teacher's salary.

But that night in 1975, we were going to see a drive-in movie about the West, mainly because someone had told us it had spectacular scenery. "Jeremiah Johnson" knocked my socks off! It was about a tenderfoot with a dream to leave civilization behind and become a mountain man.

The next day I was unusually quiet and pensive. When Diane asked what was up, I confessed that I wasn't happy working at the insurance company. She said she knew that and told me to do whatever it was that I thought I wanted. I asked her if that included being a forest ranger out West. She said yep. That's all the encouragement I needed.

I was looking very hard for something, but had no idea what it was. This was the mid-1970s, and ours was a generation intent upon exploring some of life's different pathways. And no one had ever accused me of being out of touch with my generation! I had tried the route of working in a big office building in an East Coast city, and was ready for the next course. The West was tugging hard at me. There was simply no comparison between what "Jeremiah Johnson" had shown me, and what I could see out my own back door. Diane was willing to follow me anywhere I chose to lead. Where indeed?

2

The Two Bears

(June 1975 - April 1978)

"Smokey the Bear, Smokey the Bear,
Prowling and a-growling
And a-sniffing the air.
He can smell a fire
Before it starts to flame.
That's why they call him Smokey,
And that's how he got his name"
-- ***"The Ballad of Smokey the Bear"***

The Monday after we saw "Jeremiah Johnson," Diane called my employer to tell them her husband was sick. Her husband was rarely sick and certainly wasn't this time, but instead was over at University of Connecticut trying to get into forestry college. UCONN was maybe seven miles from our cottage and was handy from that perspective. However, it was June, and the deadline for fall term pre-registration was long passed. Besides, UCONN didn't even have a forestry college. But they did have a natural resources department in their College of Agriculture. I wasn't fussy. Whatever.

I was so fixated on admission that my manner was totally ruthless. One poor admissions clerk was finally badgered into conceding the existence of an obscure category called "unclassified graduate student," where it was unnecessary to preregister. The only problem was that coursework earned while "unclassified" might not be acceptable for credit toward a graduate degree. Yeah, yeah ... shoved a check in her hands, and wham, UCONN had its newest student. Still, to have any chance whatsoever of having my coursework count toward a degree, the natural resources department had to officially accept me into their degree program. And that, despite my relentless onslaught, was simply going to take another day. Hey, no problem. That's why the gods created sick leave, especially for those with "short-timer's syndrome."

The next day I was bounced around the natural resources department until finally steered toward Dr. Henry Haalck, the only professor in his office that day. I barged in, stated my name, and thrust out my hand. And there, unpacking a box, was a huge man. Barrel-chested, 6'2", 215 pounds, he looked at me kinda funny and took my outstretched hand. Mercifully, he didn't apply much pressure, because his hands were enormous. In a loud, thickly German-accented voice, he announced that he was Henry Haalck.

Immediately the bulldozer-named-Bill was stopped dead in its tracks. Intimidation set in. This bear-like man had been focused on something else, and my intrusion was merely an inconvenient, though slightly amusing, distraction. The word "sir" started creeping into my vocabulary, as if I were a teenager caught parking with his girlfriend by a policeman. Fortunately, the bear-named-Henry was exceedingly jovial, but proved to be as clueless at university red-tape as I. This was his first day, too.

He studied my college transcript, and raised his eyebrows at the mathematics degree. He repeated the gesture when he noticed my current job was a computer programmer. He nodded gravely when told his intruder wanted to be a forest ranger out West. He laughed (I was to find he did that a lot) and said that's what he used to be, too. Henry told me to go over to the biology department and enroll in a summer course in botany or zoology or something. He admitted he had no idea what specific courses that his own natural resources department even offered, as he was so new, but that he'd agree to be my faculty advisor. He looked at a class schedule and told me the summer term started in less than two weeks, and it was going to take some smooth talking to gain enrollment at this late date. Then he laughed again. Henry became famous for that ... laughing, as he sent you after an impossible task. It was obvious even then ... it was ill-advised to disappoint this man.

Somehow I wangled my way into "Intro to Zoology," amid much eye-rolling at my unclassified graduate student status and tsk-tsking at the lateness of my enrollment. It didn't matter to me what they thought, I was in! The next day, I told my employer about my newly conceived career path and that the first day of summer school was coming up too soon to give them a full two weeks' notice. Sorry! As it turned out, zoology was rough for me. Analytical skills didn't help me memorize body parts, enzymes, or phyla. Also, five years out of school had left me a little rusty at academics. By the skin of my teeth, I was able to eke out a B-. Because of my graduate student status, anything less would have failed me.

I went to see Henry and showed him, rather humbly, my grade. He had learned the ropes a little by then, and said that he couldn't accept me directly as a graduate student, because mathematics was not considered a related field of study. He recommended my first earning a second bachelor of science degree in natural resources. That way, if something derailed me from completing the requirements for a master's degree, at least I would have something to show for my time. Henry's logic was compelling, so I signed up for the course work he wrote down.

That fall, Diane returned to teaching, I to studenting. Taking freshman courses at age 27 took some adjustment. I adjusted by going totally bonkers with the outdoors. It was impossible to fish any more than I was already doing, so I took up hunting, and became maniacal in that pursuit too. I ripped out the propane heater in our cottage, installed a wood stove, and bought a chain saw. I didn't have a clue about chain saws or hunting, but approached both at full-tilt boogie and winged it. I talked the Connecticut Department of Environmental Protection into issuing me a 25-cord firewood permit for the adjacent Nathan Hale State Forest, and started a firewood selling business.

That fall, amid the stoned-out 19-year-olds taking Wildlife 101 because they thought deer were cool, was an older guy sitting on the front two inches of his desk in the first row. Reeking of saw gas, trailing wood chips, smeared in god-knows-what's blood ... I was taking it all in. Professors were amused ... who was this guy? But at least they didn't have to wonder if they were getting their lesson across. I'd nod if I got it, frown if I didn't, and speak up if the frown didn't cause them to back up. But my loyalty lay with Henry, and we became fast friends.

Although it's hard for me to admit Henry had any flaws, he was a horrible lecturer. He'd never stick to the subject, but would digress to stories about the West when he was a ranger with the Forest Service. Other students would complain to me that Henry was a hard professor to take notes from, and I'd growl to shut up and read the text. They might be there to get an education, I wanted a job with the Forest Service. My goal was to become Smokey the Bear's right-hand man, just like Henry was.

Henry told me in private about his own Forest Service career. He hired on as an assistant district ranger, and everyone teased him because he had a master's degree. Why would anyone need an MS to work with the Forest Service? He quickly was promoted to ranger, and managed a small three-person district in Colorado, where he was an integral part of the district's outdoor workforce. He told me about being a snow ranger and skiing down potential avalanches. He regaled me with stories about three-man slash burns, when the winds suddenly picked up and threatened to blow fire all over the mountain. He laughed about watching timber cutters having to shovel eight feet of snow in the winter to get down to stump height. Yeah, me too, Henry, I wanna do that stuff.

Eventually the Forest Service asked him to move up to forest supervisor. At first he refused because he felt he wouldn't be able to continue working outside. The Forest Service assured him he could, but when the first two weeks as forest supervisor were spent in the office, he said adios. He enrolled in a doctorate program at some university in New York state and was just finishing up his dissertation when we met.

Under Henry's tutelage, I set my sights on a career as a forester with the Forest Service. Some of the other professors tried to warn me that UCONN was no longer an accredited forestry college and in fact hadn't graduated a forester in 15 years. Degrees in wildlife or fisheries biology were possible, but there simply weren't enough undergraduate forestry courses offered within the department. Henry was the only one even qualified to teach forestry, and there were NO graduate courses in forestry. They felt there was zero chance of getting the education credentials necessary to become a professional forester. Henry found a way around that ... we invented courses ... self-study, in-the-field type of courses. Basically, I became his apprentice in the woods. "Forest Mensuration" (quantitative and qualitative measurement) was taught by "cruising" trees (estimating the number of board feet) while they were still standing, then "scaling" (estimating board feet again) the corresponding logs when the trees were felled, and finally tallying the lumber when the logs were run through a saw mill. He also sent me to his alma mater, Yale University at New Haven, to check out texts on related topics from their excellent forestry library and assigned me to read them.

"Timber Harvesting" was a particularly interesting course. Henry sent me one morning (with a laugh, of course) to find the logger whose logs we had scaled and told me to simply hang around him awhile. The guy, a big redhead named Kim Sprague, was hard to track down, but eventually we hooked up on a day he was felling timber. Kim had me watch as he dumped a few trees, then handed me the saw and said to go for it. I did a credible enough job cutting the first tree, shut off the saw, and walked back toward the Kim. He simply pointed to the next tree. I dropped that one, too, and left the saw running this time. By the time the tank was empty, Kim asked me how I'd like to buy that saw and start cutting timber for him. Of course, that suited me just fine.

From then til graduation, every spare minute was spent felling timber. I bought a new Stihl 045 chain saw, and kept Kim's old saw as a backup. Working alone in isolated woodlots, I made every mistake a guy possibly could, and it's a miracle the gods spared my life. Sometimes trees would kick back after landing on the ground and thrust 5,000 pounds of angry log in my face. When I miscut a tree, it might spin 180 degrees on the stump and chase me from my chosen safety spot. Once a "widowmaker" (loose limbs hanging precariously aloft) came crashing down and shattered my hardhat. Frequently trees would land on yellow jacket nests, and the black-and-yellow demons would sting the bejeebers out of me, as I limbed the trees and bucked them into logs.

Somehow, I survived my first few jobs for Kim and then branched out onto my own. I developed a knack for talking farmers and other landowners into selling me logging rights to their woodlots. I also developed a reputation among several of the local saw-mill operators as having a good eye for timber. Consequently, there were willing buyers for all the logs I could cut.

On one woodlot I found a particularly special black cherry (_Prunus serotina_) tree and asked the owner for permission to keep the tree for myself. He listened to my plan of milling it and building a huge kitchen table on which a guy could "dump a quarter of an elk without it squatting." He called me a good worker and said he was pleased to be able to give me such a gift. I milled the logs at Kim's saw mill, and dragged the lumber all over the country before finally building what is still my kitchen table.

Falling timber so enthralled me that I momentarily considered abandoning my dream of becoming a forest ranger out West. It seemed that I could carve out a pretty good living by logging hardwoods in New England. I even thought about buying a rubber-tired skidder (tractor), and maybe even my own log truck.

One fall day in 1977, Diane's parents borrowed my pickup and left me their Mustang. I went trout fishing at a stream a few miles from our cottage, but untypically grew restless and returned home after barely having gotten my line wet. Just a few minutes after my return, my neighbor, Mary Cappiello, came pounding on my door, screamed something about her husband, Nick, and raced off. I put on my boots and followed her, finding Nick sprawled on the couch in a pool of blood. Someone shouted something about a chain saw, as I wrapped an afghan around his throat, cinched it, and sprinted over to get the Mustang.

We loaded Nick into the Mustang and roared off for the hospital. Perhaps the only thing that saved Nick's life was that he was terrified of my driving. And indeed we made the car chase in "The French Connection" look like kiddie cars ... straddled the road's center line, floored it, and laid on the horn. Once, as Nick started choking, I reached over and loosened the afghan. Blood shot out in a stream the size of my little finger and landed on the dash. We made it to the hospital, and Nick miraculously lived. As it turned out, Nick had been cutting some firewood in his yard, and the saw tip kicked back and caught his throat.

My nerves were pretty shot by the time I got back to our cottage. After a while I went out to clean up the Mustang, which looked as if someone had slaughtered a hog in it. I was emptying a bucket of gory water just as my in-laws drove up in my truck. They watched for just a second, then asked anxiously where Diane was. Because I had absolutely no use for my in-laws, I let them wonder for awhile, enjoying their discomfort, before telling them what happened.

Nick's chain-saw mishap convinced me that cutting timber was an accident waiting to happen, so I went back to my original plan and applied to the Forest Service for a temporary, seasonal job, just to get my foot in the door. Amazingly, all the federal registers for the professional forester series suddenly opened ... an event which hadn't happened in years. Because UCONN wasn't an accredited forestry college, the betting among the faculty was that I wouldn't even qualify for the forester series. In a short time, however, all three regions not only qualified me, but gave me a rating of 100. I was thrilled, and the UCONN natural resources department was quite pleased with the new feather for their own cap. Henry beamed. Now it was just a matter of waiting for job offers.

My last year at UCONN, the department hired me as a graduate teaching assistant. I taught the field portion of dendrology, which is tree and shrub identification. The southern New England forests had a lot of species diversity, and I had learned virtually every indigenous and most of the introduced species. It was so fun, taking undergraduate students through the woods and showing them what everything was commonly called, as well as its Latin name. For some of the rarer species, it was necessary for me to go alone and bring back specimens for the students. Once I almost drowned getting some black spruce from a remote swamp that was far too dangerous to be entered by a lone individual.

Henry had me help him with the field part of one of his classes, but he was there for all the outdoor sessions. Henry wasn't going to miss being in the woods, so mostly my role was to carry the gear and listen to his stories. And there was nothing wrong with that. The man was an amazing field forester, who taught me a lot every time we went in the woods together.

Eventually I completed my coursework and focused on writing my thesis and, worse, typing it. This was 1978, before word processors, so equipped with a Royal portable typewriter, I attempted to type perfect copy (erasures not permitted) with my two-finger approach. The thesis itself was abjectly unnoteworthy, but did satisfy department requirements. The day of my thesis defense, Henry had me out planting trees and waited til the last possible second to race me back to school. My hands and face were filthy, but the obligatory tie was in place. Maybe my advisors passed me just to get rid of me.

Right as planned, a job came through ... a temporary GS-3 tree planter on the Canyon District of the Clearwater National Forest in Idaho. The pay was $3.83/hour. We had our house closing one day, the thesis defense the next, and left for Idaho the day after that. Diane and I left Connecticut in our faithful Ford pickup, carrying only a few clothes, our camping gear, a chain saw, shotgun, Diablo, and a new springer spaniel pup. There was even room for us to sleep in the back of the truck. And we never, ever looked back.

3

Green Shorts

(May 1978 - February 1981)

"First to fight for right and freedom,
And to keep our honor clean,
We are proud to claim the title,
Of United States Marines."
-- "Marine Corps Anthem"

Diane and I enjoyed the long ride cross-country to Idaho, but years of logging and hauling firewood had left our faithful Ford pickup truck somewhat the worse for wear. I kept a close eye on all the critical mechanical areas, and hoped for the best. In Montana our little springer pup, Cammie, wriggled her way out the side window of the camper shell. She splatted in the highway, and in the right side mirror, I could see her crawl off the roadway. I sprinted back to her and could see she was hurting badly. I rushed her back to Diane's lap, and tearfully we fired up the Ford and streaked to the nearest town, Big Timber.

The vet at Big Timber said her left rear leg was badly shattered and she was in shock. He suggested we take her to a specialist at Missoula, so we roared westward. The vet at Missoula was expecting us when we arrived at midnight. We discussed her condition. Because Cammie was a bird dog, I insisted she be destroyed if her leg couldn't be fixed properly. Montana is hunting country, and the vet knew exactly what I meant. He let us sleep in the parking lot, and in the morning there was nothing left to do but to trust our springer pup to the vet and to continue over Lolo Pass to Idaho. There was nothing, love of a dog included, that was going to make me late for my first Forest Service job.

We got a rude awakening when we checked in at the Canyon Ranger Station in Orofino, Idaho. They assigned me to a remote backcountry work station, but because I had a wife and dog, they would not permit us to live at the station's compound, as we had planned. Furthermore, we couldn't stay at a Forest Service campground, because stays were limited to two weeks. We couldn't even make our own primitive campsite because of the same two-week rule. Where does that leave me? Up-the-creek, they said, a little too smugly for my taste.

Humph, I didn't go to grad school, sell my cottage, and drive across country to be thwarted by lack of a place to stay. After several false leads, we finally went to the timber division of Potlatch Corporation, the local timber barons. They were incredulous that the Forest Service wouldn't let their own employees stay on National Forest System lands and, after some coaxing, pointed out a nice spot to camp on Potlatch land adjacent to Soucie Creek. We thanked them and set out for our new home.

Soucie Creek was beautiful, and we made a splendid camp, which was continually improved as time passed. We bought a nice 12-foot x 10-foot wall tent and built tables and shelves for the inside. We dug a spring hole in the creek, to keep our few perishables cool. It was neat to have trout fingerlings swim around the beer stash! I built a rude woodshed and put up a couple cord of campwood. The firepit started as a simple ring of stone, and eventually grew to a seven-foot-high rock cairn.

Working on the tree-planting crew was a kick, despite the drudgery. This was May 1978 and definitely the rainy season. I'd meet my assigned crew early in the morning at the Forest Service compound, and we'd drive off in "crummies" (Chevy Suburbans) over the most god-awful, washed-out, sheer-sided roads imaginable. We'd load up our planting bags with trees, grab a "hoedag" (planting tool), and deadhead up the mountain to the planting site. My work mates said that this was the largest clearcut in the nation, and I believed them. It was huge.

Something in my gut warned me to keep a low-profile. It didn't seem wise to mention my education, as it might keep me from just being one of the gang. One day, however, I just couldn't help ask our crew foreman why we were planting western white pine (*Pinus monticola*) seedlings in the vicinity of gooseberry (*Ribes spp.*). He asked so what? I explained that there was a blister rust disease which the genus *Ribes* passed to western white pine, which ultimately killed the tree. I pointed to newly planted seedlings right next to gooseberry bushes and told him the trees were doomed. He looked at me dumbfounded.

The next day there weren't any white pine seedlings in our planting bags. The crew foreman worked next to me, and after a time asked me how I knew about blister rust. Flustered, I muttered something about graduate school, and the cat was out of the bag. My crew mates stared at me in amazement and hooted that it was pretty bizarre for someone with a master's degree in forestry to be planting trees in the rain. I was embarrassed at the attention and told them I just wanted to work.

A few night's later, my foreman showed up at our camp at Soucie Creek with a six-pack of Oly. He said he had put me in for a promotion to GS-4, but admitted it still wasn't enough. He suggested that it would be wise to keep quiet about the promotion, because some of the crew had been working at the GS-3 level for several seasons. He himself had a B.S. in forestry and had been working for seven seasons, finally achieving a GS-5.

The time at Soucie Creek passed poorly for Diane, but I was so enthralled with my new job that I simply didn't worry overmuch about her. I would get up in the pre-dawn rain every workday, and light the campfire, then head off for work. She'd be left alone for the day. Diablo was a superb guard dog, but his barking would only increase her anxiety. We had driven back to Missoula the first weekend to get Cammie, whose leg surgery came out fine, but she was left with a limp for life. And while the dogs proved some company, most days Diane didn't see another human until I slogged home at night.

One night, some of my crew mates took Diane and me to a bar in Weippe, a teeny timber town. Drinking beer, shooting pool, country-swing dancing to the jukebox ... it was great ... until I made the mistake of proudly telling one of the local loggers that I worked for the

Forest Service. Geez, my friends barely got me out of there alive! Evidently the locals took a pretty dim view of the Forest Service, and my crew mates cautioned me against ever making such a blunder again. And here I thought everyone liked Smokey Bear ...

Diane had a copy of Euell Gibbons' classic book, Stalking the Wild Asparagus, and we experimented with wild foods. The bases of emerging cattail stalks were delicious. We rolled elderberry "blows" (blossoms) in flour, fried them, and then rolled them in powdered sugar. Almost every meal included trout. We would heat water in a washtub over the firepit and take baths, but it didn't replace the desire for a hot shower. One day I decided to risk sneaking her up to the Forest Service compound for a shower, even though it was expressly forbidden to use compound facilities if you weren't living there. Unfortunately, one of my crew mates noticed me with a towel outside the women's bathhouse.

I didn't get along with this guy, and when he got in my face and threatened to turn me in, I lost my temper and decked him. He wasn't any pantywaist, so we got in a terrible brawl, which eventually got broken up with no clear victor. The guy screamed he was going to get me fired, and I believed him. So when my foreman showed up at Soucie Creek the next night, I was expecting the worst. But actually, he came to tell me that I had just been offered a full-time job as a GS5/7 professional forester on the Emmett District of the Boise Forest in southwestern Idaho. He handed me my mail, and there were job offers from the Upper Peninsula of Michigan and Colorado, too. In looking back, I think this was the most exciting moment of my whole life.

When we arrived at headquarters in Orofino to fill out the transfer papers, there was no mention of my recent brawl. After having been camped for three months, Diane and I basked in the unaccustomed luxury of sitting on a toilet seat, instead of squatting in the woods. I signed the papers for the Boise Forest, and we fairly floated downstate to my new duty station at Garden Valley, Idaho.

As we rolled down the steep, narrow Salmon River canyon through Riggins, I looked back and was horrified to see a semi trailer tailgating cars and running some off the road. I anxiously watched the rearview mirror, and soon enough the maniac was directly behind our pickup. I HATE to be tailgated, but even more so was not about to let this reckless tailgater threaten our safety. I frantically waved him back, then impetuously extended my left arm in the universal sign of brotherhood and affection. Rather than back off, the rig inched even closer, before roaring around me in a No Passing zone. As the semi pulled ahead, the driver suddenly swung the wheel and jack-knifed the trailer, blocking the entire highway. Holy schmoly!

I slammed on the not-too-good truck brakes and watched as the driver swung out of the cab and stalked back toward me, fists balled. He was huge and pissed! I was scared, but even then not wise enough to back down. So I hopped out of our Ford and walked to meet him. Diablo decided he'd come too. Just as the guy started the shouting which I knew would precede our fight, Diablo went berserk. Evidently, the truck driver had an innate fear of being disemboweled by the jaws of a large, powerful, dog with an obvious hatred of anyone who yelled at its master. The man raced back to his truck, pretty darned quickly for such a big guy, and he made it, but just barely. Needless to say, the dog ate well that night!

Garden Valley was wonderful. They had a potluck dinner for us the night of our arrival and moved us into the old ranger's house on the compound. We were utterly amazed ... in a week's time I'd gone from almost getting fired for trying to use the bathroom, to being domiciled in the ranger's house. If you were a full-time employee, I guess it was OK to have a wife and dogs.

Diane, freed from the confines of the tent, got a part-time job at the local mercantile and made friends with some of the locals. We had a huge three-bedroom house and absolutely no furniture. Our kitchen table was a Coleman cooler, and we sat on the floor. Nights would find us at 'The Joint', sipping beers and country-swing dancing.

For me, my Forest Service career began in full swing. I was assigned to the tree marking crew. There were four of us, plus two University of Idaho students who rotated between several different crews. Our boss was a journeyman GS-9 forester, named Jay Kittams, who was a Viet Nam vet, ex-smoke jumper, hard worker, excellent forester, and absolute nutcase. Marking timber entails walking through the forest and spraying paint on the trees to be cut. We'd squirt the paint through 'guns' which fit into quart cans of special tree-marking paint. Each tree to be cut would be painted at chest height on the uphill and downhill sides (so cutters could tell the tree's status no matter from what side they approached), as well as below stump height (so after the tree was felled, you could tell if the cutter was SUPPOSED to have cut it).

We covered great swatches of country, marking Ponderosa pine (*Pinus ponderosa*), Douglas-fir (*Pseudotsuga menziesii)*, grand fir (*Abes grandis*), lodgepole pine (*Pinus contorta*), subalpine fir (*Abies lasiocarpa*), and Engelmann spruce *(Picea engelmannii)*. Ponderosa, or 'P-pine', was our money tree, and we marked it pretty hard. Our objective was to lay out timber for sale, but also to make sure the remaining stand was viable. This wasn't clear-cutting, but rather selective logging. So we looked at the trees being selected for cutting, as well as the ones being allowed to grow. We covered a lot of ground that summer and marked a lot of timber.

On one particular sale designed to be helicopter logged, we were looking for a helispot (a place for the small, shuttle helicopter to touch down). Jay picked out a spot and proceeded to mark all the trees for the clearing. One of these was a huge, exceedingly rare whitebark pine (*Pinus albicaulis*), that was probably 600 years old. Just as Jay started to paint the whitebark, I asked him to reconsider. He asked why, and I said it was just to save that tree because it was so special. He marked it anyway. That weekend I took my own pickup back to the sale and hiked into the proposed helispot. With black paint, I "unmarked" all the trees in Jay's helispot, then located and marked an equally good spot that protected the 600-year-old whitebark pine. On Monday I told Jay what I'd done, but he just shook his head and shrugged. Though he never mentioned it again, I think he was pleased that I cared so much.

One day Jay said the ranger wanted to see me personally at the main ranger station in Emmett. I was afraid it had something to do with my fist fight with the guy outside the shower room up north. The next morning I showed up in Emmett, clean shirt, fresh mink oil on my boots ... the whole nine yards. My desire to please this man was so great that, while I didn't salute, I probably stood at full Marine attention. The ranger, Dick Estes, looked at me sternly and told me he had some things for me to do. Yes, sir! First, the ranger handed me a calendar, which had two-inch boxes for each day, and told me to faithfully keep a daily diary of all my work activities. Next, he ordered me to go to Boise and buy myself a pair of White boots (absolute top-of-the-line leather field boots) and, while I was at it, buy a red-and-black wool Filson cruiser jacket. Yes sir! I almost bolted out of the door in my hurry to get to Boise.

Dick called me back. Whatever test he had set up for me, I'd just passed it, so he invited me to sit down. We talked about hunting, fishing, and forestry for about an hour. Spittin' and whittlin', tail waggin' ... whatever you want to call it. Then he told me the real reason he had called me in, which was that he wanted me to start administering timber sales on the Emmett side of the district. He also wanted Diane and me to move down to Emmett and buy a house. I gulped and told him how much Diane and I loved Garden Valley, but that we'd do whatever the Forest Service wanted us to do. It was definitely the right thing to say, because Ranger Estes was firmly in my corner after that first meeting.

Diane and I went to Boise that day, and bought the boots and jacket. Later we started looking for a house. Emmett was a lot bigger than Garden Valley (4,000 vs. 150), and much hotter and drier. It was too low in elevation for timber, so the landscape was a pale, washed-out panorama of cheat grass and sagebrush. A nice plus though was the bountiful agriculture ... corn, alfalfa, sugar beets, wheat, orchards, dairy farms, and so on. We were to end up with a wonderful farm-house, way outside of town.

The next day, my new supervisor, Bill Terrill, told me there was some logging going on up at Sage Hen, and that I should get a rig and go check it out. He gave me a thick folder that had something to do with the history of the sale, then, without another word, he was gone. I didn't know the first thing about that country and had no idea where Sage Hen was. I hunted up maps, borrowed a Forest Service green rig, and took off for Sage Hen, wherever it was. It was a total fiasco. I had absolutely no idea where I was going on the spaghetti-like network of forest logging roads, most of which weren't signed. I drove around for hours. It seemed like I was getting close, but every time something started to match up with the map, I'd see the timber had already been cut.

Finally, I heard some saws running, drove toward them, and parked the green rig. I caught the timber cutter's eye, and approached when he acknowledged that he had seen me. He shut off his saw and leaned on it. We greeted each other, then I asked him if he could show me on my map just where the heck we were. He looked at me kinda dumbfounded, this tough, Idaho cowboy/logger, then narrowed his eyes and drawled, "You mean you don't even know WHERE you are?" The last thing a guy ever wants to do in the woods is admit to someone else that he's lost. The very LAST thing! But my boss had told me to go to Sage Hen, so I asked this logger if he knew where it was. He was still into the tough guy bit and asked why I was looking for Sage Hen. I returned his gaze and told him I was the new timber sale administrator. We looked at each other for awhile, and then he sadly shook his head. Clearly he didn't think much of me, but realized I had the authority to make his job tough. And that was my introduction to Idaho loggers.

Gradually I learned the ropes. The nearest point of the district boundary was a solid hour's drive from the ranger station in Emmett, and to reach any of the timber sales, was an additional 45 minutes to an hour. I started driving at least one way on my own time. I left in the morning before anyone else arrived at the ranger station, and returned at night after everyone had gone home. I became a phantom to the Forest Service, but not to the loggers.

I learned that most of my predecessors had been married to their pickups and their coffee thermoses. This meant that they seldom got out of their green rigs and into the logging units. Not me. I had to constantly remind myself that it was not my responsibility to do the logging or the cleanup work myself. This was difficult, as I was un-used to watching someone else work. In my youth, I once had a summer job with the Pennsylvania Highway Department. One day my boss had told me to go over and watch this old guy do some digging. After a few minutes of watching the poor, old guy sweat, I grabbed a shovel and started digging too. My boss came over, grabbed the shovel, and yelled that he had told me to WATCH, not dig. I quit at the end of the day.

But as time passed and I grew to understand my job as timber sale administrator, I found plenty to keep myself busy. I walked all the units prior to the loggers starting ... made sure the boundaries were clearly marked, marked some additional trees to be cut, or, if the original marking had been too heavy, nullified some of the marked trees with black paint. I then walked the unit with the "bullbuck" (boss) and we discussed how the unit should be logged. We pre-flagged skid trails (paths for the tractors to drag the logs out of the woods) and log landing (storage areas) locations. I followed the timber cutters' progress ... made sure they weren't cutting extra trees, that their stumps were low enough, and that they were directionally felling the trees so as not to damage the residual stand. I flagged locations for water bars to keep rain gullies from forming, as well as other erosion-control structures. I made sure logging debris was pulled clear of creeks. And so on.

At first, this extra attention didn't sit well with the loggers. They were used to operating on their own, with little direct oversight. Now they had to deal with someone who walked everywhere, looked at everything, and wanted everything right. There were a few blowouts, but when I didn't back down, there emerged a grudging respect. As time went by, the loggers and I started to work out a mutually beneficial system. I listened to their ideas and was willing to mark a few extra trees or to let them skid logs a different way, e.g., tree-length instead of being bucked into logs, if they could convince me it did not compromise the residual resources. Gradually, they conceded I made their job easier in some respects, but was much harder on screw-ups. When they did good work, I wrote it up for their bosses. They liked that and worked extra hard to get the smiley-faced reports.

The American logger is one of the most fiercely independent and resourceful breeds of men throughout history. They are a hard-working lot who have to deal with danger, the forces of nature, and constant breakdown of cobbled-together equipment. Many are over-capitalized, few are rich. They have a tendency to live in small towns throughout the West and drive Ford pickups with a tool box and two 55-gallon oil drums in the back. Their front yards are a tangle of junked logging equipment.

Often logging has been the traditional family trade, spanning several generations, and the right to carry on their vocation is almost as fiercely defended as their right to carry a .30-.30 Winchester in their window gun rack. In their eyes blazes a pride at their accomplishments, yet at the same time, an incredulity that mere men are able to conqueror such enormous trees. There is immediate gratification at day's end to gaze back at progress so starkly apparent, and a groan with the realization the labor must be repeated the next morning. It's a good life.

Most of the local loggers subcontracted work as "gyppos" for the actual timber purchasers, which on the Emmett District meant Boise Cascade Corporation. The BCC purchaser representative I dealt with was an older fellow named Bob Shimp. One day Bob and I got in an argument over some work I was demanding the loggers do. He finally protested that the work wasn't required in the timber sale contract. I blew up and asked him what this contract was ... I'd heard mention of it, but had never seen one. That night my supervisor called me at home and ordered me to stay in the office the next day. I figured Bob Shimp had given him a call.

The next day my boss admitted that he'd "neglected my training" and gave me a crash course in timber sale administration. He explained there was a legally binding contract governing the sale of National Forest System timber, and I'd better follow it. I told my boss that I'd had no idea there was any formal contract, and was just trying to make things look good. He stared at me and shook his head, unable to believe that his new sale administrator had spent the whole season in the woods without knowing a timber sale contract even existed, much less what it said.

One logging experience on the Boise bothers me to this day. On one of my sales, there was some timber marked in an isolated stretch of canyon along Joe's Creek, and logging it would necessitate skidding logs directly over the creek. I wasn't sure how to proceed and tried to get a more experienced forester to come out to give me some advice. No one was able to shake loose, so I analyzed the options. I could cite irreparable resource damage to the stream and delete the included timber from the sale, or I could just go for it with caution. I decided on the latter course. I had the loggers build a log culvert (Boise Cascade wouldn't spring for a metal one), to try to mitigate the effects of sediment introduction.

Just downstream from the logging "show" (site), there was a pool in Joe's Creek, with trout in it. One day, on my way home, I stopped at the pool and found it muddy. Even after the stream cleared, I never saw the trout again. I had screwed up, but learned from the experience. Sometimes it's better not to make a mess in the first place, than it is to try to clean it up later on.

That winter, just before snow shut down logging operations for the year, I was inspecting a timber sale and the bullbuck told me one of the cutters had just gotten a new Stihl 056. I asked where the guy was cutting and hiked off in that direction. After I caught the cutter's eye, I approached and told him he was shut down. He immediately started sputtering that I had no right to do that, but I told him again he was shut down. Then I added that the reason was because I wanted to try out his new saw. Well, that was different. He watched me dump a few trees, and beamed as I pronounced the new saw a honey. It was incidents like this that cemented my relationship with the loggers.

When winter finally shut down logging, a wonderful veteran forest technician, Dave DeMasters, and I talked Ranger Estes into renting snow machines for us so we could mark next season's planting and thinning units. We reasoned that it would keep us busy, and it would be easier to walk around on eight feet of snow above the brush than to wade through the brush in the spring. This kicked off some of the best times I ever had with the Forest Service.

There was never a better field partner than Dave DeMasters. He was the proverbial Idaho cowboy, lived in the area all his life, had a ranch, and was a dead ringer for Sam Elliot. We got an awful lot of work done, but we played hard too. The bosses loved to see us work together because we were really productive, but also because it was safer to send two guys out, rather than a guy by himself. Especially where we went and what we did!

We'd tow the snow machine trailers until we'd hit the end of the snow plow's path, then we'd snow machine until we hit steep country, then we'd strap on snowshoes and head out. Because I'd never run a snow machine, Dave drawled this cryptic advice, "This here is the gas. Crack it wide open. This here is the brake. Don't ever touch it. Follow me." And he was gone.

After particularly big snowfalls, our boss would send us out to shovel the snow off the roofs of the remote guard stations. The first time we got this assignment, I wondered why Dave was in such high spirits. It sounded like a lot of back-breaking work to me. He looked amused while I got out the shovels, then as I looked for a ladder, he told me not to bother, cause I'd only mess up the snow. He said we weren't going to shovel the roof, we were going to cut it off. Huh?

Dave tossed a wire over the roof, and we each grabbed an end.

We started at one end of the roof, and sawed the wire down through the snow to the roofing itself, then worked the wire along the roof toward the other end. We had to stop and go around the chimney, and a few other obstructions, but sawed through to the other side in maybe 15 minutes. Dave hit a beam with an axe, and a big chunk of snow fell off. Once it started, the other pieces came down quickly, and within minutes the roof was clear. This meant we had the rest of the day free for ... uh, reconnaissance on the snow machines.

That winter, lunch time would usually find us on snowshoes in eight feet of snow on some mountainside. We'd look for a pitch snag and torch it off for a "lunch fire." The first couple of lunch fires scared the bejeebers out of me, because we'd have flames 70 feet in the air. This didn't seem like the kinda thing Smokey would approve. But Dave finally convinced me that the fire couldn't possibly go anywhere, and I guess he was right, because none ever did any damage. But they would burn for several days and would allow us to gauge our progress for the week by observing the smoke of the previous days' lunch fires.

Finally Dave told me that he had always wanted to camp out at a guard station in the winter, and no one would ever go with him. OK, Dave, let's do it. Our bosses would agree to anything to get us out of the office, because we were too rambunctious for the pace of office life in the winter. So off we went. There were some springtime planting units which were going to be contracted, and needed to be surveyed. That was our official assignment, but we brought along the 90-proof snow snake medicine just in case there was any free time in the evenings for a poker game.

Rather than pay us per diem, the Forest Service elected to provide our meals from the district cache of freeze-dried food. Some of this stuff was REALLY old, but, hey, that stuff never goes bad, eh?

Our plan was to stay out two nights. The weather was going to be great, clear and bitter cold, with night-time lows to minus 30. Oh boy. The first night, a log with a big pitch knot jammed in the cabin's wood stove, and the fire went out. I awoke, with Dave cursing the log and trying to restart the fire. I was sure we were both going to freeze to death, but somehow Dave got the fire going again and managed to thaw the cabin.

We set out the next morning on snow machines, and of course

didn't bring any water, because it would just freeze. Instead, we ate snow. Lotsa snow. At lunch, I used my backpacking stove to melt snow for some ancient, freeze-dried goop. Within minutes of eating it, we both had wicked stomach cramps and diarrhea. We were both EMTs, and recognized the other's white-spotted cheeks, severe dehydration, and rapid onset of hypothermia. At 20 below, on a ridge in Idaho, five miles from the nearest road, 30 miles from the nearest person, this is serious stuff. We snowshoed back to the snow machines and rode down to the cabin. We built a raging fire in the wood stove, and were even well enough by evening to try some of the snow snake medicine. Yeah, working with Dave was a kick!

The next field season was a year of tight budgets, but this time with a twist. Rather than clamp down on expenditures or workforce size, vehicle mileage was going to be the restricted item. This meant we could spend all the money we wanted, but couldn't drive out to the field to do our job. At least not very often. The districts, forests, and regions with the biggest timber outputs were allocated the most miles. Although Emmett had a big timber cut relative to the rest of Region IV, the fact remained that Region IV simply didn't pump out enough timber to get allocated many miles.

We devised some interesting ways to get the job done. First we bought Honda 110 cc motorbikes, and loaded them into the back of our pickups. According to regulations, we couldn't unload them until we got to the forest boundary, but nonetheless it saved a little bit. After a few close calls driving around blind curves against log truck traffic ... geez, I almost ended up as a hood ornament on a Peterbilt ... I looked for something else. I started bumming rides up to the sales with loggers, but my boss found out about it and told me to stop. Next I simply started driving my own rig. My boss said I couldn't do that either. I told him I needed to inspect my sales and would go on annual leave if I had to. He gave up and told me to get up to my sale ... just don't get caught and don't get him in trouble.

On my way out, I heard him laugh and mumble something about green shorts. I asked him what he meant. He told me that Forest Service uniforms and rigs are green, and that extremely loyal employees are said to wear green shorts. I took it as the supreme compliment and thanked him.

Just as the fiscal year was ending, in late September, I got a call from my boss one night. He said that he had forgotten about a salvage sale target, and if we didn't meet the target, we had to give the budget money back. As he'd already spent the money to buy those damned Honda 110 cc trail bikes, he wanted us all to gang up on getting the sales laid out in the morning. In a couple days, we had them laid out, marked, and sale packages sent into the forest supervisor's office in Boise. Whew, made it.

A month or so later, I found myself administering the logging of one of these small, hurriedly thrown-together sales. The first day on the sale, I noticed a survey marker, and flagged the area and made sure the bullbuck knew to avoid any disturbance in the immediate area around it. The next night Ranger Estes called me at home. Evidently, that survey marker indicated the National Forest boundary, and the sale illegally intruded onto land owned by Sumner Holbrook. Moreover, eight trees of Sumner's had been cut and removed.

It got worse. I had heard of Sumner Holbrook and knew he owned a big ranch below the National Forest System boundary at Whitlock Gulch. I had even heard of the old Holbrook burn, but didn't know its history. The ranger filled me in. Maybe 30 years ago, Holbrook had been burning some slash on his land, and it had gotten away from him and had burned up into National Forest land. The government had made him pay for the fire suppression cost, as well as the fire-damaged timber. Sumner was not a happy camper, and now 30 years later he wanted his revenge. The ranger told me to do whatever this guy wanted and use whatever charm I had to keep it strictly between Sumner and myself. Oh yeah, and if Holbrook sued the Forest Service, to expect to be shouldered with the entirety of the blame and to have at least a letter of reprimand placed in my file.

I met Sumner Holbrook the next day. Was he ever mad! And smug. And right. I understood where he was coming from, told him he was right, that I was the guilty party, and that I was there to make things straight. Sumner proceeded to berate me, the Forest Service, and the entirety of the United States government. I listened. Finally, he got frustrated with yelling at a guy in tin pants, corked boots, and a flannel shirt. He wanted the president, or at least the chief of the Forest Service. I repeated that I was the guy responsible, and that if I couldn't resolve it, that it might cost me my job. Sumner might have been a lot of things, but he wasn't the kinda guy that wanted to see some small fish lose his job.

So instead, we inspected his damaged land and agreed what had to happen to make amends. We measured the stumps of his missing trees, and found correspondingly sized trees that were still standing. I cruised those trees and showed him the volume. I told him the Forest Service would pay him double the price we had received for the timber on the little salvage sale adjacent to his land. He agreed. He wanted some seedlings planted, and some grass seed where the tractor had run. I personally did the work, and Sumner shook hands with me at the end. He told me I had kept my word and had kept the Forest Service from getting in deep, dark trouble. He said the only reason he didn't pursue it any further was because he didn't want to see an honest man get hurt over something that had happened 30 years before his time. I thanked him and said that I loved the Forest Service and was glad to be able to keep my job. I'm not sure if I ever got a letter of reprimand or not.

Back in the Emmett Valley, Diane and I had the lifestyle we had long envisioned. The farmhouse we bought had a couple acres with it, and we had enormous, productive gardens. We raised laying hens, meat roosters, hogs, and bummer lambs. There were tons of pheasant in the valley and even more chukar and Hungarian partridges in the steep breaks surrounding the valley. My springer spaniel, Cammie, and I pursued them relentlessly. I shot huge bull elk in each of my first two hunting seasons. Life was good.

Diane began to obsess about raising a family. She was infertile, and in fact had been extensively tested at Yale School of Medicine before we left Connecticut. We even tried artificial insemination, using my sperm. I used to joke that I had given so many sperm samples, that I'd get sexually aroused whenever I saw a glass jar. Nothing seemed to work, which was fine with me, because I didn't want kids. However, at age 33, time was running out on her maternal clock. I had everything I wanted, and in a rare moment of empathy, I decided to give her what she wanted, too. We discussed adoption and quickly set up an interview with the state adoption agency.

We went to see a state of Idaho social worker on a Monday in the late summer of 1979. The case worker told us it would take several years to get an infant, and she'd keep us posted. On the way out, the social worker casually asked, "Oh by the way, would you consider multiple siblings?" I looked at Diane, and said, "Why sure. Heck, we probably want more than one, anyway." Little did I know ...

That Friday when I got home, Diane met me at the door with an ice-cold Oly. She led me over to my dad's old, red recliner and helped me off with my boots. I wasn't sure what this was all about, but was willing to soak up all I could get. Finally she said the state social worker had called and had three kids for us ... a boy aged seven, and girls aged two and one. I almost choked on my beer. Evidently, the usual several years had been shortened to four days.

When we met with the case worker, we were told the children were orphans and were currently in foster care. We were cautioned there might be some slight emotional disturbance. A visitation was set up at the foster home, quickly followed by an afternoon visit at our farmhouse, then an entire weekend.

Over the next few weeks, we received a little more insight into the kids' problems. However, it wasn't until the court date was established for the final adoption that the state finally leveled with us. The father was paranoid/schizophrenic and unable to work. He warned people that he was getting worse. Finally, one night he killed the mother in front of the kids, dismembered her, and wrote on the walls in blood. He forced the children to sleep on the bed with the body. The boy made it to school the next morning, but was covered with blood. This tipped off investigators, who found the carnage, hauled the old man off, and placed the kids in a foster home. The father immediately hung himself in prison.

We were flabbergasted, but with the final adoption date set, we felt we had no choice but to continue. Within two months of our initial interview, Diane and I were the clueless parents of three children. Within a month Diane got pregnant. Time passed and Diane got as big as a house. In November 1980, she delivered a son whom we named Jeremiah, after you-know-whom.

Around that time, I was scheduled to take a zone entomologist (insect specialist) with me to look at some bark beetle infestations. We had a bad day. First, we got stuck in some deep mud. In trying to unstick the rig, we ran out of gas ... I had forgotten to fill the spare tank. Then in trying to radio for help, the battery went dead. Oh boy, was the entomologist impressed.

Because I always worked late and never let anyone know where I was going, Diane had instructions to call my partner Dave if I weren't home by 7:00 PM. So I knew help would eventually come. We walked out to a huge slash pile, maybe 100 foot x 30 foot x 8 foot, that was bulldozed into a clearing on a barren, scab hillside. When night approached, I intended to torch it off and let my rescuers know where I was. The entomologist was horrified, because he thought I was going to burn down the entire Boise National Forest.

Dark came, and I torched the slash pile. Delighted, I had flames shooting 60 feet into the air. The entomologist was panicked, and tried to put it out before he realized this fire was way too big to be extinguished. He must have thought he was in the company of a madman. My buddy Dave came out looking for me, spotted the blaze from about 15 miles away and said, "There's Bill." When Dave got up there, I felt pretty bad, because I knew I'd screwed up big time. Nobody said anything; I was being cut a lot of slack because of the kids.

We had some personal sadness. Henry Haalck developed cancer and went quickly, at age 47. I was dumbfounded. Our beloved Diablo died unexpectedly at age five, right in the prime of his life. This was probably the worst thing that happened to me in my entire life, as I loved that savage beast. I wept for weeks. We immediately got a new puppy, a Newfoundland x Rhodesian ridgeback, which I named "Max."

The state of Idaho contacted us and told us that the children's grandparents on the father's side were looking for the kids. We asked if this was a problem and were told YES! Evidently the paranoid tendencies were congenital, and these were fairly desperate people. Never one to back down from a fight and armed to the teeth, I said I'd protect my home. They suggested I leave town.

The Forest Service has a rich tradition of taking care of their own. I had expressed an interest in going out to the coast of Oregon and working in the big Douglas-fir. When I mentioned to Ranger Estes what the social worker had cautioned, a presale forester job opened up on the Siuslaw National Forest in central coastal Oregon, and I was quickly selected.

We left town so fast, I barely had time to say goodbye. In 1978, when Diane and I had moved to Idaho in our pickup truck, we had enough room to sleep in the back. Now, in 1981, we had four kids, the biggest truck U-Haul rented, and a jam-packed trailer hooked on behind that. At the end, my Yamaha dirt bike wouldn't fit in. Dave, who was helping, said not to worry, he'd buy it. And that was that; we were Oregon bound. And we never, ever looked back.

4

Timber Beasts

(February 1981 - March 1985)

"I was born one morning when the sun didn't shine.
I picked up my shovel, and I walked to the mine.
I loaded 16 tons of number one coal,
And the straw-boss said, 'Well, bless my soul'."
-- Merle Travis, "16 Tons"

My new duty station was on the Mapleton District of the Siuslaw National Forest. Mapleton, Oregon was a tiny timber town, about 14 miles inland from the coast. The road to the coast followed the Siuslaw River valley, which snaked its way to Florence, where it emptied into the Pacific Ocean.

This was the land of Ken Kesey's Sometimes A Great Notion. It was rumored that the house that inspired Kesey was the barely erect hulk on the far side of the river, slightly upstream of where the North Fork entered. Years ago, my former supervisor at the insurance company had given me a copy of Sometimes a Great Notion as a farewell gift, and our moving here seemed another of life's circles.

My previous district over in Emmett, Idaho, had been a sleepy little place that struggled to cut 30 million board feet annually. Because it was not a big timber producer, and because much of the timber was fairly low grade, the Emmett District didn't have a big budget. By contrast, the Mapleton District on the Siuslaw National Forest was a virtual timber factory ... pumping out 90-110 million board feet annually. And we're talking about prime Douglas-fir, worth a ton of money. Make that two tons.

A "board foot" is an arbitrary measurement equivalent to the amount of wood in a 1-inch x 12-inch board that is one foot long, a 1-inch x 6-inch board two feet long, or 1-inch x 4-inch board three feet long. And so on. Because that's a fairly small amount of wood, and because foresters deal with large amounts of wood, the terms 'mbf' (thousand board feet) and 'mmbf' (million board feet) are frequently used. And 'mmmbf' (billion board feet) for when we're feeling really frisky. To help conceptualize, a log truck carries about 5 mbf, while the average stick frame house uses about 10 mbf.

At Mapleton, my job was to "layout" (mark the boundaries on the ground) and "cruise" (estimate the timber volume and value) timber sales. For this part of the operation, I had five tough, veteran forest technicians (non-professionals). The other half of my responsibility was to appraise the timber, i.e., work up a detailed estimate of the logging, road construction, manufacturing, and other costs ... and to subtract those costs from the value of the timber. This difference was referred to as "stumpage," the net worth of the trees. Then we prepared the timber sale contract (by now I knew what this was), and two forest technicians were assigned to the appraisal end of the operation.

There wasn't a lot of messing around at Mapleton, because so much money was involved. This was Douglas-fir country, and Mapleton grew some of the most gorgeous Douglas-fir on the planet. The wood was highly prized for construction, and the trees were enormous. Douglas-fir, or Doug-fir, is hyphenated, because it is not a true fir. It's in the genus *Pseudotsuga,* which means "false hemlock". Coastal Doug-fir requires wet conditions, long growing seasons, and rich soil. There was also a little bit of western hemlock (*Tsuga heterophylla*) and western redcedar (*Thuja plicata*) around, but no one really cared. Like I said, this was Doug-fir country.

Overall, the ranger station was a madhouse. It worked like this. Timber sale planners did the advance field reconnaissance for determining which areas were going to be logged next. Then the planners wrote environmental assessments, which were lengthy documents which stated that there were no negative environmental effects from logging, and that everyone was going to make a whole bunch of money. Then the engineers surveyed the road locations. Next my presale crew laid out the cutting unit boundaries on the ground, making corrections as needed, to facilitate the logging of the timber and subsequent burning of the logging "slash" (debris). Immediately after layout, my crew cruised the units, i.e., determined a statistically credible estimate of the volume and grade of the included timber. After all field work was completed, my appraisal shop valued the timber and prepared the logging contract. When the timber was auctioned off to the highest bidder, the timber sale administrators oversaw the logging (what I used to do in Emmett). When the logging was complete, fire control burned the bejeebers out of the unit, getting rid of all slash. Then finally, silviculture replanted the freshly burned unit back to Douglas-fir and monitored the new seedlings' growth and survival, so that the cycle could be repeated.

If this suggested an assembly line, then I am getting my point across. When a department finished doing its thing for a given timber sale, the next timber sale should be in front of them on the conveyor belt. God help anyone who gummed up the works, as a lot was at stake. While many Forest Service regions actually lost money on their timber sale programs, at Mapleton, we were rolling in it. When I arrived in 1981, stumpage values were approximately $500/mbf, which made each log truck load worth about $2,500, and each individual tree worth $700.

Running the district was a tough, bull-headed, cranky ranger named Mick Kessel, who dressed like a rhinestone cowboy. Mick called me into his office upon my arrival and told me that there had been some previous problems with my crew's cruising, and that he expected me to get on top of it. No problem, Mick. He growled that there better not be, and told me to get out.

My presale crew exchanged a lot of knowing looks the first day I went out in the field with them. Their previous two bosses had gone out in the field maybe two days a year. I could see why. This was a rainforest, averaging 90-100 inches of rainfall. The landscape was someone's idea of a cruel joke, with a typical slope gradient in excess of 70 percent. But the worst problem was the brush, which was unimaginably dense. For the most part, it was impossible to stand upright. Locomotion was by crawling or sliding on your belly. Salal, rhododendron, evergreen huckleberry, salmonberry, devil's club, vine maple ... sometimes I think the brush layer was more impressive than the massive trees.

The brush also made vision impossible. Sometimes you could be 20 feet from a 175-foot-tall Douglas-fir and not even know it was there. I had no idea where I was. None. My crew was used to these conditions and were "skookum" (adept) at navigating and knowing exactly where they were. They were smugly amused at my futile efforts, but they knew I wouldn't be out there long. They felt this was a good-natured token effort on my part and expected me to spend my days in the comfort of the office. Wrong!

I told them I didn't hire on to work in the office. I started an immediate running program to build my legs, wind, and stamina. And I returned to the field time and time again. Within three weeks, I had a mutiny on my hands, as my crew was convinced I was out there for the express purpose of spying on them and trying to get them in trouble for mis-cruising some timber awhile back. I let them have their say, then I had mine. I told them that we were in this together, sink or swim, and that right now they knew how to do something that I didn't. Furthermore, their job was to get me up to speed ASAP!

Lord, we had some blowouts in the woods. Just as beer sometimes encourages guys to get a little feisty, or maybe say or do something they wouldn't repeat at church, the woods gave my crew the courage to say stuff to me that they might not repeat in the office. Plus it was annoying to be soaking wet, having to wade and crawl through brush, pulling yourself up steep slopes, and, of course, falling. Especially falling. Nothing is funnier than watching someone else fall, and nothing is more maddening than falling yourself and getting laughed at. But we'd leave these battles in the woods (usually), and generally end up sharing or trading parts of our lunch at the end of the day. Because it was no fun to sit in the cold, wet rain and eat a lunch which had likely been crushed and soaked, the crew liked to eat half their lunch before starting to work and half when we got back to the rig at the end of the day.

Over the years, I made sure I went out on the wettest days, into the steepest, brushiest units, and always deferred judgment on certain things to the two senior crewmen. Gradually, I became as competent as they were. There was some healthy competition, as we pushed ourselves and each other to do more, faster, and better. If anyone dumped on my presale crew, I was all over them. The guys had never had that type of support before and ate it up.

As mentioned, the two basic functions of my presale crew were to lay out cutting units, then cruise the trees for volume and grade. The accepted means of logging the steep coastal Oregon hillsides was to construct a ridge-top road system. This meant that the roads were built at the top of the cutting units, so that the logs could be yarded or pulled uphill with a minimum of entanglement and soil disturbance. Commonly 110-foot steel towers were anchored to the earth, usually via tree stumps, and strung with cables driven by powerful diesel engines. The cables were rigged from the diesel-driven winches through the top of the towers, and then down to the bottom of the cutting unit, where the skyline cable was once again anchored to the earth. There were many variations to this theme, but this was the general configuration.

A radio-controlled carriage rode atop the skyline cable, which was suspended in the air. The carriage was pulled out into the cutting unit by the haulback cable, and could be stopped when directly over logs. There was a motor in the carriage which could be activated to spool out a steel line to workmen on the ground (choker-setters), who attached the line to logs. The motor was re-activated, and the logs were winched up to the carriage, which was then pulled back to the tower via the mainline cable. The logs were massive and the corresponding tensions and forces acting on the cables were mind-boggling. This was a slick system when it was engineered and utilized properly. It provided high daily log production, as well as minimized ground disturbance. The weakness of the system was that it was largely suitable only for clearcutting.

My crew's role in laying out the cutting unit was to ensure that all the timber could be yarded to the landing locations. Because all the yarding corridors were basically straight-line shots, we laid out the unit so that there were no dog-legs or topographical obstructions that would get in the way. We also made sure that streams had adequate protection. In a nutshell, we were the trouble-shooters.

Our other function was to get an accurate estimate of the amount of timber within each cutting unit. This was essential to determine a value for the timber, as well as to provide rigid accountability of the amount of National Forest System timber removed by the loggers.

For instance, if we cruised a unit and determined that it contained 2.5 mmbf, and the logger only presented 1.5 mmbf for scaling and payment ... we knew there was a possible log theft problem. The loggers knew that we knew how much timber was supposed to be there, and, well, it kept honest men honest.

We took our cruising dead seriously. Our established method was to walk every foot of every unit and get close enough to each tree that we could call an ocular estimate of volume to the tallyman. A sufficient number of trees were subsequently measured with a precise German instrument known as a Spiegel-Relaskop to ensure statistical validity, and to correct for ocular errors. In short, we gave a hard look to every tree on the hill, and it was rare that our volume estimates were more than plus or minus 5 per cent off what the loggers removed. We eagerly awaited the cut-out results from each timber sale, i.e., the tally of how much timber was cut and removed, so that we could see how close it was to our cruised estimate.

Despite my strong preference to spend my time in the woods with my presale crew, I had to allocate almost half my time to the office, tending to appraisals, contracts, and interacting with the sale planners. My preference for field work didn't escape the notice of my fellow assembly line workers. The ranger told me he personally would kick my butt if I ever shirked my office duties to the point I delayed a timber sale from getting sold on schedule. I told him I'd NEVER hold up a sale, but also he'd never better TRY to kick my butt. It was the right thing to say to Mick, and he became one of my staunchest supporters, though never in my presence. Spending a lot of time in the woods was also the right thing to do, as Forest Service employees have a huge respect for field "skookum," just as they deplore "office slugs."

One summer I was assigned to supervise a college student who had entered the Forest Service's cooperative education program. He and I were in the field one day, and I pointed out two trees that were rubbing together in the wind. With a straight face, I told him they were "friction trees" and were a major causal agent of forest fires, and that the ranger gave bonuses to guys who meticulously identified their locations on aerial photos. The kid kept careful notes on all the "friction trees" he found that summer and eventually reported them to the ranger. Mick knew immediately who had set up this student, and ordered me to visit him in his office ... with the door closed!

One rather non-typical assignment was the district's first attempt at commercial thinning. The Mapleton District had very little old-growth timber. A devastating fire around the time of the Civil War had consumed most of the old-growth timber, so what we had was 120-year-old second growth. Huge second growth! Our average tree was about 30 inches in diameter at chest height, towered approximately 175 feet tall, and yielded about 1,300 board feet. Coastal old growth, by contrast, was at least 300 (and often 500) years old and much larger.

After logging our second growth, burning the slash, and replanting, the trees were thinned at age 15. "Thinning" means removing some of the smaller, poorly formed trees in order to allow more sunlight and soil nutrients for the "crop trees." Another thinning was planned for age 30, at which point, we expected to be able to sell the small, thinned trees, and recover some of our costs. It didn't work out that way. We found it was much more labor intensive to layout commercial thinning sales, and ... none of the local mills wanted the timber. From the large mature trees, a diversity of valuable products could be made ... veneer for plywood, large, knot-free, dimensional lumber, etc. By contrast the thinned trees, which were ignominiously dubbed "pecker poles," were about 10 inches in diameter, 50 feet tall, and contained less than 30 board feet. They were suitable only for low-grade 2x4s or wood chips.

Ranger Mick bullied a couple mills to buy the thinning sales and give them a chance. But we never were able to generate enough money from any commercial thinning sale to cover the cost of our tree marking paint, much less our labor. We realized the forest management plan, made by the wizards in the forest supervisor's office in Corvallis, Oregon, expected to make a final clearcut harvest of the stands at age 70 years, which would make the trees a lot younger, smaller, and less valuable than the second growth we were currently logging. My presale crew and I exchanged glances, then turned our thoughts inward and kept our mouths shut.

My presale crew had a tradition of always flipping coins to see who drew what job for the day. One particular day, we were cruising timber and were flipping to see who would be the tallyman. Normally, I much preferred to cruise and hated to spend all day just recording everyone else's information. But that day I wanted to tally, and did so when I won the flip. The unit we were cruising was true old growth, which, as I've said, was exceedingly rare on Mapleton District. Trees were much older and larger than normal, with a thicker, more orangish bark. The unit also had less brush and more of a hemlock and cedar component. All in all, it was completely atypical from the normal Mapleton forest type.

When we finished, I told the guys I didn't want to screw around, but wanted to get back a little early so I could talk to the ranger. Eyes rolled and hurried "hail Marys" were muttered, as we drove back to the office. I stalked down the hall and knocked on Mick's door frame. He invited me in, and I told him that I had a problem with logging the unit we were in that day. He looked shocked, as he knew me to be a rabid "timber beast." I explained that it didn't have anything to do with fragile soils or riparian protection, but rather that the big old-growth trees reminded me of a shrine. I started to feel pretty lame, but labored on and told him that there was lots of stuff we could cut, but there wasn't much old growth, and we ought to leave this stand alone.

Mick looked concerned. He had me describe in detail what I had seen and told me he had great respect for my intuition as a forester. Then he said he was going to log the unit anyhow, but to always bring any concern I had to his attention. [As it turned out, those very trees had caught someone else's attention ... someone powerful and determined. To my knowledge, they are still standing, but I gave my word of honor to never tell that story.]

There was a well-developed Forest Service family at Mapleton. There were some wonderful guys there, and we ran around together after work. We had some pretty wild parties. We crabbed in the bays, caught salmon and steelhead in the rivers, hunted elk and deer, and, when I bought my first ocean-going boat, we roared out to sea for salmon and rockfish. These were good, honest, hard-working people ... who were united by a common goal. We pumped out timber.

My crew was expected to have all our timber sale work done by July 1, so we could join Fire Control in burning slash. If pumping out timber were our mission, burning slash was our sacred cow. There was a limited dry season at Mapleton, so when conditions were right, burning took absolute priority over everything. Mick made sure of that! The entire district turned out for slash burns ... it was hard, dangerous work that yielded wildly impressive results. In just a few hours, we could turn a steep, freshly logged hillside choked with logging debris into a charred holocaust. Flames would push a huge column of smoke 3,000 feet skyward. The sun would be obliterated. Huge "firedevils," shrieking tornado-like fireballs, would roar like freight trains. And all the while we made overtime. Lotsa overtime.

When the fires died down, we would mop up the hotspots ... a process that often took two weeks. We weren't trying to burn down the whole forest, just burn up the slash so a new crop of trees could get planted. We viewed it as essential site preparation work, analogous to rototilling a garden. And we worked 14 hours a day, seven days a week. That's 100-plus hours of overtime, per two-week pay period. We took all of it we could get, or at least most people did.

I wasn't a real gung-ho smoke horse. First, I had enough other stuff to do, without burning slash. Second, the work itself exposed lungs to intense smoke and fine particulates ... kinda like smoking two packs of Camels a day. This was not helping my running career, which was just starting to blossom. Third, I thought there was some overtime padding occurring. Not that people didn't work ... Lord, that was a WORKING district! But, some of the stuff seemed unnecessary, and I just didn't want to be part of it.

Beyond all that, I simply didn't like to work 80-plus hours per week. But to avoid burning slash, you had to have some kind of socially approved excuse. That's when I got the idea to start a forestry consulting business in my spare time. Forestry consulting in Mapleton didn't mean I came over to your house to tell you why your favorite shade tree was sick. Hardly. I was in business strictly for small landowners who had some property they wanted logged. I'd run the survey, and lay it out for either clearcut or selective logging ... my recommendation, their choice. Then I negotiated the best log prices, contracted out the logging, and made sure everything got done right.

Because this work represented a potential conflict of professional interest, I had to get approval from Mick. He gave me his best growl and asked if he weren't working me hard enough. I told him I was a timber beast, and that there wasn't enough timber in the world for me. This pleased him so much, he actually smiled. He said he wished all the other foresters on the district had my soup-to-nuts knowledge of the timber game. I told him that Mapleton District's assembly line approach prevented that from happening. He put the growl back, signed my request, and told me to get back to work. Good ol' Mick.

I didn't make my fortune at this business, but did earn some extra money and managed to avoid some slash burning. If the district were planning a slash burn on Saturday, there was no use planning a fishing trip, because that wasn't a valid excuse. But clearcutting some private land was wildly acceptable. In fact, I could return to work Monday morning a hero. Timber beasts, indeed!

Diane and I were starting to crack under the strain of taking on four kids all at once. Diane said I wasn't being an involved enough father, and I said she had become a full-time mom and a zero-time wife. All we seemed to do was cross-accuse each other, without ever treating the underlying problems. I tried to balance the diametrical feelings of fulfilling responsibilities undertaken versus having my life turned upside down by a family I had never wanted. I struggled to find a compromise and developed my first and only protracted case of insomnia. Time passed, and we didn't even try to meet the other's needs, much less our own.

In 1984, miserable and guilt-ridden, I left. We started what was to become a horribly bitter divorce, in which I got slammed pretty hard financially.

This was a difficult time for me, not only from leaving my wife of 11 years, but also having to acknowledge vulnerability in my own psyche. I didn't know which bothered me more. This was the first time that I had ever quit on anything, as well as the first time I had ever experienced abject failure and guilt. In retrospect, I think Diane and I each did the best we could, given what we each knew about relationships at the time. I think she had been taught to be a passive hanger-on to her husband's life, and that I thought working and playing hard were what men were supposed to do. I know that I was less attentive and caring to her than I could have been, and that my male-focused lifestyle must have been very hard on her. But at this point in time, I was still years away from this awareness and renaissance, and it came too late for Diane and me.

The ranger called me into his office one day, and gave me some pretty gruff commiseration. Nonetheless, it was appreciated. He told me there was a vacancy in a trailer house on the Forest Service compound. He said he wanted me to move up to Mapleton, so he could keep an eye on me. I did so. Things were starting to slide downhill for me, and I knew it. My one source of strength was my running. I started getting involved in road racing, and became seduced by the marathon. My Sunday runs started to lengthen.

My first marathon was at Seaside, Oregon. At race time, it was pouring, with 35 mph winds. Totally inexperienced at marathons, I started out at too fast a pace. At mile nine, my stomach cramped, and I threw up ... without breaking stride. I wrongheadedly decided it was a waste of time to stop for water, so I plugged on. And on. I finished in three hours, 46 minutes. At the conclusion of the race, I got an orange and started back to the locker room where my clothes were stashed. On the way, hypothermia and leg cramps overcame me. I found myself at the edge of a parking lot, with a guard rail in front of me. There was no way I could lift my legs over it. I crawled on the hood of the nearest car and tried to roll myself over the guard rail, but fell short, in a puddle. I was sitting there kinda dazed, when two cops came by. They said, "Lord, there's another one!" and half-carried me to the gym.

As soon as the cops brought me into the gym, several nurses grabbed me and started yanking off my wet clothes. Part of my brain thought, "Only in America ...," the rest was numb. They wrapped me in a space blanket, and, after taking my temperature, tried to transport me to a hospital. I stubbornly refused. The nurses gave me a cup of hot tea, but my hands were shaking so bad, I spilled the tea all over myself. In a couple of hours, after a hot shower and a pasta feed, I was a lot better. On the way home, a cop stopped me in Newport for having a container up to my mouth. I showed him my race T-shirt and an open quart container of ... granola. He let me go.

5

Greenies

(March 1985 - May 1987)

"Look at Mother Nature on the run
In the nineteen seventies."
    -- Neil Young, "After the Goldrush"

"They took all the trees and put 'em in a tree museum,
And they charged all the people a dollar & a half just to see 'em."
    -- Joni Mitchell, "Big Yellow Taxi"

Everyone knows that bad luck occurs in sets of threes. Whether the number of consecutive events is 3, 6, or 30 ... there is a virtually unopposable force which seems to develop. Just when my personal life started to fall apart, calamity befell the Mapleton District.

In 1984, the National Wildlife Federation, an environmental organization (aka, "greenies"), filed a lawsuit against logging practices on the Mapleton District. They claimed that our admittedly vanilla-flavored environmental assessments had never discussed the existence or environmental consequences of landslides. We were horrified. Our horror exponentiated when the judge presiding over the case ruled in favor of the National Wildlife Federation and slapped an injunction against further timber sales.

Like a ripe tomato splatted against a wall, the mighty timber assembly line at Mapleton slammed to an immediate, abrupt halt.

No one knew or could foresee the implications of the injunction. One thing was for sure ... we had no back-up plan. If we couldn't log, burn, and replant, there wasn't anything for us to do. Idle time, the first anyone had ever seen, enshrouded us. We did not fill it with happy, positive thoughts.

Strangers in dark suits started to appear at the ranger station. Rumors flew. Finally, we were told to finish up the sale we were on, but not to start any new work. Little by little, we were told that our position did not look good. Andy Stahl, a forester for the NWF, was spearheading the litigation, and he was using his professional knowledge to tear out our guts. We were horrified. Here was a professional forester, who had formerly worked for the Association of Oregon Loggers, trying his best to halt logging. Conclusion: he was a traitor! Moreover, we had heard that Andy Stahl admitted he was a hired advocate for the NWF and was selective in his veracity. Conclusion: he was a liar! No one could even conceive of a forester turning on his brethren like that. Little did I know ...

Upper management within the Forest Service was determined to keep the lawsuit from spreading to the rest of the Siuslaw, or worse to other National Forests. To keep the damage more or less localized, they abandoned fighting the lawsuit and essentially hung Mapleton out to dry. The district went from an annual timber sale program of about 100 mmbf, to not being allowed to sell anything but personal- use Christmas trees, greenery, and a limited amount of commercial thinning.

Landslides didn't exactly take us by surprise. This was exceedingly steep country, we practiced clearcut logging exclusively, and burning killed the brush layer. The naked hillsides were then exposed to the torrential fall and winter rains, and gravity worked its way. "Headwall" areas, the dished-out tops of streams, were particularly vulnerable to slides. We practiced some mitigation measures of leaving buffer areas around these headwalls, in other words leaving some trees, but these were largely ineffectual.

I remember laying out a small salvage sale on the south part of the district one day. I had laid out the boundaries in the morning and was enjoying the luxury of eating lunch in my pickup. I looked out at the sea of adjacent clearcuts and, to pass the time, started to count landslides. When I got into the 20s, I momentarily got nervous that I was in such an unstable place that the truck would be swept over the edge in a massive torrent.

But for the most part, landslides were just considered a necessary cost of doing business. The fact that the slides had potential to impact downslope salmon streams did NOT escape our attention. To mitigate this damage, we were starting to expand the width of buffers adjacent to the streams, in an attempt to intercept and halt the slides. But the slides themselves remained. And we were shut down by the judge's decision.

It didn't take long for the effects of losing our timber program to impact the workforce. Funds to pay salaries dried up, and workers were given mandatory temporary details to other locations. Ultimately, the district workforce shrank from 110 to 28 workers. The blackboard in the coffee room carried the cryptic message, "Will the last person out, please turn off the lights!"

My presale crew was scattered to the winds immediately. But Mick kept me around as long as possible, just in case there were changed circumstances and our timber program needed to get cranked back up in a hurry. Nonetheless, my time came too, and I was shipped out to LaGrande, Oregon, on the Wallowa Whitman National Forest. LaGrande was dry, "eastside" (east of the Cascade mountains), cowboy country. The district had a chunk of uncharacteristically steep ground to log and wanted a "westside" forester, who knew how to layout cable logging systems. Just as I was struggling to regain some consistency in my life, I was faced with potential job loss and being uprooted from my beloved coastal Oregon.

There was a good bunch of people at LaGrande, another extended Forest Service family. I threw myself at my work, and tried to earn a permanent spot on their workforce, but they simply couldn't swing a slot for another forester. Summer dragged into fall, then winter. I had no idea how long I was going to stay at LaGrande, and the ranger there had no idea either. Every Friday, it seemed, I would ask whether or not to buy groceries for the next week. I went back to being a phantom again ... leaving early, returning late, keeping too much to myself.

Finally in early winter, Mick called and told me to get my butt back pronto. He wouldn't say anything more, except that my trailer house was vacant and ready. Typical Mick.

As it turned out, it was a false alarm. The timber program was not restarting. The local community started to feel the same pinch as the Forest Service. Loggers got laid off, mills shut down, families broke up ... it was pathetic. We held a demonstration in front of the grocery store in Florence, where we vilified the National Wildlife Federation, and hung their forester spokesman, Andy Stahl, in effigy. I wanted to burn and dismember Andy's likeness and then drag it behind my truck. Unfortunately, someone beat me to it.

Career counselors told us that foresters were a dime a dozen and to look for something else. Some do-gooder looked at my record and saw I knew how to program computers. The next thing I knew, I was detailed into doing some industrial strength FORTRAN programming in support of the forest silviculture program. I was a little rusty, but got up to speed pretty quickly.

The saving grace of this assignment was that I was able to wheedle my way into becoming the Siuslaw Forest's aerial photographer. This was a ball! We fabricated a special door which would fit a Cessna 185 and house a top-end Hasselbladt 70mm camera. The program was to overfly recent clearcuts and take high-quality photos to be used for silvicultural purposes. I knew where the recent clearcuts were, as I had laid them out and burned them.

What amazed me, though, was getting a bird's eye view of the district. When I was laying out sales, I was so focused on each individual sale that I didn't notice how close the current sale sat to existing clearcuts, or to the next sale scheduled to appear on the assembly line. Now I could clearly see how close the clearcuts lay to each other. Sure, there was a lot of standing timber left, but at the rate we were going through it, there was no way it was going to last until the plantations were ready to be logged. I was shocked.

When I was a presale forester, you didn't want to get between me and my timber sale. I was abjectly fixated on getting the cut out, and never considered the overall landscape. This was a literal example of the old can't-see-the-forest-because-of-the-trees adage. One day I caught up with my presale crew foreman and told him what I'd seen in the air. He just looked at me and said, "Billy, everyone knew that. It just couldn't last forever." This shook me because the whole precept of timber forestry is that it DAMN WELL BETTER last forever.

The enforced time in the office, away from the woods, gradually changed my personal outlook. My divorce from Diane was finalized, which cost me my house and half my monthly salary. As I struggled to reinvent myself, I moved to Eugene, which was renowned as a runner's mecca. It was said that if you drew a chalk line in the street, in 15 minutes, 100 runners would line up waiting for the gun to go off.

One day the doorbell rang at my newly rented house, and at the door was a GreenPeace canvasser soliciting funds. A goddamned greenie! I told the guy to wait, but something in my expression must have tipped him off. By the time I was able to get Max out of the kennel in the back yard, and race back to the front door, the Green Peace guy was running down the street. He had a good lead, but Max and I made it pretty close. Unfortunately, the greenie escaped in a waiting car.

Along this time, Mick sent me over to work with the genetic scientists at the Pacific Northwest experiment station in Corvallis. The first day at work at the PNW lab, I was shown to my office. It was reminiscent of high school chemistry lab ... with a sink, black counter tops, even a place to plug in a Bunsen burner. In a big box was the first personal computer I had ever seen. They told me to get the thing working ASAP and start writing FORTRAN. Then they shut the door.

I wasn't particularly thrilled about programming in a little room by myself, but I did enjoy listening to the forest geneticists at lunch breaks. These men were all PhDs, and I respected them immensely. One thing I remember their telling me, because I found it so shocking ... "It is biologically impossible to increase the inherent productivity of a forest. While it is possible to grow the same amount of fiber more quickly, the amount itself may not be increased. Furthermore, there has never been a forest, anywhere on the planet, that yielded as much timber volume in the third rotation as it did on the first. Never. Site productivity simply decreases." This was in direct contradiction to every Forest Service analysis of timber supply I ever read.

One day I got a call from Mick, telling me to show up at Mapleton in the morning. I purposely parked in the visitor parking spot out front, just to annoy him. I intended to visit some of my old buddies, but no one was there. I finally walked into Mick's office and was ordered to sit down. Bad sign.

Mick asked me if I knew who Jeff Sirmon was. I said he was regional forester of Region IV when I was over in Idaho and that he had been regional forester of Region VI when I came to Oregon. I joked I was kinda following him around. Mick gave a rare smile and said that was good. Then he said Sirmon was now a deputy chief in D.C, and he'd run into Jeff at a meeting. Sirmon had mentioned that he was looking for a forester who knew the woods dead and could make a computer hum. My mouth went dry. Then Mick asked how I'd like to go back to Washington, D.C. I managed to croak that I wouldn't like that at all.

Mick got up and went over and closed the door. Then he said, "Let me re-phrase that question."

6

The Bad Place

(May 1987 - April 1990)

"Lullabies, look in my eyes.
Run around the same old town.
Doesn't mean that much to me,
To mean that much to you."
-- Neil Young, "Old Man"

It was the spring of 1987. My district had been shut down, and, while I still drew a paycheck, I didn't really have a job. I was a GS-9 forester, and there was little job security in this field, and virtually no chance of career advancement. The job in D.C. was a GS-11/12 position, which meant immediate promotion to GS-11 and, one year later, an automatic promotion to GS-12. Plus, as Mick pointed out, when you complete your assignment back there, you will have a rocket tied to your career. With the support of those heavy-hitters, you can go anywhere you want.

The U.S. Forest Service, under the Department of Agriculture, has three main branches: the National Forest System, State and Private Forestry, and Research. There are approximately 191 million acres of National Forest System lands and grasslands throughout the United States, with most of the larger forests located in the West. Like all federal agencies, the organizational hierarchy resembles an inverted pyramid, ascending from 600 districts to 155 forests to nine regions to a single national headquarters, the Washington office. Districts are run by "rangers," national forests by "forest supervisors," regional offices by "regional foresters," and the Washington office by the "chief." Most of the actual field work is done at the district level, with each successive organizational level having less to do with the field and more to do with oversight and bureaucratic embellishments.

In 1987, there were approximately 30,000 full-time Forest Service employees, as well as an enormous number of seasonal workers during the field season. As federal employees, salary is determined by "GS-level" or "grade", and there is a direct proportion between grade and organizational level, i.e., workers in D.C. tend to be of higher grade than those working in Bumfididdle, Montana.

The trend throughout the years had been for professionals to start out on the districts at the GS-5 to GS-7 level and to make a series of moves every two to three years. Generally their careers followed the Peter Principle, rising within the organization until they reached their level of incompetence.

On the Mapleton District, Mick ruled supreme, and he was nothing, if not a good salesman. I guess you don't get to be a ranger by being a complete knucklehead. Or so he said. He told me Jeff Sirmon cautioned him about having "his man" camp on the job. This meant the position was a two-year assignment, and not the start of a permanent series of positions in D.C. Mick told Sirmon that wouldn't be a problem with the guy he had in mind. Mick finally brought out the big guns and told me there were four single women in D.C. for every guy. I think he even yarded out a newspaper article which showed that D.C. had the best gal-to-guy ratio in the nation. Big promotion, more money, two years, go where you want afterwards, lotsa women, whatcha say? Sure, Mick.

Even with the deal allegedly sealed, it was months before I was selected for the position, and apparently it was touch-and-go until the last second. But in the heat of summer of 1987, I left Oregon for D.C. I was once again driving a faithful Ford pickup, this one an eight-year-old 4x4, with two dogs chained to the huge doghouse on the back, and my 22-foot C-Dory fishing boat in tow.

I somehow managed to coax my menagerie to D.C. I had previously flown back for a house-hunting trip, and had secured a rental lease on a townhouse apartment (had never even heard the term "townhouse" before), at one of the few places that would allow two dogs. I made myself at home and listened soberly to my new neighbors' instructions on how to commute to USDA headquarters in downtown D.C. Go to New Carrollton, get on the Metro, take the Orange Line to the Smithsonian exit, then ... whoa, back up. What's the Metro? I was so nervous, it's amazing I didn't end up in Cleveland!

For my stint in DC, I had purchased six white, oxford-cloth, button-down-collar shirts, five ties, two pairs of Dockers, a sport coat, six pairs of black socks, and a pair of leather lace-up shoes. A veritable fashion statement! I wanted to look just like the other kids on the block, but my first morning, I never made it past the security station at the front door of USDA headquarters. What ID badge? Fortunately, I had an extension number written in ink on the back of my hand, and called someone to come down to rescue me.

I made a conscious effort to keep my mouth from hanging open. I was sweating like a pig. I had a get-acquainted meeting with the staff director, a GS-buhzillion PhD, who made no real effort to put me at ease. The only thing I even recall about the meeting was a reinforcement of the warning to not expect to camp on the job. Not to worry said I (hell, can I leave NOW?). Also, where did I want to go when I left? Southeast Alaska! Little did I know, but that made it a done deal ... if I did my job and kept my nose clean.

I shook hands with a nameless sea of male ties and female power suits, then was ushered into my office. Now what? My new supervisor came and visited with me. He used so many acronyms and such strange language (never once mentioned Douglas-fir), that I had no idea what he was saying. But he was nice. His name was Adrian Haught, and he became the force that held me together back there.

I slowly discovered the way things worked in D.C. It was obvious that there was no way I could phantom my way through this job, i.e., avoid people by arriving early and leaving late, because there was no forest to escape to. The chief's office (that's THE CHIEF of the whole Forest Service) was right down the hall. Meetings, that's how things worked, meetings. It was hotter than a firecracker that summer, but I had to drink gallons of hot coffee to stay awake. Nothing made any sense, wasn't this still the Forest Service? At one particular meeting, where I was struggling to figure what was going on, I finally asked, "Do you mean that the intent of this meeting ... the sole intent ... is to decide if we should hold another meeting?" Well, yes. Oh, I get it ...

Go to meetings, then go back to your office and do a little work on some nonsense project that was barely worth doing, much less talking about. Then it was time to think of something profound to say at the next meeting and practice saying it in front of a mirror. The rest of the day was spent flouncing around trying to impress your mentor. I knew as much about mentors as I did about townhouses.

The Washington office was purposely overstaffed, so that they could swarm and quickly answer congressional inquiries or other hot-ticket items. To be honest, there were frequent bursts of intense effort. But for the most part, it was the biggest bunch of overpaid, underworked employees I had ever seen. Even after my promotion to GS-12, I was the lowest grade male employee, not only on my staff, but in the entirety of the Programs and Legislation Department.

I was assigned to the RPA staff, which stood for Resources Program and Assessment. Every five years we were required to produce a Plan (note the capitol 'P') which governed how all the national forests were to be managed. Huh? I had worked in the woods for almost 10 years and had never even heard of the Plan, much less used it as a blueprint for my daily forestry activities. Oh well, just tell me what I'm supposed to do?

It turned out I was supposed to be a computer specialist (although they agreed to let me keep my professional forester classification). There was some information that needed to be gathered and analyzed, and some tabular and graphical output produced. For the previous Plan, there were two GS-13s, a GS-11, a GS-9, and two GS-5s handling the computer stuff. Now there was me and a GS-7 assistant. Yeah, but I had a then state-of-the-art Compaq 286 12 mHz micro-computer, 1MB of RAM, 20 MB of storage, some database software, and a compiler. I stripped the incoming data into an ASCII file, jammed it into a database, fed it into some custom programs I wrote, and sent control characters to the laser printer which ensured pretty output. Piece of cake.

There were some periods of intense work, and some of it was challenging, but it probably kept me full-bore busy about 50% of the time. Occasionally, I would get a call from some bigwig that his computer was broken. Uh, your monitor isn't turned on. Oh, I was a horrible failure at sucking up to the brass. First, it is not my nature to be ingratiating, and second, aside from Adrian, most of the upper management were jerks. Evidently you don't get to be a mover and shaker in the Forest Service by being a nice guy.

I started goofing on them. Someone would want a report from the database, that I recognized would take about an hour to run. I'd shake my head, massage my temples, while I listened to them whine. Finally, I'd tell them that their request was difficult (this actually pleased them), and that I was busy, but that I'd be able to get it in about a week. Greatly relieved, they'd shake my hand and thank me. Other times, I'd hand them their output while they waited. I would flip a mental coin ... hard or easy. What did he tell you? He said it was hard. What did he tell you? He said it was easy. Damn, this computer stuff sure is confusing. They never seemed to have a clue, and I sometimes wonder if they ever caught on.

I remember one particular meeting where our staff director, Tom Mills, was making a presentation to George Leonard, the associate chief, i.e., the second-in-command of the entire Forest Service. George was a big, hulking, ill-tempered career bureaucrat with a decided timber bias. Our director was at the point of his presentation where he showed how his ace computer analyst had summed up all the individual National Forest plans and got a composite logging level of something like 9.2 billion board feet. Leonard exploded, glowered at me, and shouted that I damned well better recalculate it into double digits ... no, make that at least 10.1 mmmbf. Leonard didn't impress me, so I shot back that my responsibility ended with accurately adding up the logging levels and had no wherewithal to change the input.

For just an instant the world stopped. Then everyone pounced on me to shut me up and assured George Leonard that what I really meant to say was that the problem could be corrected by more judicious rounding algorithms. Not liking to be shut up, I managed to insert, "Yeah, like rounding 0.3 up to 1.0, eh?". Geez, I was hustled out of there in a hurry, amid much hand-wringing and head-shaking. Didn't I know that it was suicide to piss off someone like Leonard and to embarrass our director? I said that if that's all the logs the individual National Forests thought they could produce, then who were we to up that number from the non-forested halls of the Washington Office. No one even had a clue what I was talking about and looked at me like I was nuts. Even Adrian shook his head.

It was common practice to occasionally go up to "The Hill" for a look-see, when your work was all caught up. I wasn't much interested in Congress, though I'd occasionally sneak off to the National Conservatory and look at the pretty plants. That, and run. Oh my God, did I run! D.C. is a gorgeous place to run. There was a fitness center in the basement of the USDA Building where you could grab a locker and a shower. My everyday running route was along the Mall up to The Hill, down past the Washington Monument, along the reflecting pool, up to the Lincoln Memorial, cut across to the Viet Nam Memorial, then past the tidal basin and down to the tip of Hains Point, then up the other side, past the Mint, and finally back to the gym. It was a nine-mile loop, which I ran four times a week, and required a two-hour lunch break, allowing time for pre-run stretching and a nice shower.

On Sundays, I'd typically run 12 miles, unless there was a marathon to train for. And there were lots of them. It was during my final training stage for the Virginia Beach marathon in March 1988 that I met Yvonne.

Until then, I found that most D.C. gals simply weren't interested in a guy from Oregon, who drove a pickup, and wanted to move to Alaska. I combed the singles ads and went on a lot of "interview dates" ... where you met in a bar and quizzed each other. Some gals actually pulled out an embossed card containing a list of questions and jotted down my answers. Let's see ... How old are you? How much money do you make? What's your favorite color? Most of the time, the gals never even got to the end of their list, before I was dismissed amid ponderous head-shaking and crossing out on the note pad. In most cases, after tossing down the remnants of their drink, their first word was "Look ..." I never went out with any of these gals twice and never saw any of them in the daylight. I started to think I was dating a coven of the undead.

And then along came Yvonne. She was gorgeous, an intelligent psychotherapist, and a terrific singer. I was smitten but badly. I tore myself away from her and ran a personal best 3:11 at Virginia Beach, then hurried home.

In retrospect, Yvonne and I had little in common other than an over abundance of hormones. She was a long-term urbanite, a staunch feminist, and an anti-gun liberal far to the left of Ted Kennedy. I was a hillbilly forester who wanted to move to Alaska. I tried to convince her that I didn't share her love of the city, and she'd respond by buying me a new pair of Dockers.

We bought a new house way out on Chesapeake Bay, and then, wham, Yvonne was gone. Not to worry, in a couple of months she was back. Then wham, she was gone again. My mind kept playing that wonderful Jackson Browne song, " ... she wasn't much good at sticking around, but that girl could sing. She could sing!"

It was expensive to live in D.C., and I found it hard to make ends meet, especially with a house payment of $1,200 a month. I bought a commercial crab permit, a whole gob of crab pots, and started a crabbing business on Chesapeake Bay. There was no problem selling every crab I caught, and it made a big difference financially in getting me over the hump. Plus it provided some semblance of sanity for a West Coaster trapped in D.C.

My two-year anniversary at the Washington office passed, but RPA wasn't ready to turn loose of me yet. I grew restless and realized I'd blown my big chance. I watched other people move in. They followed the established pattern for success ... move to Alexandria, dress well, be nice to the bigshots. They didn't necessarily sell their soul, they just kinda tucked it away in reserve. They were sent back out in ranger and forest supervisor positions.

By now, my six shirts were tattered, my ties were stained, and I was commuting on my motorcycle and parking by the gym. I lived as far away from downtown as I could get, and endured the 28-mile, 32-stoplight commute. I wore my emotions on my sleeve, and made no bones of the fact that I was ready to leave. Unfortunately, the RPA Plan was in the final stages of preparation and no one else had a clue how to run the computer systems I'd designed.

I came home from work one day, and Yvonne asked me what I'd done at work. I spent all evening thinking of something to tell her. I'd been busy as heck actually. But I didn't really DO anything. It started to eat at me, as I wondered if I'd truly made any progress in the 14 years since I'd left the insurance company in Hartford.

To mollify me, I was given a short-term detail to the timber management staff. Of course, the timber shop wanted me to cozy up to a computer. For several years they'd had a team of contractors unsuccessfully working on a timber sale accounting system called TSPIRS, which was some acronym my mind has mercifully forgotten. On the first morning of my assignment, I strafed off some of the TSPIRS input, jammed it into a database management system, and started firing queries at it. Is this what you want? They looked at me like I was from outer space. I decided that trying to upstage the contracting team was the wrong approach, so I feigned being baffled. Geez, this stuff is really hard. That brought them back around.

Some of my co-workers had served time in Alaska, and we had long talks about how things actually ran there. One of the guys, my temporary supervisor, John Wells, told me that going to Alaska was like going back in time 50 years. He told me the Tongass National Forest was considered the outlaw of the whole National Forest System. There were two long-term timber contracts up there, which took priority over everything. Moreover, the contracts were uneconomical, unsustainable, and pretty soon there would only be one of them. He said that the biggest snake pit was in Ketchikan, and if I ever got there, to watch my butt. I took it all in and filed it away. But it meant nothing to me, and did little to dissuade me from pushing for a transfer to Alaska.

Finally, the RPA Plan was published, and I was presented a coveted Certificate of Merit award for my contribution. Mission accomplished, I was free to leave. Miraculously, a GS-12 interdisciplinary team leader position opened up at Ketchikan, Alaska, and I was selected. People joked that I'd better enjoy my last few women, because there were none in Alaska. I took them seriously and asked Yvonne to marry me. She said yes, and we had a quickie wedding at a friend's house. Gulp!

Yvonne decided to stay behind in D.C. and close her psychotherapy practice, while I went on ahead to Alaska. I came home from work for the last time and took my six shirts, five ties, two pair of pants, six pair of black socks, and ratty leather shoes out to the driveway ... and poured kerosene on them. I touched them off, and it was one of the most satisfying moments of my life. I was going to be leaving in the morning, and I never wanted to see a city again.

7

The Dream

(April 1990 - August 1990)

"Ah, to be up and leavin' this town,
Headin' down an open road.
With all that you own
Kinda thrown on the back seat,
Thinkin' 'bout where you'll go."
-- Jerry Jeff Walker, "Maybe Mexico"

Before leaving D.C., there was a sad chore to do. My springer spaniel was 13 years old and starting to fail. Her old leg injury was bothering her, and rather than subject her to the rigors of the move to Alaska, I had her put to sleep. I had been in a quandary about what to do and had agonized over my decision. This seemed the kindest thing, and also eased my own burden somewhat. I felt pretty terrible.

Just as I was pulling out of my driveway for the trip to Alaska, the one friend I had made in D.C., a roofing contractor who had been my best crab customer, flagged me down. He installed some flashing on the roofline on Max's doghouse, which was once again riding in the back of my pickup truck. My buddy and I hugged each other, and off I went.

When I got on the highway, the devils in my head overtook my steering wheel. It was morning rush hour, as I had faced for the past two years, eight months, and four days. Whereas I had always been compelled to drive too fast, I now decided to go too slow. With the boat in tow, I was 40 feet long and had a chance to deliver a final fond farewell to D.C. drivers. As I got to the west side of the beltway, I heard the traffic report actually talk about a slow-moving truck towing a boat. For me it was uncharacteristically mean-spirited, but it did offer a measure of pay-back. I only hope it gave a coronary to some of those jerks who tailgated me while I was commuting on my motorcycle.

Oh what the hell, I just can't pass on without a final comment on D.C. drivers. The final year in D.C., the Forest Service sent me to a computer training session somewhere west of the city, over in Virginia. It must have been summer, because it was brutally hot. Traffic was in complete gridlock, and my motorcycle was on this little hill, facing down slope. You could see traffic backed up for at least a mile. My engine was shut off, and my bike was backed maybe a car-length off the car in front of me, so I didn't have to breathe his exhaust. I sat there for maybe four to five minutes, when the car in front idled ahead maybe 10 feet.

Suddenly the guy behind me started blowing his horn. I had my helmet off and turned around and looked at him. He was waving me forward and giving me the finger. When I turned around to think about this, the guy pulled his car off the roadside (we were in the left lane), swung around me, and managed to shoehorn his car in front of my bike. We sat there, completely immobilized. Most of the time, this kind of in-my-face action would have bought this guy a fist facial, but this time I was stunned. It absolutely nailed my opinion of the essence of life in D.C.

I was SO glad to leave D.C. But I wasn't going just anywhere, I was heading to Alaska. I sang the old Johnny Horton song, "North to Alaska" so many times, that Max, never the deep thinker, started to think it was his new name. Max lay sprawled across the front seat, with his head in my lap, gnawing huge knucklebones into dust. My jeans were soaked in dog-slobbered bone meal, but I didn't care. I was in great spirits, really enjoying the trip. I thought of the John Denver song, " ... going home to a place he'd never been before." It felt like I was truly going home.

It was spring 1990, and my Ford pickup was now 11 years old. I had never bothered registering it in Maryland, because it seemed important to make an identity statement with my Oregon tags, which had long ago expired. Ditto the boat and trailer ... no current registration. No auto insurance either. I also had a .357 magnum, because people told me you had to shoot halibut before landing them on board. And I expected to catch halibut before my personal goods were shipped up. My truck was in fair shape mechanically, but probably wasn't up to the rigors of a cross-country trip. I realized that I could be in big trouble if I got pulled over, but maybe I liked living near the edge.

I moved a little closer to life's edge in Sydney, Nebraska, when I heard a siren and, sure enough, a cop was behind, flashing his lights. I pulled over, took a deep breath, and told Max to be a good dog. I walked back, and the cop was staring at my boat. He told me his brother in Oregon had a C-Dory like mine and that he'd gone out in the Pacific Ocean on his brother's boat. I told him I used to live in Oregon and was on my way to Alaska to be a forester, official orders from the Government. We looked at each other in silence, while the cop's whole soul was virtually screaming, "Take me with you." The moment passed, and he shook my hand.

He told me proudly that Sydney was the home of Cabela's, the outdoor gear outfit. I grinned and said half the stuff I owned came from Cabela's, and it was true. He suggested pulling off the highway to a motel parking lot, which we did. We talked a little more about guy stuff, then he wished me well, shook my hand again, and hustled back to duty. I felt like I'd made a friend, but moreover it reaffirmed that I was doing the right thing with my life. A guy kinda needs that every now and then, eh?

We made Bellingham, Washington, and had some time to kill before we caught the ferry going north to Ketchikan. After a week of sitting on my butt in the truck, it felt great to get in a coupla runs. When the ferry left Bellingham, the ship wasn't the only thing casting off its mooring lines. It felt like I was stepping through Alice's one-way mirror into Wonderland. My whole life had been a steady progression west. The greenies had derailed my plans by shutting down my district back in Mapleton, Oregon, and I rationalized D.C. was just a detour to Alaska. I vowed it was going to take more than greenies to make me return "Down South" again. How true that proved to be!

The waves slid under the stern of the *M/V Malaspina*, as we motored north. I was to find that riding on an Alaska ferry is always fun. There is a roofed, sun-deck, with heat lamps on the ceiling. Chaise lounges are provided that can be positioned underneath the heat lamps, and with your sleeping bag stretched out, it is a comfortable and highly prized spot. The ferries have lots of other decks and lounges in which to curl up. Every hour of the day, there's a mixture of people sleeping and others wanting to chit-chat, in a quasi-Woodstock type atmosphere. Twice a day, passengers are allowed to go to the cargo deck to visit their rigs and attend to their pets.

As the hours passed pleasantly, I read some of my research materials about Southeast Alaska, the Tongass National Forest, and about Ketchikan. For the most part, SE Alaska and the Tongass were synonymous. About the only non-federally owned areas were adjacent to the few scattered towns, the largest of which were Juneau, Ketchikan, Sitka, Petersburg, and Wrangell. SE Alaska consisted of an archipelago and a narrow strip of mainland, nestled against British Columbia, Canada. There were few points which boasted a tie-through highway to the rest of the North American continent, so access was primarily by boat or plane.

The climate was temperate marine, which meant it was cool and rainy most of the time. Ketchikan's annual rainfall was an amazing 160 inches. A nice day in the summer might reach 65 degrees, and winter lows seldom dropped much below 20. Snow came and went quickly, as the rains melted it off, but at only slightly higher elevations the snow-rain mixture changed, and an impressive snowpack could develop.

The forests were ancient old growth, meaning there had been virtually no vegetative disturbance since the last ice age, approximately 10,000 years ago. Individual trees would come and go, within the generous natural life-spans Nature bestows upon her trees. Especially these trees. Alaska yellow-cedar (*Chamaecyparis nootkatensis*) and western redcedar (*Thuja plicata*) had been documented at 1,800 and 1,400 years old, respectively, and commonly reached 1,000 years. The other common species, western hemlock (*Tsuga heterophylla*) and Sitka spruce (*Picea sitchensis*) were the teenagers, seldom exceeding 500 years. Douglas-fir didn't grow in SE Alaska, which made me momentarily consider jumping ship and returning to Oregon. Because wildfire was virtually non-existent given the prodigious rainfall, the overall forest was primeval, with only windthrow creating relatively small patches of occasional disturbance. Fatal insect or disease epidemics were exceedingly rare. This was not to say that the Tongass was an unbroken sea of old-growth forest composed of huge, old trees. A great deal of the soil was thin, infertile, and simply too water-logged to grow much in the way of trees. Shore pine (*Pinus contorta*) and yellow-cedar might cling to life in these wet areas, but didn't develop into impressive specimens. Also much of the area was too steep, rocky, and avalanche-prone to develop dense forests of big trees. And everything grew slower because of the shorter growing seasons and less fertile soils, which were leached of nutrients by the endless rain.

Oh, I could read about trees forever, but there were other things to learn. The entirety of the state had less than a million people, half of whom lived in a single city, Anchorage. Brown bear were common on the mainland and on the "ABC islands" (Admiralty, Baranof, and Chichagof), but not on the other islands. Ketchikan was on Revilla island, and there were no brown bear there (whew!), but lotsa black bear. There were approximately 30,000 nesting pairs of bald eagles in SE. There were six species of salmon in mind-boggling numbers, halibut, crab ... I was overloaded. I was sold, this was the place for me.

Demographically the population was about 30% Alaska Native, a few Filipino, and the rest "honkey" (mostly Norwegians, and almost everyone not born there came from Minnesota). The main industries were timber, fishing, and tourism. I hated tourists, but two out of three ain't bad. That was enough fascinating facts, and I buried myself in James Mitchner's Alaska like everyone else.

I arrived in Ketchikan April 15, 1990, about 9:00 on a sunny Sunday morning. My new boss-to-be, Walt Dortch, met me at the ferry dock and welcomed me to town. It was a nice gesture, which was a Ketchikan tradition. I was booked into a bed and breakfast north of town, and drove up there to check in. On the way, I passed the Ketchikan Pulp mill, which seemed an inspiring sight.

The next day at work I quickly found out, once the introductions and handshakes were over, that the Ketchikan Area wasn't really ready for their new planning team leader to arrive. Apparently they had just finished some enormous project called "1989-94" that had drained the whole workforce, and there was nothing for me to do. Great! I found some shelves that needed to be built for a filing room, and started bolting them together. Damnit, I was going to do something! A lot of people stopped in to meet the new guy. They all seemed pretty impressed that I'd come from D.C. and wondered what the heck I was doing building shelves?

Yvonne flew into Ketchikan, for a look-see and to help me pick out a new house. Property was even more expensive here than it was in D.C., as Ketchikan had the highest cost of living of any town in the nation. The first day we went house-hunting, we bought a gorgeous house south of town.

Before going inside, I checked out the grounds and was amazed at the orchards and gardens. Pear, apple, cherry, plum trees, red raspberry bushes, rhubarb, kiwi, and so on. The foundation was equally impressive, with 6-inch x 16-inch western redcedar girders seated on Doug-fir pilings pressure-treated, copper-capped and drilled to bedrock. The floor joists were full dimension cut 2-inch x 12-inch old-growth Sitka spruce. There was an enormous two-story shop, with a double carport. On the way inside, I noticed about 12 cords of firewood stacked under the wrap-around solid cedar decks.

Yvonne was all smiles and slid her arm through mine. The living room was 35-feet x 24-feet, with floor to ceiling windows, skylights, a 16-foot ceiling, and an enormous stone hearth with a huge wood stove. The kitchen/dining room was monstrous and all fancy-schmancy blue tile. I could look out at the ocean. She took me off to see the solar-heated hydroponics room, which attached to the master bedroom. As I tried to figure out how the hydroponics system worked, I looked out on the deck and pointed to something. Yvonne said it was the hot tub.

At that point, I was almost dizzy. We tracked down the realtor, said it was a deal, and bought the house then and there. As I was reading the realtor's description of the house on the drive home that night, I saw mention of an upstairs. I asked Yvonne and the realtor if the place had an upstairs? Yvonne said it sure did, that it was gorgeous, and she had already claimed it for her office. Shoot, I bought the house thinking it was one-story.

Yvonne told me it was going to take her quite a while to close down her D.C. psychotherapy practice, because she couldn't simply abandon her long-term clients. When I enthused about Ketchikan and the house, I made some comments to the effect, "I want to die here." She looked at me kinda funny and warned me sternly not to make such a long-term commitment, because it was scaring her. She flew back to D.C. a couple days after we bought the house.

Back at the office, the forest supervisor had enough of my building shelves, and told my boss to get me going on something else. I was turned loose on an old environmental impact statement (EIS), which had never gotten past the draft stage. It had been five years since anyone had even looked at it, and it was all thrown together in a box. Anyone who knew anything about it had already left Alaska. It was my job to finish it, but to even get started on it, I needed to get up to speed on what made Ketchikan and the Tongass tick. I started to do my research.

Things worked a little differently on the Tongass National Forest than on the other forests I had worked on Down South. The Tongass was the largest of our country's national forests. Matter of fact, at 17.1 million acres, it was more than twice as big as the one in second place. It was the only national forest that was so big that it was broken into three administrative areas ... the Chatham Area located at Sitka, the Stikine Area at Petersburg, and the Ketchikan Area at ... well, Ketchikan. Each of these administrative areas operated like an independent national forest, although there was some degree of overall coordination.

I learned that during the post World War II and ensuing Cold War years, Alaska's proximity to the Soviet Union caught the attention of military strategists. Concerned that the territory was populated largely by Native Americans and seasonal fishermen, an effort was made to establish a year-round industry which would sustain a stable economy and population. To this purpose, the Secretary of Agriculture entered into two long-term timber contracts with multinational pulp corporations. These contracts established that, in consideration for building and operating then-state-of-the-art pulp mills, the corporations would be given access to a 50-year-supply of timber to feed the mills, at guaranteed bargain-basement prices.

And so it was. Prior to the establishment of the contracts, there had been little logging on the Tongass, and it was largely a vast, unexploited resource. The corporations built the mills, and the logging of the world's largest temperate rainforest began in earnest. The lower half of the Tongass became the province of the long-term contract with Ketchikan Pulp Company (KPC), a subsidiary of Louisiana Pacific, and commenced in 1954. The northern Tongass was assigned to the Alaska Pulp Corporation (APC), a wholly Japanese-owned corporation, and commenced operations in 1962. The contracts were a huge success in jump-starting the local economy. Loggers, road builders, and mill workers flocked to SE Alaska, along with a plethora of support service workers. In order to pump out the required amount of timber, the Forest Service experienced a huge boost in budget, manpower, payroll, and clout.

There was enormous support for these long-term contracts ... from Alaska's congressional delegation, from the local media, from the timber industry, from the town, and from the Forest Service itself. If the slash burning program at Mapleton were a sacred cow, the long-term timber contracts on the Tongass were the Holy Mother herself.

The 50-year long-term contract was divided chronologically into five-year operating periods. The Forest Service was required to write an environmental impact statement for each of these five-year periods. In fact, the Forest Service had just belatedly completed an EIS for the current 1989-94 operating period to KPC, and was far behind in its contractually required timber releases (almost a billion board feet). Both KPC and the Alaska congressional delegation were screaming bloody murder. The entire Ketchikan Area, as well as countless foresters and engineers brought up on detail from Down South, were frantically trying to layout roads and logging units for the long-term contract. Unfortunately, the logging plan for the 1989-94 sale wasn't working out. Planned logging roads were found to be infeasible on the ground, i.e., they couldn't be built where they were supposed to be located. Worse, the logging units themselves were yielding far fewer acres than had been planned.

It was already time to start the EIS for the next five-year operating period, but, having just struggled to complete the 1989-94 EIS, no one had the stomach to even consider the next one. It was going to take a huge effort to pull off this next EIS, and I was the interdisciplinary team (IDT) leader with responsibility for completing the entire project. Because the recently completed 1989-94 EIS was causing so much frustration, people were already anxious about the job I was going to do, even though I hadn't started yet. I wasn't concerned ... I just wanted a chance to get at all that timber!

8

Back to the Woods

(March 1998)

I took a break from packing cardboard boxes to change into my running gear, stretch, and go for my run. I opened the wolf's kennel and snapped on his leash, as he likes to run, too. Perhaps running together symbolizes the hunt to him. Who knows? Running provides my best opportunity for self-reflection, and I wanted to see what I had discovered so far in my search for the events or character make-up that was responsible for my declaring all-out warfare against the U.S. Forest Service. It still wasn't clear to me.

I recalled that I was a child of the 1960s and had been profoundly opposed to the Viet Nam war. I had petitioned for conscientious objector status, but had been turned down by my local draft board. With a draft lottery number of five, I had been nervous when I was called in for my pre-induction physical exam and determined to keep a low profile. We were taken to a locker room and ordered to strip to our shorts. A drill-sergeant came in and started yelling for us to line up by height, heel-to-toe. The guy in front of me had a big, saggy rear-end, and I wasn't about to put my toes next to his heels. So I gave him a little room. The sergeant screamed at me to move up, but I wouldn't budge. In my mind, I was still a civilian, and he had no authority over me. At the end of the day, I was classified 1-A, but ultimately was granted conscientious objector status and later received a medical discharge.

My mind turned to some of the fights I'd been in, including the one that never happened with that huge truck-driver in Idaho, who had run me off the road. Those events reminded me that I had a tendency to stand up for what I believed in and also to somewhat foolishly refuse to back down from harm's way. But these were just personality traits, they weren't all-consuming passions. I didn't see myself as someone with a chip on his shoulder, but rather as a guy who tried to avoid trouble until his back was against the wall.

The blackest mark on my soul, the deep guilt over leaving Diane and the kids, was being erased through my gradual self-awareness that my decision to leave had been an agonizing balance of goods and harms. We had been in an impossible situation, not wholly of our own creation, and continuing the marriage would have done no long-term good to Diane, the children, or my own soul. Yet the scar of that decision impressed upon me the need to do the right thing by dismissing ideology and acting upon the facts at hand. It also taught me that the "right" thing often carries a steep price.

When I first arrived on the Tongass in 1990, everything was going my way. I was 41 years old, had a gorgeous wife, a wonderful house, a prestigious job with an agency that I loved (I was renowned for my "green shorts"), and was living in a place I considered to be paradise. There was nothing wrong with this picture, as it looked remarkably like the American dream.

I finished my run, showered, and returned to my packing. Whatever time bomb lay ticking within me was hidden around the corner. I plowed onward.

(August 1990 - November 1990)

"Dance hall girls were the evenin' treat.
Empty cartridges and blood line the gutters of the street.
Men were shot down for the sake of fun,
Or just to hear the roar of their .44 guns."
-- Marshall Tucker Band, "Fire on the Mountain"

I started work on the old EIS I was assigned to re-write, which was called North Sea Otter Sound. It was a timber sale project to log about 40 mmbf of timber scattered on a group of islands off the west coast of Prince of Wales island. It was largely a grope in the dark for me, because I had never even seen the area out there, much less had any extensive field knowledge of it. Moreover, there was no one around to help or fill me in. Still I tried to do the best I could.

I got to know my boss, Walt Dortch, who was the planning staff officer. I also became well acquainted with the timber staff officer, Gene Eide (the guy responsible for all aspects of the Ketchikan Area timber program), as well as Mike Lunn, the forest supervisor (big enchilada). Their primary concern, other than how to catch halibut on the weekends, was how to get enough timber laid out fast enough for the pulp company. Things were not going well.

They told me it was taking an average of two to three weeks to lay out each logging unit, and that each unit was ending up much smaller than it was supposed to be. Too little, too late was the sad truth. When I suggested I might be able to help a wee bit, they were all ears. I told them that before I went to D.C., I had been a presale forester in coastal Oregon and had probably laid out half a billion (yep, with a 'b') board feet of timber. Furthermore, I was a distance runner and probably still able to get around in the woods pretty well. Besides, there was absolutely nothing I would rather do more than grab my field gear and go layout some timber.

They went bananas! This would get some timber laid out, maybe I could figure out some things that would help speed up the other foresters' efforts, get me some field exposure to the Tongass (which they assured me is like no other), and make me known around the area as the kind of guy who likes to help out. They quickly decided that they'd just been handed a win-win-win-win proposal. I told them I couldn't start until my wife arrived and got settled. Fine, fine, no problem. Hey, Bill just leave when you can. Boy, this was great news. Lotsa smiles.

Yvonne finally arrived, along with our furniture and personal effects. I took some administrative leave to do some much needed nesting, as well as to reunite with my new wife, who was much less impressed with Ketchikan than I was. Yvonne started her female net-working and explored the hoops she needed to go through to start up her psychotherapy practice. In a short while, she was seeing a steadily increasing number of clients out of her office in our upstairs.

I was anxious to get out to the woods, but by then, the bosses were feeling the first pangs of pressure for me to get going with the next EIS for the long-term contract. We negotiated three weeks in the woods for me. Most of the logging unit layout was being done on the Thorne Bay District over on Prince of Wales island. The ranger over there was a jolly guy named Pete Johnson, who seemed impressed both by my Washington office credentials, as well as by my willingness and ability to help with layout. Over the phone, Pete assigned me a single unit to layout during my three-week stint. I asked for six, and we settled on four.

I kissed Yvonne goodbye, and hopped a float plane for Thorne Bay. When I arrived at the ranger station to meet my assigned work partner, I found the poor guy, a young forest technician named Chuck Klee, was a wreck. Chuck was nervous about working with a high-powered forester from D.C. I was sure he felt the same way I did when, as a rookie forester, I was summoned to the ranger's office in Emmett, Idaho. I tried to put Chuck at his ease, but couldn't quite pull it off, because I found myself in a new and strange place too. There were a lot of people craning their necks to catch a glimpse of me. Chuck told me there was quite a bit of resentment toward me because I'd suggested that two to three weeks to layout a unit was way too long. Chuck said we'd never get four units done in three weeks. I gave him my best conspiratorial smile and whispered, "just watch."

We grabbed a Forest Service green rig, and headed for Coffman Cove, a small logging camp about 1 1/2 hours north of Thorne Bay. I was fascinated by the landscape, and had Chuck pull over a few times so I could examine some large old growth, some freshly logged units, some older units which were starting to regrow, and some streams. Lots of things caught my forester's eye, as I tried to assimilate the complexity of the Tongass landscape. We stashed our gear at the Forest Service trailer house where we'd bunk at Coffman Cove, and headed for the woods.

The first step in timber sale layout is to locate the precise stand of timber that's scheduled for logging. At the initial planning stage, proposed units are drawn on topographical maps (the kind with contour lines) and aerial photos. Layout foresters then use these maps and photos to orient themselves on the landscape. I wasn't familiar with the local road system and key landmarks, so it took us awhile to find our first unit. But by the time I laced up my corks (spiked logger's boots) and transferred gear into my cruiser vest, I felt like I was home again.

Foresters mark logging unit boundaries by tying brightly colored plastic flagging (1.5-inch-wide ribbon) to tree and shrub branches. This process is called "flagging." A lot of times, you find you didn't flag the boundary in the proper location, and you have to rip down the flagging and establish a new flag line. This process is called "aggravation." When you're pretty sure the flag line is correct, you reinforce the boundary by using a staple hammer to affix highly visible boundary cards. This final process is called "tagging." The goal is to make sure the boundary is highly visible, and I flagged and tagged the hell out of my units.

Chuck and I worked steadily, and got to know each other. He relaxed visibly when I cussed after taking a hard fall. He started to realize that, Washington, D.C. be damned, Bill was just another forester ... and a fair-to-good one. The first unit fell into place in several days, and we headed off in search of our next unit. This unit was numbered 577-107 and was much more difficult.

We found the general location for our unit, just beyond a unit which was currently being logged. It appeared the unit being logged was much closer to our unit than it was supposed to be. We spent some time scrutinizing this, using the maps and aerial photos and matching them to landmarks on the ground. We were then SURE that the in-progress unit was too close to ours, but decided to proceed anyhow.

We had other problems to face. Part of the timber that was planned to be included in our unit was non-commercial scrub land, composed of small, widely scattered trees, on a very wet site known as "muskeg." After a lot of walking around and taking measurements, Chuck and I decided to exclude this portion of our unit. There was simply no reason to include "dead ground," which didn't have any trees on it, because there was really nothing there to log. Moreover, these muskeg sites were obviously fragile and could be severely, if not permanently damaged by an unprofessional decision to cut a few trees simply because some office planner included them in the unit. I explained to Chuck that we were here to get some logs, not to make a mess. He agreed.

Our next problem was a biggie. The unit was planned to go to the banks of a large salmon stream, as well as one of its major tributaries. The map indicated that this was Logjam Creek, and Chuck said it was one of the most important salmon streams on the whole island. It looked like it to me, too. We noticed the map's narrative, which described the unit boundary, discussed a wide buffer strip of uncut trees adjacent to the creek, but the map showed no buffer at all. It was confusing, but there was no doubt in my mind that we were going to put in a buffer, and a big one at that. We were definitely going to protect a major salmon stream!

As we continued flagging the boundary of the unit, we discovered another unmapped tributary which flowed into Logjam Creek. We examined this stream and discovered salmon smolt in it, which meant we were going to have to flag a buffer on this small creek, too. As we ran our flag line along this "new" creek, we discovered that it branched, and that each of the branches also contained salmon smolt. By then, we were both thoroughly pissed and had given up flagging a boundary for our unit and were just walking to see what lay ahead. Finally, we decided to truncate the unit boundary on one side of this unmapped tributary, and to re-establish a new boundary on the other side.

What was planned to be a contiguous 103-acre clearcut unit, ended up as three individual chunks (separated by stream buffers), and only totaled 40 acres. It was the best I could do with the ground, given my 15 years experience as a professional forester. Nonetheless, I wanted a second opinion and requested a fisheries biologist come meet us out on the ground to see if he agreed with what we did. We worked on our other assigned units until the fisheries guy could schedule a visit. When he came out, we spent a lot of time walking and looking. He bought into our work 100 percent and complimented us on having done a good job of protecting the streams.

While working on one of our remaining units, I noticed some flagging hanging outside the area where our unit was supposed to start. Curious, I walked over to it and read what was written on the flagging. What I was looking at was a cruise plot for our unit ... one single plot which was supposed to be representative of how much timber was in our unit. And the plot wasn't even inside the unit boundary!

I called Chuck over and demanded an explanation of the district's cruising program. He hung his head and admitted that the district didn't cruise timber. What? How the bloody hell is the Forest Service supposed to know how much National Forest System timber is being sold to KPC, if they don't even perform a cruise? Where's the accountability? Chuck was horribly embarrassed and said that the cruise plot represented a half-hearted attempt to comply with the required national cruising standards. The idea was to place a single cruise plot in every unit, and that taken as a whole, there should be sufficient statistical credibility to make a volume estimate for the entirety of the 1989-94 sale, though certainly not for each individual unit.

I explained to Chuck the seriousness with which we used to take cruising on the Mapleton District ... how we tallied a volume estimate for every single tree in our unit. All of them! I pointed out that this cruise plot wasn't even within the unit boundary. He said it was a slip-shod, crash project, and that people helicoptered somewhat close to the expected unit boundaries and slammed in a plot wherever. I tried to cool down, as I knew this wasn't Chuck's fault ... that he wasn't calling the shots for the Tongass timber program.

I told Chuck this was a serious problem. If the Forest Service didn't cruise the timber, then it had no idea how much wood was supposed to be in each unit. KPC logged the unit, hauled the logs to the log dump, where they transferred them to salt water, and towed them to Thorne Bay, where they were sorted and scaled. That was a long time for "them" to have "our" logs, without our knowing how many logs they had. Suppose something happened to some of the logs? How did the Forest Service know some of the logs didn't disappear? What was going on here? Chuck just kicked the dirt unhappily and waited for my anger to pass.

We finished our final two units, and pretty soon my three weeks were up, and I had to return to the office. Although I felt refreshed from having once again spent time in the woods, I was somewhat humbled by our performance, knowing we were really strapped to finish those four units. Furthermore, I had a much better appreciation of the problems which the Thorne Bay layout foresters were facing. In a nutshell, the units the foresters were trying to layout on the ground had been poorly planned in the office. I was also concerned about the lack of a cruising program and its implications for potential log accountability violations which could promote wholesale timber theft.

My greeting back at the Ketchikan office was something like the Chicago Cubs would experience if they ever won the World Series. I had laid out 12 million feet of timber in three weeks and was the new fair-haired darling. Suddenly everyone had a lot of confidence in the new EIS I was going to produce, and they were eager for it to start. I told them I was ready to start immediately, but first needed them to authorize me to assemble the required interdisciplinary planning team and also to issue my official management direction. None of the bosses were ready to make any decisions or commitments, so nothing happened.

I returned to my office and wrapped up work on the North Sea Otter Sound EIS. I was uncomfortable with the product I was turning out, because I'd had to do it without help from any other professionals and without ever having visited the ground. But it was done and the forest supervisor, Mike Lunn, signed it. I was told to expect an appeal of the timber sale from the greenies. Grrrr!

One day I got a call from Chuck Klee. He asked me if I remembered unit 577-107? Oh, yeah. He said he and the fish biologist returned and widened the buffer along Logjam Creek. Evidently, the biologist got second thoughts about the importance of Logjam and about some previous windthrow in the area. Chuck explained exactly where the new buffer was placed, and I told him that it sounded good, and that I would support it 100 percent. He sounded relieved.

About a week later, I got another call from Chuck. This time he was really upset. He told me that one of the KPC foresters didn't like our boundaries and bullied the fisheries biologist into going out with him while he changed them. I counted to 10, then went to see the forest supervisor, Mike Lunn. I told him about KPC's changing the boundary, and asked him if that was the way he ran his Forest. Mike came absolutely unglued. He ordered me to get back out there the next day and resolve it, then to report back to him. Furthermore he ordered Gene Eide (the timber staff officer) and Mark Voight (the planning coordinator) to fly out with me and for the Thorne Bay ranger, Pete Johnson, and his staff to meet us on site. As I was boarding the float plane the next day, I noticed Eide was a no-show. Mark Voight told me he didn't expect Gene would want to get involved in any confrontation with KPC. Then Mark said that if Gene wasn't going, neither was he. So I went alone. The pilot flew me to Coffman Cove where I met Pete and his staff. I drove them out to the unit where we met the KPC forester, Jerry Kilanowski. I was pissed. Straight off I asked Jerry to walk down the road with me and told him I'd thrash him if he EVER touched one of my boundaries again. Jerry was obviously used to being the one doing the bullying, and started to bluster. He stopped short when he realized I was flat serious and was ready to have him right there and then.

We looked at the boundaries, and Ranger Johnson said he agreed with my original work. Jerry complained that we had excluded some nice Sitka spruce that he wanted to log, but Pete stood firm. We spent the day tearing out Jerry's flag line and putting the boundary back in its original location. Pete worked right along with me and asked me what Jerry and I'd talked about on our little walk. I figured what the heck, and told him. He laughed and then told me some of the history of the Forest Service's relationship with KPC.

In the early days of the contract, KPC simply put the access roads and logging units where they wanted them. The Forest Service made no attempt to even get involved in the process. When the Forest Service would send some 22-year-old newly hired forester out to inspect the logging, KPC would be notified of the incoming flight carrying a Forest Service guy. The KPC bunch would meet him at the float-plane dock and summarily throw him in the water. Before letting the poor scared kid back on the dock, they would make sure that he realized how things worked. Then the forester would go up to the cookhouse to dry out and drink coffee until it was time to fly home.

Things had changed gradually over the years, and the Forest Service had eventually redeemed their responsibility of doing their own field work. But KPC still got their way, almost all the time ... no matter what it was. Pete also explained that the mindset of many of the veteran Forest Service personnel was that their main mission was to please KPC. I told Pete that wasn't the way I worked, and he chuckled. Then he told me to watch my butt.

The summer was slipping away. Yvonne and I explored the waters around Ketchikan and did a bit of fishing. The word "bit" in the previous sentence could probably be interpreted by others as "a lot." It was the peak of the salmon run now, and we soon had a freezer full of coho. I had planted a big garden which was doing quite nicely. Green beans, broccoli, snow peas, zucchini squash, cukes, potatoes, carrots, beets, Swiss chard, and herbs. Plus the orchard was producing much better than we ever expected. The hydroponics room had tomato plants to the ceiling, covered with red fruit. I was putting my tap root down to the bedrock of the island, and wanted my wife to be happy and content here. But you can't really control someone else's happiness, eh?

In the early fall, Mike and Pete suggested that I take a float plane out to Sea Otter Sound and visit with one of the potential appellants of the North Sea Otter Sound EIS I had written. There was a staunch environmentalist, a woman named Sylvia Geraghty, who lived alone on a remote island in the middle of Sea Otter Sound. It was rumored that she wasn't happy about the plan I had written, so we scheduled a little visit. Damned greenie, was all I could think. God-damned greenie!

I hopped a float plane to Thorne Bay, where we picked up Pete and one of his staff. They were in uniform. Though I loved the Forest Service, I had never worn a uniform in my life -- ever! Just wasn't my style, I guess. I had on my usual rubber boots, jeans, and wool shirt. It was a gorgeous flight over, and Sea Otter Sound was spectacular. The islands were a mosaic of old-growth forest and regenerating clearcuts. Separating the islands were a succession of sheltered waterways. It was a picturesque fairyland.

The pilot landed the plane, and we taxied to a dock where a stout, no-nonsense-looking lady met us. I was introduced to Sylvia Geraghty, and we warily, but studiously sized each other up. My impression was of a Woodstock momma who had been toughened by living a back-to-the-land existence in a beautiful, but unforgiving locale. Pete and his staff headed up the ramp to Sylvia's house, where she had laid out some coffee and cookies.

Sylvia and I started up after them, when I noticed a small shed that seemed unusually tall. I asked her what it was, and she said it was her smokehouse. Naturally, I wanted to see it, and quizzed her on its design and function. We finally headed up the ramp again, when I spotted the chickens. Then the rabbits. We had to see them, too. And what's that over there? Oh, that's the old ice house. Well, can I see it? Why sure.

We almost made it to the house, but had to pass in front of the garden. Uh-oh. Pete finally came out to see if Sylvia and I had killed each other or what, but instead found us chatting away like bluejays. I wanted to see what else her homestead contained, but realized we were being rude to Pete. So we went inside. Our conversation made a gradual transition to the EIS, and she politely and articulately detailed her concerns. Sylvia seemed quite nervous to me, despite being in her own house, on her own land, and in the company of someone who obviously admired her lifestyle and was doing his limited best to be charming.

The day passed quickly, and soon it was time to leave. Sylvia smiled sweetly and said she was going to file an appeal. I was crushed and felt I'd failed. On the plane ride back, Pete asked me what I thought of Sylvia. "Damned greenie," was all I muttered, and looked out the window at the magic that lay below.

9

The Pleasure Palace

(November 1990 - September 1991)

"The big fish eat the little fish.
The little fish gotta be fast.
That's the law of the fishes, Momma.
You gotta move your ass.
Move your ass."
-- The Radiators, "Law of the Fishes"

"Hide it in a hiding place, where no one ever goes.
Put it in your pantry with your cupcakes.
It's a little secret, just the Robinson's affair.
Most of all, we've got to hide it from the kids."
-- Paul Simon, "Mrs. Robinson"

By Thanksgiving of 1990, the end of my first year in Ketchikan, I finally pestered my boss, Walt, into giving me the green light to start planning the EIS for the next KPC five-year operating period. There was unanimity that I should get started, but Walt hedged because there were a lot of questions still unresolved ... like how big the timber sale was supposed to be and where it was going to be located. And who was going to be assigned to my planning team. I was anxious to get going because a day's delay at the onset is effectively the same as one lost at project's end, or crunch time. And a false start could actually be more costly than doing absolutely nothing. So I was pretty insistent about getting some basic ground rules established.

I showed Walt that the first step of the planning process, according to the Alaska Regional Guide, is the development of a Multi-Entry-Layout-Plan (MELP), which is a logging and road plan for ALL the logging units that can be made out of the forest planning base. I convinced Walt and Gene Eide that I better get going on this because it was the framework for the rest of the planning process. And I reminded them of the continuing disaster they were facing on the 1989-94 sale because of the poorly planned units. They nodded soberly. They assigned a GS-11 forester, Bill Nightingale, to my supervision. I also temporarily borrowed a soils scientist.

Walt had placed me in charge of Ketchikan's Geographic Information System (GIS) shop. GIS is a high-tech computer system that blends conventional tabular database information with mapping coordinates. It has the dual capability of performing numerical analysis, as well as producing high-quality maps. I had never taken the time to learn the software, but could grasp its potential. I had my eye on a talented Native Alaskan analyst working in my GIS shop, a Tlingit Indian named James Llanos, and stole him ... well, from myself, I guess, and assigned him to my new planning team.

It was a humble, rag-tag collection ... and we weren't really sure of any of the details of what we were supposed to be doing. But it was a start. The first morning, we were hunched over a drafting table, looking at maps and aerial photos, trying to design a couple of decent timber sale units. We sweated, we swore, we shouted, we soared. Damnit, we got excited! Other people walked into my office to see what we're doing. And they got excited, too. Some of them stayed. Pretty soon the whole Ketchikan Area was abuzz that Shoaf had started planning the next long-term sale.

Within a month, the project took off like a fire running upslope through dry timber. There were Forest Service-wide vacancy announcements soliciting professionals for my planning team ... soils scientists, landscape architects, wildlife and fisheries biologists, writer-editors, and more foresters. Walt rented us a suite of offices across the street from the main office, because he didn't want anything to disrupt our work. Computers were being set up and phone systems wired. I was ensconced in a huge private office, replete with its own conference room. People who a month earlier didn't want to have anything to do with the new EIS were falling all over themselves to see what was going on. Big-shot managers from the regional office in Juneau showed up for a show-me tour. Alaska Sen. Ted Stevens even sent his staffers to get an eyeful of the operation.

And this is what we had to show them. I had James download the Tongass Forest Plan database and extract the timber base. This showed the precise location of all the timber that the Ketchikan Area of the Tongass was supposed to be able to feasibly and legally log. I then had him plot this timber base on the same scale as our high quality topographical maps, which were themselves computer generated from precise orthographic aerial photos. We carefully aligned these topo maps with James' plots of the timber base, then placed them on a "light table," which is a big flat sheet of frosted plexiglass, with fluorescent light bulbs underneath. On top of these paired maps, we'd lay the corresponding colored aerial photograph. With the light shining through from underneath, we could simultaneously see all three map layers.

This process allowed us to specifically delineate the entire timber base on fixed scales maps, with topographic and aerial photo collaboration. So, as we examined each acre of the timber base, we were able to see its topography, vegetation, and a host of other features. We then engineered logging units and road systems on these composite maps, using visible, tangible ground characteristics.

It was a neat setup. Logging system engineers took the first pass at designing the units and roads, then passed the proposal on to the other resource specialists for their review. Designs were checked for fragile soils, unstable slopes, fisheries impacts, visual disturbance, and a whole host of concerns. It was our intent to ground truth our planned units out in the woods to make sure they were truly viable. In other words, we had to check that what we were "seeing" back in the office matched what that particular piece of forest really looked like on the ground, and that our proposed logging plan could be carried out.

At this point in the process, nothing else really mattered. Our mission wasn't to build campgrounds or to protect Bambi ... we were there to clearcut the forest. ALL of it! And in fact that's the whole essence of what we were doing. This was a composite plan to clearcut every acre that we were legally entitled and physically able to log, within the confines of forestry science, law, policy, and regulation. It could be cut slowly or quickly, but we had no doubt that it all would get cut.

Our visitors were generally impressed. In essence, we showed them where and how much timber our project area contained, as well as a viable way to log it. When we'd receive a stern reminder that the last logging plan proved to be non-viable on the ground, we'd nod our heads and show them why. We'd 'light-up' the previously planned units on our composite maps and point out roads that were designed to be built right up the gut of salmon streams, of logging proposals to yard logs down vertical cliffs ... of all sorts of problems that should have been eliminated by taking a hard look, such as we were doing.

Nonetheless, the visitors would reiterate the need to make sure our logging plan was feasible. The whole Ketchikan Area had a bellyful of out-to-lunch logging plans, and ours damn well better work. We assured them they would. Just before the office door would close, a head would invariably pop back in and tell us to make sure to find plenty of timber. Lots of it.

In order to determine just how much timber we were finding, James digitized our planned logging units back into the computer. This meant that he used geographically precise control points on the map composites to input the units' shape, size, and location into the GIS database, and then interface it with the tabular portion. He then queried the database and made reports of unit size and approximate volume of loggable timber.

But all wasn't happy at Mudville. The people who had done the office planning for the 1989-94 operating period were not at all pleased to hear me say they had done a shoddy job. And the use of innovation was a departure from the good ol' way of doing things at Ketchikan. And was all this scrutiny really necessary. Just who was this guy from Washington, D.C. anyhow? And why did he have his planning team over there all by itself in that fancy office? Paranoia, jealousy, and fear brewed into a bitter stew in a very hot caldron.

The Tongass had been squarely in the public spotlight for years.

To conservationists, it represented the jewel of our National Forests and was like the Holy Grail to the faithful. Championed by George Miller (D, CA), the chairman of the House Natural Resources Committee, there was a hue and cry to save the Tongass. In opposition was the timber industry, stung by the spotted owl defeat in the Pacific Northwest. Championing their cause was the powerful Alaska congressional delegation, consisting of Senators Frank Murkowski and Ted Stevens, along with Alaska's single congressman, Don Young.

I made it very clear on which side of the issue I stood. I told one and all that I had logged my way through forestry school and wanted permission to cut the first tree on my timber sale. There was unanimity that I would be awarded this privilege.

In November 1990, a compromise bill was written into law, the "Tongass Timber Reform Act" (TTRA). This was the first and only piece of environmental legislation enacted for the management of a single National Forest. As Forest Service legal beagles figured out how the new law would change the way things worked on the Tongass, rumors were rampant, but clear management direction and decisions were curiously absent. My team received increasingly urgent encouragement to go-go-go, but correspondingly decreasing instructions on where or how to go.

Yvonne became increasingly unhappy in Ketchikan and was clearly annoyed that I liked it so much. We planned a one-year anniversary trip to Hawaii, and on our flight, she took my hand and said that life was short, and that she didn't want to spend any more of hers in Alaska ... or with me. After my initial sense of betrayal passed, I was more chagrinned with my own naivety than overwhelmed by grief. In truth, I probably had longer and more meaningful relationships in junior high school.

When we returned, she moved out, and I never saw her again. One day I came home from work, and the only thing in my living room was a lawn chair. The next day at work, I tried to find some humor in it and told some of the members of my planning team that at least I had ended up with both of the pyrex measuring cups. The next day I came home from work, and there was only one cup. I took this as an indication that she was staying with one of my employees.

Yvonne was long gone when I attended court for my divorce

hearing before the judge. After meeting the obligations imposed by the court, I had a grand total of $101.52 to my name, a $1,100/month home mortgage payment, and a $300/month divorce loan payment. I went back to my use-it-up, make-it-do, wear-it-out philosophy and survived the next six weeks on a diet consisting largely of rhubarb and fish.

But the Forest Service wasn't about to give me time to grieve. As Ken Kesey said in Sometimes a Great Notion, "... there's cats to kill, and contracts to fill."

The first crack in the Tongass wall occurred in the early summer of 1991 when the timber staff officer, Gene Eide, sauntered over to our office and asked me exactly how much timber we were finding. I had by now downloaded all James' information to a micro-computer and showed Gene, watershed-by-watershed, how much viably loggable timber we had identified in our MELP. He nodded, then pointed to a second column on the computer screen and asked me what that was. I explained that was how much the Tongass Forest Plan timber base said was there. Only about half of the timber base was loggable when looked at on a site-specific basis.

We exchanged a long, knowing look. Then silence. I told him that he was looking at the real reason the field layout foresters were having such a hard time making the 1989-94 logging units work on the ground. It wasn't inexperience or incompetence on their part, but rather that much of what they were being ordered to include within their units was simply unloggable.

I got out some aerial photos and maps and showed Gene why much of the ground was inappropriate for logging ... too close to salmon streams (which were everywhere), too steep, too wet from muskegs, not enough merchantable timber, not suitable for road construction and too isolated to make helicopter logging economical, and so on. I told him that the previous EIS simply had failed to examine the proposed logging units in sufficient detail to weed out these unloggable areas. After another protracted silence, Gene asked if anyone else knew this. I said no, and he left.

Within 10 minutes, Gene returned with Walt in tow. He told me to show Walt, and I did. Walt was floored. Gene didn't stay around for a re-hash of the information, but gave me a wink as he left, and told me to keep this under my hat. Walt stayed to discuss it.

The level of logging permitted on any national forest was calculated by dividing the estimated volume in the timber base by the rotation age (the time interval between successive "crops" of trees). By federal law, this logging level was supposed to be fixed, non-declining, and capable of being maintained indefinitely into the future. Furthermore this logging level was not allowed to cause declines in other forest resources, such as wildlife, fish, water, range, and recreation. This law, the Multiple Use Sustained Yield Act of 1960, was to modern forestry what Einstein's theory of relativity was to nuclear physics.

The whole thing was analogous to a person's going on a vacation for 10 days and having $1,000 to spend. Obviously, if they were required to spend a sustainable, non-declining daily amount, then that amount would necessarily be equal to or less than $100 per day. Same thing for the annual logging level, which was formally called the "allowable sale quantity" (ASQ).

If my team's data were corroborated in other areas of the Tongass, then there was some pretty conclusive evidence that the current logging levels on the Tongass were too high ... in fact, almost double what they should be. I told Walt that everyone I had talked to elsewhere on the Tongass had run into the same phenomena. Walt gulped and a thin sheen of sweat appeared on his forehead.

Moreover, the Tongass allowable sale quantity (ASQ) presupposed a rotation age of 100 years. I pointed out that Forest Service data showed that Tongass trees grew so slowly that at 100 years the average tree was only projected to be 10.8 inches in diameter. Not only would it be infeasible to log such small trees (they wouldn't be strong enough to support the necessary logging rigging), but it would be difficult to manufacture them into any type of product that could compete economically within the world market. Furthermore, my team could find no units where the recommended rotation age was less than 120-150 years. Even then, the unit was not expected to BEGIN to exhibit old-growth characteristics until an age of 250 years.

In the scope of the vacation spending metaphor, this was like spending $100 per day, when the trip was really going to last 25 days, not 10. Walt's forehead started to drip. Mine was a torrent.

And just like Star Trek's Captain Kirk needed warp speed to

evade the Klingons, the Forest Service needed a high logging level to meet the demands of the two long-term contracts. Less was not an option. From there on in, I felt like Scotty on the Enterprise. Captain Kirk: "Take her to warp speed, Scotty (find more timber, Shoaf)." The engineer: "She'll nae take the strain, Captain (do you want out-to-lunch logging units that won't work on the ground, Eide?)"

Around this time, forest supervisor Mike Lunn was reassigned to the Siskyou National Forest in Oregon. In his stead was Dave Rittenhouse, a guy I knew from D.C. Lunn's deputy supervisor, Joy Berg, was also reassigned and replaced by Bob Vaught. To complete the house-sweeping, Thorne Bay Ranger Pete Johnson was also transferred Down South and replaced by Anne Archie. It was inconclusive whether heads were rolling or rats were leaving the ship.

Some of my employees sensed that something weird was going on and realized that my planning team was going to be a brutal, thankless hotseat. I threw an alleged fisheries biologist off the team for abject non-performance. Another fellow, a landscape architect named Michael Terzich, felt he should be on the fast-track and received a transfer. Michael's claim to fame on the Ketchikan Area had been to select the color of paint for the refurbishing of the outside of the Federal Building in which the Forest Service was housed. For some inexplicable reason, he chose a god-awful shade of pink, which earned the building the nickname, "The Pleasure Palace."

Landscape architects were hard to come by, so to replace Michael, I reluctantly had the landscape architect from Thorne Bay temporarily transferred to my team. This guy's name was Robert Wetherell, and his reputation preceded him. Robert insisted that 1989-94 logging units be reduced in size so that they would meet the modicum of visual management standards and guidelines dictated by the forest plan. He was right, but nobody liked it, because loggable timber was hard enough to come by and his insistence on playing by the rules was making it even more difficult to get enough timber to KPC.

I remember walking into my office one day, and seeing Michael there with a tall, woodsy-looking guy. Michael introduced me to Robert Wetherell ... all 6'6" of him, with a long blonde ponytail and piercing eyes. Robert and I glowered at each other. "Damned timber beast" daggers leapt from his eyes. "Damned greenie" from mine.

We made no attempt to shake hands. We just stared.

[Several years later Robert said that Michael had told him that there was absolutely no chance that he would ever get along with Shoaf. To forget it, that I was just a rampant timber beast, with no regard for visual niceties. Ironically, Robert went on to become one of the closest and dearest friends I have ever had in my life.]

A few of us flew up to Juneau for a timber meeting. At the end of the day's session, Gene and Walt headed off to the bar to cry in their beer over their frustrations at having the 1989-94 logging units failing to meet planned timber volume expectations. They had an idea and wanted me to join them. I told them I was going for my run, but would meet them later for dinner.

That night they explained their idea. They wanted me to do an extensive, precise study of how much falldown (or underrun) was occurring on the 1989-94 sale. In other words, the sale had been planned for 960 mmbf ... almost a billion board feet. How much would it actually yield? I told them that I simply didn't have time to do such an involved study, especially if I was supposed to continue to go-go-go on the new environmental impact statement.

Walt looked at me, basking in the glow of a coupla Millers. Shoaf, do you understand what I've just asked you to do? Do you understand I am your supervisor? Do you understand that you have just been given a direct order by your supervisor? Do you understand that if you refuse to execute this order, that you are subject to ... OK, Walt, I get the idea. He beamed.

Gene was in his late 50s, or early 60s then. He had thinning, red hair, a beer gut, and smoked like a chimney. He played a corn pone, good ol' boy act, but had a cunning mind. He wore double layers of green underwear. Walt, on the other hand, was 30-something, with intense hazel/green eyes, and blazing sharp intellect. Articulate, fun-loving, and wholly irreverent, Walt made more than a few of the hard-line old boys within the agency just a trifle nervous. Walt and Gene hung out together, but there were periods when it was apparent there was some conflict between them.

My team and I started the infamous "Falldown Analysis" on July 8, 1991. We started by mapping the planned locations for all the 1989-94 logging units and overlaying them with the actual location of where they were finally laid out on the ground. We used the same basic process we were using on our MELP, i.e., high-quality aerial photos and topographic maps. We called in field layout foresters, timber sale administrators, and other personnel to make sure we had the best available information. What we found was that falldown, or underrun, was clipping along at about 25 percent. But we found something else. Something bad.

Someone apparently issued direction for the field layout foresters to make up for falldown by expanding the units into areas that hadn't been planned for logging in the EIS process. My whole team was shocked, as there were a number of problems associated with this practice. I flat out asked the Ketchikan planning coordinator Mark Voight if this so-called unit expansion policy were even legal, and he emphatically said it was not. As Mark explained, the sole intent of the National Environmental Policy Act of 1969 (NEPA) was that for all significant proposed federal actions, the government was required to formulate alternative actions, disclose the environmental consequences, and inform the public throughout the entire process.

The unit expansion policy, which appeared overnight on the Ketchikan Area, was a covert operation. There was no analysis of environmental consequences and no public disclosure. Mark said he was aware it was going on but didn't know how widespread it was. I told him it had covered 5,000 acres so far. He looked at me incredulously.

I buttonholed Walt, and we had a long, private heart-to-heart talk. I told him what I'd found out about the unit expansion problem. I told him about my conversation with Mark Voight and his conviction that it was illegal. I explained that the salient item here was not that the boundaries were being changed, but that the expansion constituted a borrowing of future timber supplies to make up for current shortfalls. I told him that if we were to discount the 5,000 acres of expansion which had been included into the layout, that overall falldown was approaching the 50 percent predicted by my team's MELP. This meant we were logging the Tongass at twice the rate which could be sustained ... even faster given that the 100-year rotation age was bogus. This violated policy, regulation, law, forestry science, and most of the Ten Commandments.

Even worse, because each successive timber sale proposed to

log the "best of the rest," the substandard timber was simply being pushed farther into the future. When the time came to log the substandard stuff, which might prove to be almost entirely unloggable, there would be no more good stuff to expand unit boundaries into to make up the shortfall. It was a very grim look into the future.

Walt asked me if I remembered the unit I had tagged where KPC had tried to move the boundaries. I grimaced to indicate I did indeed remember 577-107. He said Eide sent a coupla foresters back to the unit to expand it by 30 acres, and in doing so had reduced the size of some of my fish stream buffers. He said Ranger Pete Johnson had come unglued and had refused to sign off on the changes. Then he said that Pete was gone now. Mike Lunn was gone, as was his second-in-command. Dave Rittenhouse, Bob Vaught, and Anne Archie were the new centurions, and they weren't nice people. Walt said to watch my back, and I echoed the warning to him.

My planning team was pretty spooked. They could see what was happening, but didn't want to get involved in something that might get them in trouble with management. These people had families and careers to think about. Nonetheless, we published the Falldown Report as requested and called for an immediate cessation of further unit expansion. We said it was illegal.

> "The planning team strongly recommends that the Forest Supervisor reconsider the decision to expand 1989-94 units outside the boundaries established by the ROD [Record of Decision]. This unit expansion policy has dubious NEPA [National Environmental Policy Act] sanction ... and will ultimately lead to less volume available to KPC during the life of the long-term sale."

Tongass management was caught in a bad place. There was no way they could continue to supply the amount of timber necessary to meet the obligations of two long-term timber contracts and at the same time comply with environmental law, much less honestly disclose to the public the true consequences of unsustainable logging practices. So local Tongass managers seemingly made the conscious decision to elevate contractual compliance above both environmental law and honest disclosure. And who can blame them? Alaska's congressional delegation was applying white-hot pressure to keep the Forest Service's nose to the long-term contract grindstone. Sen.

Ted Stevens went so far as to require weekly briefings on how many logging units and how much timber volume were released to KPC. Caught between the twin grist stones of the timber industry and the congressional delegation, local managers prepared to swat the planning team leader who had caught them with their hand in the cookie jar.

In August 1991, two weeks after my team published the "Falldown Report," I was asked to prepare a briefing for the managers. The presentation was to focus on the status of my team's project, as well as the resources and management decisions needed to deliver the project on time. I prepared some graphical handouts and had a semi-rehearsed speech. I had involved my team in the preparation of the presentation and had secured permission for them to attend the meeting.

The U.S. Forest Service was nothing, if not a paramilitary organization. The management team consisted of the forest supervisor, deputy forest supervisor, and the three district rangers. These people were considered "line." Also included were the forest staff officers, including timber, engineering, administration, planning, fish & wildlife, and recreation. There were about 12 members of the management team, all at or above GS-13. My own rating was GS-12, so I guess I was considered sub-staff.

I was semi-nervous about the presentation. I had spent most of my Forest Service career either in the woods or programming computers. I had never been to charm school and was in no way a polished public speaker. The meeting was being held in a conference room of the fanciest hotel in town, as the Forest Service didn't have a large enough meeting room of their own. When my employees and I arrived, they dispersed to seats around the table, while I made my stand-up talk. I was at one end of the table, and forest supervisor Dave Rittenhouse was at the other.

I finished the presentation, which lasted 10, maybe 15 minutes, and breathed a sigh of relief. I thought it had gone OK, as I remembered to make eye contact with the audience and hadn't swallowed my tongue. Moreover, my talk hadn't dealt with any of the timber supply issues which were of such concern, but rather focused on timelines and necessary personnel, office space, computers, and things like that were needed to enable us to meet our deadline.

All of a sudden Rittenhouse verbally ripped into me with a ferocity and anger that was shocking. He started shouting and attacked my professional credibility by claiming that I was doing a terrible job and had a bad attitude. As his tirade exploded, I was taken back, because it was totally out of context with my rather boring, matter-of-fact presentation. I barely heard his words, and actually they didn't matter, because it was so much, "Blah, blah, blah, BAD DOG, blah, blah, blah!" As Rittenhouse ranted, I looked around the table and everyone was frozen in place, shocked. My employees were horrified, but I noticed smug smiles on the faces of some of the management team members. Rittenhouse went on for maybe five minutes, then my boss, Walt, came to my rescue. I don't remember what Walt said, other than to call a time-out, as I hurriedly gathered up my stuff to leave.

I was absolutely humiliated, as I felt that my Forest Service career was now unofficially over. Rittenhouse had publicly denounced me as a worthless cull, in front of the entire management team and all my employees. Everything good I had ever accomplished in my career, every chance for advancement had vaporized in the hotel meeting room. I was crushed.

As I rushed for the exit, deputy forest supervisor Bob Vaught caught up and followed me out the door. Vaught was really upset, and he put his hand on my shoulder and said that "Rittenhouse was totally out of line." He said I was "being set up for something," and that he would try to find out what it was. Those were his exact words. It was amazing that I couldn't remember exactly what Rittenhouse had said ... maybe because I was so taken back. But Vaught's words were so welcome that I remembered them verbatim.

The next day was my regularly scheduled day off, and I tried to put the shellacking out of my mind. A few people called at home to console me, but there wasn't anything anyone could do. The damage was done. To this day the incident is referred to as the "OK Corral."

Walt met with me on Monday behind closed doors. I asked him what I had done to precipitate Rittenhouse's tirade. Walt said that maybe I failed to complete all the politically astute kowtowing and groveling at the get-go, but that there was nothing contentious in anything I had said. Then he said he was having trouble with Rittenhouse, too, as well as with the top brass at the regional office in Juneau. He said they were uncomfortable with making any decisions and were getting pissed because Walt (and I) kept pressing them. I told Walt I couldn't do my job without some basic direction ... like WHERE and HOW BIG the timber sale was supposed to be. He just shook his head.

A few days later, Vaught called me into his office and was very much the cold fish. He told me he felt Rittenhouse's blowup resulted from communication shortcomings on my part. I told him that it was important to me to do an excellent job ... that merely doing an OK job wasn't enough. We discussed some communication briefings I could do.

A short time later, Vaught called Voight and me into his office. He was on the phone when we walked in, so we seated ourselves in the chairs at the far end of his office. When he hung up, Vaught turned and stared out the window, away from us. After maybe 30 seconds of silence, Bob said quietly that he had found out that his career was tied to doing everything that the regional office asked him to do. And that was exactly what he intended to do. Then he was silent.

Mark and I just looked at each other and waited. After maybe three to four minutes of silence passed, with Vaught still staring out the window, Mark and I realized that the meeting, such as it was, was over. Unsettled, we walked out. There is a saying on the Ketchikan Area that he or she, "has had a sip of the water." Many come to the Tongass with ideals of ethical professional conduct and resource stewardship, but once they realize how irrevocably their careers are controlled by the power brokers of the agency, they go with the flow. Vaught didn't simply have a sip of the water, he was baptized in the stuff. Our paths seldom crossed after that.

Within weeks, I was removed from responsibility to supervise the GIS shop. Bill Nightingale was removed from my supervision and promoted to the same position as mine, and placed in charge of another project. Another planning team leader, Larry Lunde, was quickly hired ... so that where I had previously been solely in charge, there were now three of us.

10

Good Soldiers

(September 1991 - July 1992)

"Onward Christian soldiers
Marching as to war,
With the cross of Jesus
Going on before."
    -- Sabine Baring, Arthur Sullivan

"So I told him, that he'd better
Shut his mouth,
And do his job like a man."
    -- Peter, Paul, & Mary, "The Great Mandella"

Ironically, as plans for my timber sale firmed, questions surfaced more quickly than they could be resolved. The newly passed Tongass Timber Reform Act (TTRA) had seemingly dictated that individual timber offerings be smaller than the five-year, 960 mmbf behemoths of the past, of which 1989-94 was the most recent. Consequently, rather than write a single EIS for 960 mmbf, the local managers decided to have four individual sales: Lab Bay (85 mmbf), Polk Inlet (125 mmbf), North Revilla (200 mmbf), and Central Prince of Wales (290 mmbf). Lab Bay and Polk Inlet were contracted to private consulting firms which specialized in the production of environmental impact statements, with Larry Lunde acting as the Forest

Service representative. Nightingale was responsible for North Revilla, and I led the CPOW effort, which at 290 mmbf, was the largest timber sale in the nation.

Eide told me an interesting story about the derivation of the 290 mmbf target for the CPOW timber sale. He and Walt had gone up to Juneau to meet with the regional forester, Mike Barton. Walt made a pitch for a single 600 mmbf timber sale, to be led by me. His rationale was that it would be much cheaper and expedient to do one environmental impact statement than four. Barton allegedly hit the roof and told Walt that his big sale, CPOW, would be less than half that amount. Walt said OK, 300 mmbf. To which, Barton screamed, "I said LESS than half that amount!" Walt said, "OK, 290 mmbf." Some science, huh?

Because everyone knew that the 1989-94 long-term offering was going to yield much less than its promised 960 mmbf, it became necessary to place one of the new sales on the fast track to ensure KPC would receive its contractually mandated supply of Tongass timber. CPOW was chosen to be first out of the gate, and the pressure to complete it in a timely manner was enormous.

The contract between Ketchikan Pulp & Paper Company and the U.S. Forest Service was signed July 26, 1951. The basic intent of the contract was that KPC would construct and operate a pulp mill, with operations to commence July 1, 1954. In return for this, the Forest Service agreed to provide sufficient Tongass timber to run the mill at "full scale operation" for a period of 50 years, ending June 30, 2004. The caveat was that the Forest Service was not obligated to provide more than 8.25 mmmbf over the course of the 50-year contract. When this amount was reached, all bets were off. Furthermore, "full scale mill production" was defined as a 27.5 mmbf annual minimum and a 192.5 mmbf maximum.

TTRA was passed in November 1990 and made unilateral modifications to the long-term contract. Unfortunately, contractual law doesn't support unilateral modifications. I remember having a discussion with Alaska regional timber director Gene Chelstad and commenting that this unilateral contract modification in essence gave KPC a "golden parachute," meaning that KPC could sue the Forest Service for breach of contract anytime they felt like it, and virtually be guaranteed a victory. Chelstad agreed, with a sparkle in his eye. He told me he had a recent conversation with KPC's timber manager, Owen Graham, in which Owen said, "It's not a question of IF the Forest Service is going to buy our pulp mill, it's WHEN."

One of the unilateral contractual modifications made by TTRA was a clause which required the Forest Service to "seek to specify sufficient Offerings to maintain a Current Timber Supply in all Offering Areas that totaled at least three years of operations..." According to the contract, this could range from a minimum of 82.5 mmbf (three times their minimum production rate of 27.5 mmbf) to a maximum of 577.5 mmbf (three times their maximum production rate of 192.5 mmbf). In other words, the Forest Service had to write enough EISs to build up a shelf-stock of timber equal to three years of KPC's pulp mill production.

Instead of following the contract, the Forest Service took it as a given that they would supply KPC with their maximum entitlement of 8.25 mmmbf over the life of the contract, even though this amount was clearly a ceiling and not a floor. Furthermore, to meet this amount by June 30, 2004, they decided they were duty-bound to provide KPC an average of 205 mmbf per year, even though this amount clearly exceeded the 192.5 mmbf maximum annual amount allowed by the contract. And nothing less would do.

It seemed the Forest Service was placing KPC's interests above the government's, and was willing to operate outside contract specifications to do so. I don't know who was making these decisions on the part of the Forest Service, but it sure wasn't anyone that I talked to on a regular basis.Except for Dortch, everyone agreed with me in private that the Forest Service was outside the contract, but in public would back the Forest Service policy to the hilt. Walt and I were of a common mind, and he agreed with me both in private and in public. As Walt spoke with more senior level people than I, he paid a more immediate price for his dissent.

What I became steadfastly incapable of absorbing was why the Forest Service would build a series of timber sale EISs upon a foundation that was so blatantly flawed. It made no sense. The Forest Service continually wrung its hands over litigation by greenie organizations, but nonetheless seemed determined to produce a series of timber sales that were dead-on-arrival in the 9th Circuit Court of

Appeals. My planning team wildlife biologist, Norm Matson, continually told me he thought the Forest Service was trying to "throw it." I recalled Gene Chelstad's telling me that he was going to let the National Environmental Policy Act (the law that requires EISs for major timber sales) break the long-term contract.

This was an exceedingly high-stakes game. KPC was a multinationally owned corporation that delivered most of its product to the Pacific Rim nations. During the cold war years, the United States definitely preferred Japan's getting its raw materials from Alaska, as opposed to Siberia. Now that the cold war had thawed, the new buzz phrase was the "balance of trade with Japan." There were powerful international, national, and local forces competing to influence the outcome, which was not just maintaining commerce, but also the management and welfare of our country's largest National Forest.

My marching orders were to produce a timber sale totalling 290 mmbf from my 520,000-acre project area. While my team and I had found only about half as much timber as the Tongass computer models had predicted, we had a solid, feasible logging plan for each unit, all mapped and drawn in great detail on high-quality topographical maps and aerial photos. We felt confident we could deliver 290 mmbf and still avoid logging the 35 percent of the available timber that the Forest Service had promised would be set aside for the management of wildlife and scenic viewsheds.

Not only had the Forest Service promised the public that these wildlife and visual reserves would remain unlogged, but Rittenhouse, Dortch, and Eide, as well as the staff officers for recreation, fish and wildlife, and engineering, signed written direction to my planning team to avoid these areas.

Everything was skating along relatively smoothly until I read the Labor Day, 1991, edition of the "Ketchikan Daily News." That was the day the formal, legal Notice of Intent to produce an EIS for CPOW would be published, and I wanted to see what my sale looked like in print. What I saw blew me away! My project area had been reduced by 200,000 acres. I was now going to have to come up with 290 mmbf from 320,000 acres, instead of from 520,000.

I stewed the whole holiday weekend, then stormed into Walt's office Tuesday morning. What happened to my project area? Where did the 200,000 acres go? Walt told me it was all a mistake, and just to proceed as if my project area were still 520,000 acres. He'd get it corrected. But he didn't. So I asked others. Eide, Vaught, Rittenhouse, the regional office ... what's going on? How big is my project area really? Everyone, but everyone, assured me it was 520,000 acres, and to just ignore this little mistake. Great, correct it in the newspaper. But they wouldn't either.

I kept pushing for a resolution to the problem of the missing 200,000 acres, finally scheduling a meeting with Rittenhouse and Vaught on November 25, 1991. After listening to my pitch, they made a decision, which I wrote up and filed in the official Planning Record.

> "The new decision is to eliminate volume from contingency areas [the deleted 200,000 acres] for Alternatives 2-4, which will cause these alternatives to fall considerably below target volume of 290 mmbf. The team will then develop a new alternative which would get the target volume from the reduced project area, but would yield at best marginally acceptable environmental consequences."

In other words, they conceded that my team simply couldn't lose 200,000 acres and still achieve the targeted 290 mmbf without substantially degrading the environment. I told my team and implemented the bosses' orders for the new EIS alternatives. A few days later, December 2, 1991, Rittenhouse and Vaught changed their minds. Maybe those environmental consequences wouldn't be so bad after all. They rescinded their instructions of the previous week and told me that all the CPOW alternatives had to produce 290 mmbf from 200,000 fewer acres.

Mark Voight's was the next head to roll. The Tongass was still using 1979 aerial photographs, which were simply outdated. On all other National Forests that I had worked on, photos were updated every five years or so. There was simply so much logging and road building, which modified the features of the landscape, that it was necessary to schedule a new set of photos. There was a lot of expense in new photos, but they were used in many aspects of our activities ... from orienteering in the woods to the type of logging systems planning my team was doing.

Mark had been pushing the regional office to secure new photos, but was meeting stonewall resistance. Mark was brilliant, articulate, and extremely knowledgeable in his position as GS-12 NEPA coordinator. He could also be tactless and abrasive. He finally bullied the regional office into obtaining new photos, but shortly after found himself demeaned into taking some basic entry-level NEPA training. Mark not only could have taught the course, he could have taught the instructors. Mark took personal affront and refused to attend. Vaught told him to go or it was his job, and Mark told him to shove the job. He was gone.

When the new photos arrived, my planning team started transferring our planned logging units from the old 1979 photos to the new 1991 ones, so as to use the most current information available. We set up light tables all over the office, and all of us pitched in for the task. I can't remember who was first, but within minutes of starting, someone yelled for everyone to come take a look. There was one of our newly planned units looking oh-so-good on the 1979 photos and already clearcut on the 1991 photo. What? We looked at it and discovered it was immediately adjacent to a 1989-94 logging unit which had been expanded to gobble ours up.

We went back to our respective tables and pretty soon someone else hollered out. Same thing. From there on, it sounded like someone was making popcorn ... pop (a unit's gone), pop-pop (two are gone), pop-pop-pop-pop (they're all gone!). No wonder the regional office had dragged their feet about getting new photos ... they simply didn't want anyone to see what was occurring on the ground on the Tongass. For years, KPC had run amok, and the Forest Service hadn't seemed to care, as long as KPC and Alaska's congressmen stayed off their backs. Well, the hawk was coming home to roost.

I called Walt and Eide over and showed them the situation. Walt got quiet and nervous, while Eide made a great display of e-mailing a plea to stop the unit expansion because it was compromising the new logging units. I told them it was like eating all the cookie dough before any baking got done, and to not expect many freshly baked cookies.

On Christmas Eve 1991, I received written notification that my project area was officially 320,000 acres ... another timber sale (Control Lake) for 187 mmbf was going to be planned on the 200,000-acre annexed portion. There was to be no relief in the 290 mmbf target. In fact, I was not permitted to develop any alternative below that level. Furthermore, I was directed to pursue logging units on the wildlife and scenic viewshed reserve areas which the Forest Service had promised would be deferred from logging. Merry Christmas, Love, Walt. Actually, to Walt's credit, someone higher up had drafted this direction letter for his signature, and Walt refused to sign it. Mark Voight, shortly before he resigned, signed for him.

This was a whole new ball of wax. For one thing, this revised direction meant that my planning team had just wasted four months of time on a project with a tight timeline just because management couldn't make up their mind WHERE the timber sale was supposed to be. For another thing, we were now ordered to implement logging in wildlife and scenic viewshed zones which the Forest Service had promised would be deferred from logging. But most important of all, this new timber sale (Control Lake) was going to take another big bite out of the area's remaining timber supply.

Little towns had sprung up on Prince of Wales island as a natural succession to the original KPC logging camps. These towns' fates were ultimately tied to the local logging industry. Nearly everyone in those towns rode to work in a crew crummy, spent the day in the woods, and came home at night. There simply wasn't any other work to be had. There was enormous local pressure to keep logging levels high to ensure community stability. Nonetheless it was becoming increasingly apparent that the logging levels couldn't be maintained for long. But no one dared to mention a reduction in logging in order to save something for the future. People were figuratively burning their walls to heat their house. The general response to this obvious paradox was right out of "The Emperor's New Clothes."

The new management direction drove my planning team nutso. I gave everybody a coupla days to 'kick the dirt' and complain about wasting all that time, then convened everyone, and restarted from scratch. Or rather scratch minus 200,000 acres.

One of the new problems my planning team now faced was how to come up with the necessary volume. We had our comprehensive logging plan which identified all the specific logging units that were available. There were big units and small units, but basically the individual units averaged about 40 acres in size. Our logging plan consisted of spatially isolated units, as well as clusters of adjacent units. The National Forest Management Act (NFMA) required that clearcuts in Alaska be limited to 100 acres or less in size. This meant that if we had a cluster of three adjacent units, each of 40 acres in size, that we could log zero, one, or two of these units. A proposal that would log all three of these units would create a contiguous clearcut of 120 acres, which was outside the mandate of the NFMA.

This was a problem. And unfortunately a problem for which there was no solution. It became a shell game in which the objective was to avoid creating a clearcut in excess of 100 acres, either by avoiding existing clearcuts or by avoiding adjacent units from our logging plan. As a matter of fact, we called it the "Penny Game," because we used pennies laid on the map to spatially keep track of which units we were proposing to log. There was no way we could reach target volume and keep our unit sizes under 100 acres, and there was no way management would allow us any slack on volume attainment. This was the proverbial Catch-22, but we had our orders and had no choice but to do as directed.

Walt was in the hotseat from running interference for me through the Forest Service timber bureaucracy. The stress was causing him personal problems that I feared might be affecting his work. Because I personally liked and respected Walt, I discussed my concerns for his welfare with the administrative officer, Lee Nightingale (Bill's wife), a GS-13 member of the management team. Lee explained that the Forest Service had a Concern Program, where supervisors could refer their employees to professional counselors. She got me an immediate audience with Walt's supervisors, Rittenhouse and Vaught, to whom I reiterated my concerns. They told me they had heard the same thing from others and would take steps to see Walt got a referral. Naturally, I was assured my coming forward would be held in strictest confidence, and they told me I had done the right thing.

A few days later, Walt called me over and slammed his door shut, positively glowering. He said that Rittenhouse had told him that I had ratted on him, and if that weren't a stab in the back. He was under a lot of pressure and the only hope for either of us was to stick together and present a united front. As much as I agreed, I told Walt I was nonetheless concerned about his personal welfare. He finally calmed down, and we talked about proper diet, rest, and exercise as holistic means for dealing with stress. But our relationship was never the same. God damn Rittenhouse!

Around this time, Walt was written up for a minor Fish & Game violation. Walt had a habit of tossing a crab pot over the side of the Forest Service parking lot, which abutted the harbor, and hauling it in the evening. I teased him about eating crabs from the harbor, of all places, but, hey, he liked to do it. A fish cop checked Walt's crab pot and allegedly found a whole pink salmon in it for bait. Pink salmon come into the adjacent Ketchikan Creek in the tens of thousands and are so plentiful they are considered a nuisance. Hell, I fed the damn things to my dogs! But Alaska has a "wanton waste" law, so it was technically illegal to use a whole pink salmon for bait, without first filleting the flesh for personal consumption. So Walt got busted, even though he denied putting the pink salmon in his crab pot. Knowing Walt, he was probably using Cheez-its or something like that for bait. Walt appealed the charge and was given permission to delay his hearing.

When the original date of his hearing found him not in court, a cop arrested him at work. Walt was in a management team meeting, and for some reason, he was paraded through the office in handcuffs. He must have been totally humiliated, because he immediately resigned from the Forest Service. His former supervisor, Mike Lunn, intervened, and Walt was whisked from Alaska and reinstated in a Forest Service job Down South. And just like that, he was gone, too.

Over the next several weeks, my team and I made field trips to Thorne Bay to ground truth some of our new logging units. I had developed a solid professional relationship with Robert Wetherell, the Thorne Bay landscape architect who had been told he would never get along with me. One night Robert waylaid me outside the bunkhouse and asked me to take a walk with him. He was scared. He told me that it was widely held that my job was next on the chopping block and to watch my back. It was an obvious heartfelt concern on Robert's part, and I believed what he told me. Because now I was alone.

Enter Dortch's replacement, Dave Arrasmith, around April 1992.

The whole planning shop held a little ice-breaking, get-acquainted meeting for our new boss down at the Ketchikan Yacht Club. At the end of the session, Dave and I talked for a few minutes outside the yacht club. I asked Dave what all he'd been briefed on. With a grin on his face, he told me that management had advised him to consider removing me from my job. Ah, the hatchet man cometh. Rittenhouse, apparently no longer willing to get his own hands dirty, recruited a henchman, and a willing one at that.

The first few weeks, Arrasmith shadowed me as I made presentations to the public and special interest groups, like KPC, Alaska Department of Fish & Game, the greenies, and so on. As soon as he felt up to speed on the issues, he started to micro-manage every facet of my job performance, down to changing my work schedule. Because he had never worked a day in the woods in his life, and didn't know a spruce from a hemlock, he represented everything that I felt was wrong with the Forest Service. He had a degree in agricultural economics, with a specialty in the profitability of growing tomatoes. He once told me that he believed that forest management was a lot like raising tomatoes, but I walked away without giving him the courtesy of an audience.

My team and I took to calling him "Spot." I would ask him a direct question which he would be unable to answer. Pretty quickly, he'd leave our office to go ask his masters for an answer. As soon as he left, I'd make a throwing motion with my arm, and say, "Fetch, Spot, fetch."

The Thorne Bay Ranger District, only having recently completed logging unit layout for the last of the 1989-94 timber sale, started focusing their attention on CPOW. Where they wouldn't have touched CPOW with a stick when they still had 1989-94 units to work on, CPOW was now their focus, as it would provide their field workload for the next several seasons.

In the spring of 1992, the entire district layout and road crew made an extensive office review of my team's logging plan. When the field season started in full swing, they started field verifying our proposed logging units and roads and provided us with feedback as to what worked and what didn't. Jack Oien, an engineer, sent a note to Eide, stating, "In general the reports indicate that the units looked at so far can be implemented as planned with little change only. There is general agreement that we feel better about layout on CPOW than we did on 1989-94 units." Eide responded, "This is some of the best news I have heard since CPOW started. This really excites me."

My team was pleased to have our units ground truthed and to make them more readily implementable. However, I wasn't thrilled about everything that was being done. The field recon reports were coming in on a pre-printed form that contained a slot to document unit expansion possibilities, i.e., whether the planned unit could be enlarged to rob timber from adjacent National Forest System land.

I was on pretty good terms with a lot of the field foresters, and several of them mentioned they were uncomfortable with continuing this carte blanche unit expansion policy. They asked my opinion, and I told them that as far as I knew, willfully moving the boundaries after the Final EIS was produced, was not supported by NEPA, because it avoided assessment of environmental consequences and public disclosure.

They also told me that they were being directed to do something beyond reconnaissance. They were also doing some hardcore logging unit layout. I explained that this was also outside NEPA, because it constituted a predecisional commitment of National Forest System resources which inherently biased the decision-maker. I called up the regional NEPA coordinator, Tom Sheehy, and asked him about it. He assured me that it was way out of line and had never occurred on the Tongass. I told Tom to make sure he was seated, and then explained what was occurring. Later I discussed Sheehy's comments with Pete Griffin, Mark Voight's replacement as NEPA coordinator. Pete said he was aware of the apparent predecisional work, but that "it's a real world." A few months later Tom Sheehy took early retirement.

It didn't take long for it to get back to management that I was advising field foresters that what they were being directed to do was illegal. Not surprisingly, this was not the role Rittenhouse had envisioned for his planning team leader, and like Nixon, he only wanted to escape his term without a scandal. I wasn't a dummy. I had watched the Tongass witch trials, which eliminated anyone who opposed the logging-without-laws approach. I didn't want to be the next on the hit list, but I also didn't want to be the fall-guy for condoning illegal forest management activities. For their part, management didn't want to have it substantiated that they had direct knowledge of these illegal activities, so in August 1992, Arrasmith gave me a direct order to have no communications with any member of the Ketchikan management team. As I watched the agency I loved behaving so shamelessly, my green shorts started getting awfully itchy.

I kept returning to my team's logging plan which showed that less than half of the timber base we had analyzed was suitable on the ground for logging. I discussed my concerns with one of the other IDT leaders, Bill Nightingale, who shrugged and said HE GOT THE SAME THING on his project! We compared facts and figures in great detail and saw his results were within a few percentage points of mine. Larry Lunde told me the private contractors were finding the same thing on their projects. This was something that everybody knew, but nobody talked about. Tongass logging levels were based upon more hot air than a loaf of cheap, white bread.

One of the requirements of TTRA was for the Forest Service to make an assessment of the amount of available Tongass timber and to present their findings to Congress. The Forest Service hired the Irland Group, a forestry consulting firm from Maine, to produce the report. The Irland report concluded that the Tongass forest plan timber availability estimates were overstated by approximately 44 percent, which basically corroborated Nightingale's, Lunde's, and my own findings. The Forest Service peer reviewed the Irland report and said the forest plan timber predictions were too high by 31 percent.

It was impossible to be responsible, as I was, for the delivery of such a high-powered environmental document and not be aware that the REAL issue confronting the CPOW project was unsustainable logging levels. However, Forest Service officials did not want this issue to surface. After a few "fatherly talks" and "wink-wink-nudge-nudges" failed to put CPOW back on track, the Forest Service wheeled out its damage control specialists, and the game began to get ugly indeed.

11

Weeklong Days

(April 1992 - August 1992)

"And she made me
Apple cider and homemade bread,
To make a man say grace
In a house she built by hand
With a warm feet fireplace."
        -- Jesse Winchester, "Yankee Lady"

Almost all of the Forest Service travel in SE Alaska is done via float plane or boat. The Forest Service takes safety very seriously and has an excellent record. To that end, they hold several mandatory safety/survival-type courses every year for all people whose jobs require them to go into the field. One of these courses is called "PIG," or "Personal Immersion Gadget." The training is held at the local high school swimming pool and is intended to teach you how to get out of a float plane, if it ends upside down in the water.

The PIG is a simulated float-plane seat into which the trainee is strapped with a safety harness. The PIG is then tossed in the pool upside down, where two spotters await any unforeseen emergency. Trainees are taught to release themselves from the seat, take off their helmet, open the door, and follow their bubbles to the surface. It's a good session.

A couple of us were standing around the pool awaiting our turn in the PIG, when I recognized a gal I had recently met. I slid over and reintroduced myself, and soon we were chattering and shivering merrily. Her name was Debi, and she was a seasonal archeology technician. Before I could stop myself, I impulsively asked her over for dinner on Saturday night. Saturday came, and indeed Debi showed up. It turned out she had a master's degree in recreation and was a veteran white-water raft guide and ski bum. We hit it off and started seeing each other on a regular basis. She and her son were living in a tiny apartment, and to help cut down on her food budget, I brought her frozen coho salmon and blueberries from my own freezer. She dropped hints that she'd promised to take her son camping, so we started planning a trip over to the Forest Service cabin on Phoecena Bay. I was in the final stages of marathon preparation, and our trip had to fit into a scheduled rest period in my rigorous training regime.

We left on a Saturday morning and boated maybe three hours to Phoecena Bay, which was on the back side of Gravina Island, the island immediately west of the one Ketchikan is on. Her son, Aaron, brought his school chum, Mike, along for the trip. Just outside the entrance to Phoecena Bay, we jigged a small halibut for camp meat, and I hurriedly dressed the fish with my pocket knife. We motored into the bay and beached my dory next to the cabin, unloaded all the gear, then tied the boat up to the mooring buoy, and rowed back ashore in the rubber raft.

A word about Forest Service cabins, which are among the best kept secrets in the world. Well-maintained Pan-Abode structures, with either a wood-burning or a diesel stove, they are nestled in truly spectacular sites. Some are solely fly-in, some boat-in, while a few can be reached via hiking. At $25/night, they are a prized recreational steal. The cabin at Phoecena Bay is one of my personal favorites. A heavily forested slope is the entirety of the eastern viewshed, to the north is the bay itself with forested beach beyond, to the west is a fringe of timber, then the open Clarence Strait, which is big water. Then to the south, is more forested beach.

After setting up camp, the guys went off to explore, while Debi and I took a walk along the beach. We sat on a rock watching an otter play, when I felt a pinch on my right foot. I took off my rubber boot and sock, and there was a big blister. Damn! After thousands of miles of running, my feet were pretty tough, and I didn't blister easily, especially in my rubber boots, which I wore daily. As I started to lance the blister, Debi grabbed my hand and stared at me in disbelief. "You're not going to use that pocket knife you just used to clean our halibut." Tough, macho, stupid ... you bet I did.

Our intent was to spend three days and two nights at the cabin, but a 35 mph gale was forecast for our final day. Being a cautious skipper, I decided to leave a day early, while the getting was still good. The guys were kinda disappointed, so on the way back to town we stopped at a pretty good halibut hole I knew about. Within 10 minutes, Mike hooked an enormous halibut, which decided to make a brawl out of the struggle. Mike turned out to be an experienced fisherman and got the fish up from the depths in maybe 20 minutes. I harpooned it, and we watched in amazement as the halibut dragged the big buoy underwater for a moment. Shades of Jaws! We recaptured the buoy, then I shot the halibut with my .357 magnum. That really pissed it off, and it dragged the buoy under again. By now we had cut the fishing line and were just following the buoy.

When we caught the buoy, I blasted the halibut again, which seemed to calm it considerably. We managed to wrestle it aboard, then ran into the wheelhouse, closed the door, and left the fish to thrash on deck. A wild halibut is nothing to mess with (as I was to find out), and is more than capable of breaking a guy's leg. By the time we docked in Ketchikan, the fish was ready to be dealt with. It wasn't that big, maybe 100 pounds, but was a nice fish nonetheless. Debi went to the store and bought some ziploc baggies, while I filleted it. It was pouring, and everyone ended up getting thoroughly soaked. We went out to my house and had a huge halibut feast.

A few days later, my foot swelled so badly that I couldn't put weight on it. With my race that weekend, I panicked and went to the doctor (a huge concession of fundamental life values) and was diagnosed with acute fish poisoning. Duh! They gave me medication but shook their heads at its effecting any overnight cure. On the day before the race, my foot was still so painful that I couldn't stand on it. One of the guys on Bill Nightingale's planning team was an ex-commercial fisherman, and he gave me some Buckley's ointment, which was an old, out-of-production fish poison balm, made from God-knows-what. The swelling went down almost immediately, and that night I ran three miles and pronounced myself fully recovered.

Race day was pleasant and rainless. Outside of the fish poisoning, I had trained hard and was in excellent shape. The gun went off, and I ran according to plan until mile 14, when my poisoned leg started to cramp. I had no choice but to slow down. It became excruciatingly painful, and forced screams of agony from me. I looked down once and saw a divot in my right calf that could hold a small hen's egg. At mile 20, the leg buckled, and I took a hard fall. I couldn't get up, and onlookers came over and called an ambulance. Within 30 seconds, I recovered my feet, fought off my well-intentioned benefactors, and hobbled another four miles, before the race director and Debi came over and grabbed me and ended the nightmare. We were all crying, them from having to witness my agony, and me from the humiliation of not being able to finish my marathon. Debi dragged me home, helped me into the shower and to bed.

True to her word, Sylvia Geraghty appealed the North Sea Otter Sound timber sale. The Forest Service didn't think the government case was very strong, so Bob Vaught gave me carte blanche authority to attempt the first-ever negotiated settlement of a Tongass timber sale appeal. I asked Bob what the ground rules were, and he told me anything I was able to get was better than nothing. He had heard from ex-ranger Pete Johnson that I had gained a rapport with Sylvia, and he wanted me alone to deal with her. Because it involved decision-making, a Forest Service line officer had to be present at all times I met with her, but I was to do the wheeling and dealing.

We met a couple of times in Ketchikan, and even though she was a greenie, it was hard for me to hate Sylvia. For one thing, I really liked her as a person and admired her lifestyle. For another thing, her suggestions mostly made sense. On some of her requests, however, I wouldn't budge, and she smiled and told me my BS meter was well-tuned. We hammered out a good settlement, which reduced the size of the sale from 45 mmbf to 28 mmbf, but made it a much better sale. I wrote up an agreement, we both signed it, and shook hands.

One of the items Sylvia asked for by way of settlement was a copy of my planning team's "Falldown Analysis." I logged onto the Forest Service computer system to print out a copy for her, and when I located the document, I saw that it had been recently edited. Curious, I called up the document's history to see who had been the last person to edit it. Imagine my surprise at seeing Bob Vaught listed as the last individual to make changes in the falldown report! Gone was the recommendation to discontinue the unit expansion policy. Gone was any reference to poor logging systems planning on the 1989-94 sale. What I was looking at was totally censored ... not at all what my planning team had written.

Sylvia, who had a lot of environmental experience, was not at all surprised by these shenanigans, but doing her best to remain deadpan. She was failing miserably. I was trying just as unsuccessfully to mask the embarrassment I felt at the realization that my agency was so blatantly trying to whitewash information. I asked her which version of the report she wanted ... Bob Vaught's or mine. She said she preferred mine, so that's what she got.

I was pleased at negotiating the settlement. A few weeks passed, then I heard Rittenhouse refused to sign off on it. I was horrified! I told my boss that I considered that to be a major breach of trust, a breaking of faith, an outright lie. I refused to have any further part in the negotiations. I called Sylvia and apologized profusely for my agency's betrayal of trust. She told me she expected it, and actually seemed amazed at the force of my emotion. I told her that I didn't lie, and when I gave my word I meant it.

Negotiations with Sylvia dragged on for over a year at a "more senior" level. After an agreement was reached, but before everything was signed, the Forest Service sold and logged part of the timber. I was shocked, as that was a flagrant violation of law. But things worked differently in Alaska. Boy, did they!

The short Alaska summer of seemingly weeklong days hurtled by. James Llanos, my Tlingit computer analyst, and I had started fishing together the previous year and had become exceedingly close. From May 15 until we were sick of catching cohos in late September, we fished every Friday and Sunday (Saturday was chore day for me) without fail, unless it was too stormy. We didn't even discuss time, as we always left at 0630. I provided the boat and gas, James the bait. A typical conversation would be, "Halibut or salmon?" That was all it took.

One weekend we decided to donate our catch to local Tlingit elders, who weren't able to get nice, fresh fish on their own. We caught our limit of halibut and brought them back to the dock, where I filleted them and packed them in ice in my big cooler. James distributed the fish, and I guess they were a big hit. Later James got real serious and asked me who he should say was responsible for the fish ... in other words, how did I wish to be commemorated. I just said that James and his friend wanted to thank the elders for letting us fish their waters. That seemed to work.

My friendship with James became a sore spot with people at work. Some members of my planning team jealously felt it gave him an unfair edge to gaining the boss's ear. And they were right, it did! But others in slightly higher positions saw it as the formation of solidarity, and that scared the bejeebers out of them.

Even given all the weird events at work, the highlight of the summer of 1992 for me was the arrival of my new wolf cub. For about a year, I had been searching for a wolf cub, but didn't want one from a game farm. Someone finally put me in touch with a gal from Soldotna, who had a litter from a 97 % black father and a 87 % grizzled mother, whose own father had been a 167-pound giant. This was just what I was looking for! The gal accepted my deposit and put my name on a grizzled male, but when someone else failed to come up with deposit money, she gave me pick of the litter ... a huge black cub with white stockings.

Prior to the cub's August arrival, this gal and I talked almost nightly, getting me prepared for life with a wolf. It was necessary to get the cub at age four weeks, because hybrids with such a high percentage of wolf in them have great difficulty bonding to humans. So the theory was to place them with their human pack even before they were fully weaned. "Chacon" arrived on the jet, in a tiny dog cage. By the time I got to the airline freight office, the gals in the office had already taken him out of his cage and were playing with him. Oh my, he was gorgeous, resembling a bear cub more than a wolf, because he was so fat and roly-poly.

Of course, he woke continually the first night, with frightened howling. Each time I came to his rescue. The next night, I just tried to sleep through it. The third night, he went into the kennel with Max, with whom he became fast friends. Debi had left for Utah, which left the wolf and me, and, Lord, did we bond.

Watching him grow was like watching someone blow up a balloon. At two months, he was 15 pounds, 40 pounds at three months, 59 pounds at four months, 84 pounds at six months, and 92 pounds at 6 1/2 months. Chac is now 7 years old and is wraith-like at 120 pounds. He has brilliant amber eyes, with yellow eyebrows that make it appear that his eyes are open even when he's asleep. When affectionate, he'll place his paws on my shoulders, peer down on me, then throw his head back and howl. He's been timed at five minutes on his hind legs.

It was amazing the number of people who made up an excuse to come visit me while Chacon was a young cub. For his part, he was terrified of strangers and it was difficult coaxing him into the house the day AFTER someone stopped over. He would invariably slink over to where they had been sitting the previous day, and, weight on his back paws, tail between his legs, he'd take in their scent. Once two Girl Scouts came to the door selling cookies, and he got so terrified at the 11-year-old girls that he peed.

Wolf hybrids are less like dogs than cats are. They have no inherent sense to please man and do not often bend to their will. Chacon has learned to sit and give his paw, but only obeys half the time. On the rare occasions when he gets loose, he seldom allows me to approach more closely than five feet. This makes recapturing him difficult, to say the least. He's happily adapted to kennel-life and walks fairly cooperatively on a leash. After years together, I have concluded that hybrids are a mistake, and had him neutered so he couldn't breed. But despite his weirdness (and mine), he remains my steadfast friend.

Debi and I kept in contact after she went back Down South to Utah. She even made a few return visits. But life on a remote island in Alaska is unlike the rest of the world, and it presents barriers that no amount of phone calls, letters, and occasional visits could remove. We drifted apart. Perhaps it was just as well, as I had troubling things on my mind.

12

Expatriates

(March 1998)

Daylight was fading, and it was time to stop packing and release the wolf from his kennel and vigil of overseeing the dismantling of our home. Concern was in his eyes, as I snapped on his leash. We headed out for a walk on the tangle of logging roads behind my cabin. As we walked in the gathering dusk, I reflected on the events of 1992, when I had been two years in Alaska. During that time, I had observed a wrongness within the Tongass which I had never seen at my other duty stations. I didn't know if it simply didn't exist elsewhere, or if it were there all along, but my time in the woods prevented my noticing it.

Of course I knew about some of the more publicized government scandals ... Watergate, Irangate, Abscam. But that was the government, not the Forest Service. It was then that slow realization dawned. The farther from the woods and the deeper into the federal bureaucracy you drew, the more the Forest Service ceased to be the Forest Service, and the more it became the government. And for upper level bureaucrats, it was just as easy to attempt to cover up overcutting of National Forests as it was illicit arms deals.

It seems that my career had taken me high enough within the agency ranks that I now stood at the very edge of the Forest Service, at the cusp between the field crews who rode in green rigs and the men who wore dark suits, where I could peer into its government underbelly. I didn't at all like what I saw, but more importantly, once I had that glimpse, there was no way I could slam the lid shut on that

Pandora's Box. For to deny it was to accept it and to accept it was to become part of it. I couldn't do that. But why? Everybody else did. I wondered what my forestry professor Henry Haalck would have done. Once again I asked myself, "Why me?"

I wondered if the reason I couldn't turn a blind eye was that something had changed inside me. For 14 years I had been doing the Forest Service's bidding, without ever really thinking of the consequences. While I had loved all of the forests where I had lived and worked, they were merely waypoints on my journey home. Alaska was my home now, and I wonder if that didn't make all the difference. A good animal simply doesn't crap in its own nest.

(August 1992 - December 1992)

"Behold the fisherman.
Mighty are his preparations.
He ariseth early and disturbeth the whole household.
And when he returneth, late at night,
Smelling of strong drink,
The truth is not in him."
-- Mark Twain

The pace was frantic at planning team central as we raced to complete the draft EIS. KPC was rapidly logging its way through the 1989-94 offering, and there was tremendous pressure on the Forest Service to have new timber available for KPC before the end of the 1993 logging season. It typically takes a year to convert a draft EIS into a final EIS and an implementable record of decision, so we needed to have CPOW's draft EIS on the street in the fall of 1992.

The draft EIS went to the printer and was distributed to the public, who had 60 days to comment. Boy, did they comment! Despite pressure from Arrasmith, I made sure that the timber and socio-economics sections showed the results of my team's comprehensive logging plan. This highlighted the certainty that timber supplies were running out much faster than the Forest Service had been saying previously. The document made it brutally clear that loggers could expect to be out of work pretty darned quickly, because they had been duped into cutting themselves out of house and home in the government's futile attempt to buoy the economic stability of SE Alaska by clearcutting the Tongass at a grossly unsustainable rate. Greenies and loggers alike were pissed.

I don't think the Forest Service in Alaska had ever before put an honest evaluation of their actions in front of the public. The local managers didn't like it, but weren't quite sure what to do about it.

The CPOW draft EIS was a document whose singular premise was that Alaska was going to fall into the sea if the Forest Service didn't rush massive quantities of National Forest System timber to KPC in order to meet the terms of a contract that went into effect 10 years before "Leave It to Beaver" first appeared on TV. And even though it anticipated losing millions of dollars of taxpayers' money in having the Tongass clearcut, and that virtually the entirety of the forest environment would be degraded, this was still a noble and wise thing to do.

It was right here that I started to lose it. There was absolutely no way CPOW should be allowed to continue, yet I knew without a doubt that the project WOULD continue, because the industrial-military complex, the Alaska congressional delegation, the timber industry, and the Forest Service WANTED it to continue. It was obviously go along with the program or get crushed.

As public reaction to the CPOW draft EIS poured in, my planning team was required to conduct a series of subsistence meetings in the local communities to record public comment on how clearcutting another 10,000 acres of the Tongass National Forest would affect people's guaranteed Alaskan right to shoot/catch/trap/cut/gather subsistence resources which they needed in the conduct of their rural lifestyles. The Forest Service was concerned about what I might tell the public out in remote communities, so they sent Arrasmith to preside over the meetings.

One meeting I recall was in Coffman Cove, the small logging community where I had worked a couple years previously when I laid out those logging units. We even stayed in the same bunkhouse as before. The meeting was up at the local community hall one evening. There were a bunch of drunk loggers in the hall, chewing up Arrasmith, who was unwise enough to wear his Forest Service uniform. I stood over in the corner in my jeans, wool shirt, and rubber boots. My hair was long and pretty grey. The loggers had seen me around before and exchanged nods with me. I listened to them rip into Arrasmith, noting with satisfaction that his parroting of Forest Service buzz-phrases, heavily punctuated with Government-speak, was inciting the drunk loggers to the flash point.

I don't know what made me do it, but I strode over and fairly yelled, "Hey, how would you guys like to cut some 8-foot-thick spruce?" There was a roar and the small community hall shook. I held up my arm, and the guys quieted down. Then I said, "Well, you cut all them about ... what ... 15 years ago?" Dead silence, sullen eyes. "Hey, how'd you guys like to cut some 6-foot spruce?" Big roar again, but not quite like the last time. Once again, I spoke, "Well, you cut all them ... what ... 10 years ago?" Dead silence, downcast eyes. "Hey, how'd you guys like to cut some 3-foot spruce?" Maybe a whoop or two. "Well, they're gone, too."

In 10 minutes, the hall was empty. No one even stayed to present comment for the record. Arrasmith and I exchanged a long look, then I left and walked back to the bunkhouse. In retrospect, I should have let those loggers lynch him.

After the subsistence meeting in Thorne Bay, Robert Wetherell came over to the bunkhouse where I was staying and invited me to his cabin on South Arm for some killer spaghetti. It was a 10-minute skiff ride in the dark, and provided yet another glimpse of real Alaska. Robert had a rustic cabin and generated all his own power. He was also concerned about mismanagement on the Tongass and had felt the sting of reprisal for his professional stand on the necessity to protect the visual beauty of the landscape. In the course of the evening, and with the help of a few beers, we laid the groundwork for a solid friendship. It felt good to have a professional ally and friend.

The subsistence meeting in Hydaburg was also pretty memorable. Hydaburg is a small Native Alaskan village of Haida Indians, with a pretty militant bent. James cautioned me to watch my butt over there, as he had heard through the Native grapevine that trouble was brewing. It was an evening meeting at the town hall. Arrasmith was talking to an elder, then suddenly cut him off dead and walked away. I watched the elder react as if he'd been slapped, then walked over next to him and looked down respectfully. It was how I would approach a wolf.

The man acknowledged me and we introduced ourselves. Although he gave me his first and last names, I addressed him as Mr. He and I ended up in a corner and had a long conversation in which I talked 20 percent and listened 80 percent. At one point, I remember asking him if he believed that trees had spirits. He glanced at me quickly, looked away, then really looked at me ... kinda like he was doing a double take. He asked me why I would bring up such a subject, and I told him about a tree that was on the ridge several miles above my house. It was a distinctive hemlock that had a massive "witches broom" (a growth disfiguration caused by parasitic mistletoe) in its top. I could see the tree through my window at home when I was standing directly in front of my wood stove. I spent a lot of contemplative time standing in that spot, staring at that tree. I had taken to referring to that tree as my 'power tree,' a la Carlos Castenada's The Teaching's of Don Juan. I felt the tree and I had some kind of connection, which was pretty darned vague on this level, but I had a sneaking hunch that if I were able to explore other conscious levels, I would find a much deeper connection.

The elder was quiet awhile and then we really started talking, in a manner much unlike our previous conversation. I made no attempt to divert my attention from him the rest of the evening, and recall almost nothing of the formal testimony. I do remember that when we returned to Ketchikan, James gave me a long look and a smile.

Back at the office, my planning team labored to produce the final EIS. We went over the public comments and started the process of drafting the agency response to the public comments, which would be printed in the final EIS. Another huge source of input were the field reconnaissance reports that the Thorne Bay layout crews sent in to support their field verification of our proposed logging units and roads. As the team logging systems specialist and resident timber beast, I personally made the field recommended changes on our master map of the comprehensive logging plan. I invited Jack Oien to work with me. Jack was an engineer with a wealth of field experience in road location and logging systems. We spent weeks updating our comprehensive logging plan to include information from the field reconnaissance reports.

One of the recon reports documented extensive wolf dens dug into Alaska yellow-cedar rootwads immediately adjacent to one of our proposed logging units near Trumpter Lake. This information struck a cord within me. Because of Chacon, I had developed a fondness for the wolf ... maybe even to the degree of being unprofessional. But the Alexander Archipelago wolf was proposed to be listed as a threatened species, and it seemed skookum to bring this information forward and to attempt to protect identified wolf habitat.

I asked Doug Larsen, a wildlife biologist with Alaska Department of Fish & Game, what it would take to protect this area so that wolves might continue to use it. He suggested leaving an uncut buffer of trees around the den site or maybe even prohibiting logging and roading during the denning season. I asked him how effective that would be, and he laughed, "Bill, you live with a wolf and know how skittish they are. Multiply that by 10 when they're denning." I asked Doug if it would be best to just not log that unit. He looked surprised and said he wasn't aware that was an option. I told him it was always an option, and that I would personally push for it.

Another of the issues my planning team had to wrestle with was the recent emergence of the significance of the cave resources (karst) on Prince of Wales island. It wasn't a secret that there were some caves on the island, but no one had ever looked at how many, where, how come, and what they meant. Nobody ever cared before, as Prince of Wales was largely a place to cut timber. Most of the best timber on the island grew on soils which were derived from limestone. As the 100-plus inches of rain poured down each year, it flowed through the peat-bog-like muskegs and picked up a distinctly acidic tinge. When these acidic runoffs flowed over the limestone, they dissolved the carbonate and ate their way into the earth, producing a honey-combed labyrinth called karst.

The deepest pit on the North American continent rested within the CPOW project area. Previously undiscovered species of animals were found, as well as ancient bones of creatures never believed to have inhabited SE Alaska. Cave art and human remains were found which changed the way scientists theorized the Americas were colonized by our ancestors. Limestone-enriched streams produced the best runs of salmon, and the soils produced the most nutritious foods for wildlife. Trees grew well and this, of course, spelled the doom of the above-ground portion of the karst ecosystem. On Prince of Wales, the prevailing axiom has always been good trees equals clearcut. Cave entrances had been used extensively as convenient dumping grounds for logging slash and road construction debris.

Shortly after returning from the subsistence hearing over in Coffman Cove, I got a call from forest geologist Jim Baichtal. He had found some karst features in some of the CPOW units, in an area which had previously been presumed to be karst free, and invited me over to field recon the area with him. It was December 1992, and when I showed up at the float-plane dock the next day, the weather was pretty snotty. The pilot looked at me and asked if I were sure I wanted to go? You bet, sez I. He sighed, then said, "Well, let's throw her up and see what happens." What a ride!

Somehow we made it over to Coffman Cove, and the pilot cautioned me not to stay too long, as the weather was rapidly deteriorating. Baichtal met me, along with Robert's girlfriend Cat Woods, who was a highly accomplished caver. We drove near the proposed units and then hiked in. We noticed exceptionally nice timber and lots of deer sign. Suddenly something wasn't right. I slowed, then continued, then slowed again. I shouted out to Cat and Baichtal that something was wrong. They came back and looked at me like I'd lost my mind. Suddenly we realized that the tiny stream we had been following had suddenly disappeared. Huh? Where did it go? Cat and Baichtal got excited and started looking for the insurgence and resurgence because that spelled C-A-V-E. Sure enough, they found one.

Baichtal and I decided to go have a look and wriggled into the hole. Cat grudgingly stayed out for emergency backup. After a lot of grunting and scrunching, Jim and I emerged from the other side of the hill, sweating like pigs. Jim was pumping his arms in the air, shouting that we had made a through-climb of a previously unexplored cave. I was looking dejected because I had torn my rain gear.

Nonetheless, this jumble of big trees, productive fish creeks, deer sign, caves, and disappearing streams was unlike anything I had ever seen. The float-plane ride back to Ketchikan was particularly awful, but I was lost in thought.

The 60-day period for the public to comment on the CPOW draft EIS was rapidly coming to a close. Arrasmith kept continually lobbying me to defuse the timber supply issue by removing the results of my team's comprehensive logging plan, which showed that only about half of the Tongass timber base was loggable. He recommended using information from the forest plan's computer models. I told him that would constitute substituting bad, generalized information for good, site-specific information. He urged me to do so anyhow, but I just stared at him and challenged him to put it in writing and make it a direct order. Well, he wasn't quite prepared to do that ... yet.

I could see the writing on the wall. Arrasmith was being used as the bully-boy to try to get smiley-faced stickers pasted all over the CPOW EIS. He was like a snake-oil salesman who claimed his elixir might not cure cancer, but rather changed it around so that the cancer was actually good for you. I was determined that CPOW would present the honest-to-god skinny.

On Sunday, Dec. 13, 1992, the day before the public comment period closed, James came over to my house and told me he was going to submit a personal comment letter. I told him I was thinking the same thing, and we went upstairs to my computer and wrote our letters. As an afterthought, I cc'd myself at the bottom of my letter. When James asked why, I told him it was to ensure Arrasmith didn't somehow cause the letter to disappear. James smiled and said he wouldn't put it past him. I told James that we might get in trouble for this, but he wasn't the type to back down either. The next day we logged our comment letters into the planning record.

December 13, 1992
David Arrasmith
IDT Staff Officer

Thank you for the opportunity to comment on the CPOW DEIS. I wish to comment as a United States citizen and resident of Alaska.

My first comment is very site specific. Please do not harvest unit 583-258. There is a significant wolf-denning area adjacent to the unit, near the northwest corner of Trumpter Lake. There are extensive areas of karst within the project area. Very recently (since publication of the DEIS), karst has been discovered near Luck Lake -- in areas where it had not been anticipated. There is a very complex ecological relationship of hydrology, fishery productivity, wildlife use, timber productivity, world-class cave resources, and archeological significance within karst areas. Science is only beginning to understand some of these relationships. I am in favor of a five-year moratorium of timber harvest within all karst areas, until such time as the Forest Service can more fully assess the effects of intensive management activities on karst features. I would like to see the Forest Service pursue funding for an interdisciplinary study of ecological relationships within karst areas, with a focus on the effects of timber harvest and road construction.

I am deeply concerned with the stated purpose and need for the project, i.e., to provide 290 mmbf to KPC as part of the long-term contract. This very narrow purpose and need has severely limited the range of alternative actions considered in the DEIS. With all due respect, the 290 mmbf figure was purely a management decision and was not based upon the biotic capability of the land to produce timber on a sustained yield basis. I am in favor of a more generic purpose and need for the FEIS -- to provide timber to KPC, without specifying a target volume. I am also in favor of a wider range of alternatives. I propose an alternative at the current sustained yield level of 20 mmbf annually (or 60 mmbf for this three-year project), another alternative at the 150-200 mmbf level which would utilize site-specific public comment, and another alternative at the full 290 mmbf level. There may be additional alternatives in-between.

As a professional forester and Alaska resident, I am deeply concerned with the harvest level associated with the project. Given the extensive past harvest within the project area (approximately 2.5 mmmbf), the current proposal (290 mbf), and the proposed future entries by 2004 (270 mmbf), there will be an unacceptable reduction in sustained yield of timber within the project area. Because of the immensity of the project area (321,866 acres) this is not an incidental example of accelerated harvest. I believe the same situation of departure from sustained yield is occurring on the adjacent Lab Bay, Polk Inlet, and proposed Control Lake project areas. I am in favor of the CPOW FEIS using site-specific data from the MELPs for these aforementioned projects (not TLMP data) to analyze whether there is an apparent departure from sustained yield on all these project areas, which account for the bulk of economically viable commercial forest lands on Prince of Wales Island. This would focus analysis on whether the timber schedule to complete the long-term contract (Appendix A) is within the tenets of sustained yield timber management principles.

Since the CPOW DEIS has been published, I have listened to many people's views on community stability. I recommend that community stability (perhaps in conjunction with sustained yield) be elevated to the status of significant issue and be fully analyzed within the FEIS. I feel it is important to clearly display the reduction in timber employment associated within the CPOW and adjacent project areas, after the implementation of the timber schedule shown in Appendix A. The long-term contract was established in 1951 to provide (among other things) community stability for SE Alaska. I find it contradictory that continued execution of this contract may have a negative impact on long-term community stability within SE Alaska.

A major concern I had with the implementation of the 1989-94 ROD was the widespread practice of expanding harvest units into adjacent stands, when there was some reason the planned area could not be fully harvested. I feel this practice is damaging for several reasons: (1) there was no chance for the public to comment on this displaced harvest, (2) it gives an overstated factor for timber implementation,and (3) often the expanded areas disrupt subsequent and long-range timber planning efforts. I am in favor of the CPOW ROD restricting harvest to within the boundaries of the selected units and not permitting wholesale generic unit expansion.

NEPA requires an EIS to disclose social and environmental consequences of alternatives to a proposed action. Sometimes there is so much political pressure to justify an action ("put the best foot forward" approach), that full disclosure suffers. I feel the CPOW FEIS needs to more objectively display analysis, especially on issues which may question the proposed action. There are some very difficult decisions ahead. I hope the Forest Service wisely reviews the analysis to choose the best course of action, instead of selecting a preconceived, politically-correct course of action. Thank you for the opportunity to comment.

Sincerely,
Bill Shoaf

cc: Bill Shoaf, IDT Leader
    Mary Carr

I'm not sure whether the 'No Fear' or 'Just Do It' slogans had come out yet. Or if they'd caught on Down South, whether they'd made it to SE Alaska yet. Maybe 'No Brains' was more applicable. But damnit, I felt that CPOW was being wrest from my control by Forest Service officials who seemingly didn't feel constrained by the covenants of forestry science, environmental law, or basic honesty. I knew that, by commenting as a private citizen, the Forest Service now had to deal with my concerns and could no longer sweep them under the rug. I made sure my letter was logged into the planning record, but didn't go to any lengths to advertise the fact. As far as I knew, James was the only other person who was aware of it.

James and I frequently exchanged small gifts, particularly food or something we had made. Once he gave me a German beer stein that had belonged to a favorite uncle. James said I reminded him of his uncle and told me some things about his life and spirit. Then he told me that I could keep his uncle's stein for a while, but that I had to pass it on eventually when I found someone with similar attributes. I was honored and agreed.

That Christmas, James gave me a handwoven cedar basket that his wife had made. We were at work and everyone gathered round to ooh and aah at the gorgeous and obviously valuable present. Arrasmith said it was inappropriate for a supervisor to accept such a gift from an employee. Everyone was shocked, and it put a wet blanket on the moment. To give it back to James would have been an insult, and I guess I made a from-the-hip decision to honor friendship over government protocol. One person said it was probably worth $250, but James maintained that it had cost him nothing and was worth nothing. No one wanted to challenge his Native reasoning, and the incident blew over, but it made me realize the necessity of watching my p's and q's.

A couple days later, one of the local greenies, Dave Katz, was perusing the CPOW planning record, as he had a perfect right to do. Suddenly, he gave a yelp and raced into my office. He started pumping my hand and thanking me. I wasn't sure what he was going on about, until he requested a copy of my public comment letter. I made a copy for him and shooed him out.

Arrasmith's office was right next to mine, and he asked what Katz was going on about. I told him, then showed him my letter. Arrasmith looked at it, then asked me why I had done it. I told him it was the only way I knew to force the Forest Service to heed my concerns. He nodded, then headed across the street.

Fetch, Spot, fetch.

13

Tied to the Whipping Post

(January 1993 - July 1993)

"What we got here, boy, is failure to communicate. Failure to communicate."
-- **Warden in "Cool Hand Luke"**

I had never been in a situation even remotely like this. My first inclination was that my facts were wrong. I talked to everyone within the agency who was willing to discuss it, and tried my best to truly hear what they had to say. There was almost unanimity that the Ketchikan Area was being logged at an unsustainable rate and that logging was being allowed to bowl over concerns for other resources. Some people detailed irregularities of which I wasn't aware. Almost everyone had some sordid story of mismanagement to throw on the heap. The more I listened, the more my facts were substantiated.

The most amazing fact was that no one had ever brought any of this stuff out in the open. But it seemed the urge to speak out was right in the back of people's throats, on the tips of their tongues. But no one ever did. Why not? I had never been aware before that the Forest Service maintained a Gestapo or branch of the KGB. This was "my" Forest Service, the agency I worked for and loved. It was hard to know what to do, but I guess I finally decided to just be 110 percent honest. It was simple, if not pretty, after that.

Never in my wildest nightmare, did I ever imagine the furor that would be generated by my public comment letter. About a week after Dave Katz had discovered my letter in the planning record, an Anchorage reporter called and asked me about it. I had no idea how he had gotten hold of it, but answered his questions nonetheless. Several days later there was a story on the front page of the Anchorage Daily News blasting the Forest Service.

The day after the story was printed in Anchorage (December 27, 1992), I was summoned to Rittenhouse's office. There was an obviously orchestrated statement on the ethics of personal and professional communication. The presence at the meeting of the forest administrative officer, Lee Nightingale, told me that the script had originated in Washington, D.C. I listened to what they had to say, and told them I had been contacted for an interview by a Juneau TV station. Rittenhouse, Arrasmith and Lee visibly paled. They rather timidly requested I delay this interview, and I agreed. Later that day, Arrasmith placed the request in writing.

I went over to the library to read the Anchorage newspaper to see what had caused such a hub-bub. Holy schmoly, the article described Forest Service intimidation and harassment of agency wildlife biologists who had published a report critical of Tongass management. Some comments from me were at the tail-end of the article. Two simultaneous slaps in the agency's face.

On January 7, 1993, Arrasmith issued a memo which forbade not only myself, but the other IDT leaders and members from speaking to the media. I reminded him that I had, until then, been responsible for all media contacts associated with my project. He told me I wasn't anymore, and that Rittenhouse wanted to see me again.

On January 12, Arrasmith told me that management was now faced with the burden of addressing timber sustainability for the first time. In order to more or less defuse the issue, they were considering replacing my team's comprehensive logging plans results with computer models developed by the Tongass Forest Plan. This was getting to be a monthly discussion between us. I pulled out some maps and showed him the huge difference in site specificity between the detailed logging plan and the forest plan computer generalization, which hadn't made any attempt to design even a single logging unit or road. I also showed him places where our best units had considerable falldown, based upon field review by district personnel. He said the regional forester didn't believe the logging plan. I responded that the regional forester had never even seen it. Dave shook his head and said, "Yeah, the decision was kinda risky." He then told me that the General Accounting Office (GAO) was coming up the first week in February to conduct investigations of alleged violations of TTRA, and I was scheduled to be questioned.

Congress was looking hard at the Tongass, yet the local managers were sending down orders to willfully cook the books. How could they be that arrogant? Or stupid? It seemed like a football coach was sending in plays for his quarterback, but the plays didn't fit the situation, because he was watching an entirely different game ... like baseball. End: "Pant, pant ... Coach sez to bring the infield in to double-play depth." Quarterback: "What? It's third down and 6 yards to go!" I knew it was damned if I did and damned if I didn't. But I'd be damned if I'd be damned for being dishonest.

That night, I made a call to a Forest Service employee support group that I had heard about. It was called the Association of Forest Service Employees for Environmental Ethics (AFSEEE). Amazingly, AFSEEE had heard all about me, and in a few minutes their organizer, Brian Hunt, returned my call. Brian warned me about Forest Service reprisal against me and advised me to contact Sarah Levitt, a D.C. lawyer with the Government Accountability Project (GAP). He told me in confidence that Congressman George Miller (D, CA) had a copy of my public comment letter and was launching an investigation. I told Brian that I didn't want the Forest Service embarrassed, but only good resource management on the Tongass. He said he would come to Ketchikan with an attorney the next weekend, and I invited them to stay at my house.

The next morning, I called Sarah Levitt in D.C. When I explained my situation, she said I was in deep trouble and to start documenting everything that occurred. That certainly turned up my paranoia meter. Next they'll be taping recorders to my chest and embedding location transmitters in my ear. I told her I had been maintaining a professional daily diary for 15 years, but she wanted more than that. She told me GAP would provide assistance if things got more repressive at work or if I wished to pursue further disclosures. I didn't even have a clue what she meant.

On January 14, Congressman George Miller, chairman of the House Committee on Natural Resources, wrote to Secretary of Agriculture Mike Espy and Alaska regional forester Mike Barton.

"I have also been informed that a key Tongass timber sale planner has come forward to his superiors with concerns that harvest rates in the region are unsustainable. In a December 13, 1992 letter, Bill Shoaf wrote that the timber harvest plan for CPOW, which he was in charge of, 'was purely a management decision and was not based upon the biotic capability of the land to produce timber on a sustained yield basis.' Mr. Shoaf also cited potential illegalities in the 'widespread practice of expanding harvest units into adjacent stands' rather than limiting harvest to the approved plan areas.

I respectfully request that you ... determine how the Forest Service plans to respond to Mr. Shoaf's allegations."

Whoa, whoa, whoa, Congressman Miller, this was just a dinky public comment letter from a podunk forester on a little island in Alaska. Suddenly the letter took on a life of its own. AFSEEE sent out a press release the next day, which, along with Miller's letter, came to the attention of the only daily newspaper on the southern Tongass, the "Ketchikan Daily News." The paper's publisher, Lew Williams, was a staunch supporter of the timber industry. The "Daily News" ran a front page lead story the next day titled "Miller Requests Tongass Probe." My name was liberally splashed throughout the article, which didn't please me, especially in the role of slamming my own agency.

I was scared of the consequences, because I was in over my head, and the situation was wildly out of control. Things went to hell for me pretty quickly after that ... not in a handcart, but in a race car. Incoming USDA Secretary Mike Espy said he wouldn't comment until his nomination was confirmed, but stated that he "wanted to be an honest broker between commodity producers and environmentalists." The Forest Service issued a terse reply to Congressman Miller that I had made a personal comment and that mine would be analyzed along with all the other public comments.

On January 19, Rittenhouse called me in for another carefully rehearsed speech on Forest Service policy on public expression of personal views. He emphasized that "there was nothing personal in this" and told me there would be no retaliation against me for writing my public comment letter. He then gave me a letter outlining ways personal opinions given on personal time were against agency regulations ... such as if they negatively affected employee morale. Basically, a Forest Service employee, standing out in the rain getting soaked, can't professionally assert that it is raining, if the official Forest Service position is that it is NOT raining. The employee's getting soaked is rather a 'personal opinion,' and can only be proffered if three or more of the planets align. This was madness!

Carolyn Minor, a news reporter for the local radio station, came over to my office to see me on January 15. I told her I couldn't talk to her. Undaunted, she turned on her tape recorder and marched into Arrasmith's office demanding to know why she couldn't talk to Bill Shoaf anymore. What's going on, Dave? He's always been my contact on CPOW before? Arrasmith made Carolyn a copy of his gag order to me, as well as a copy of my public comment letter, which she hadn't seen. She walked into my office and made herself at home at my desk in my chair, while she read them. Part way through, she started laughing, then got kinda serious at the end. She looked at me for a long time, then asked, "You can't talk to me anymore, huh?" I told her not on government time. She kept looking at me, then asked, "Wanna go have a beer tonight?" Yeah, I did.

On January 20, Arrasmith told me that he was going to call a meeting of IDT employees to discuss the potential negative effect my public comment might have had on employee morale. Moreover, I was to be excluded from the meeting. I refused to dismiss myself from any meeting involving my own employees. Moreover, I told him that it was a blatant retaliatory attempt to misconstrue the facts to conclude my comment letter violated agency regulations. He relented to my presence, but called the meeting nonetheless.

Arrasmith presented the reason for the meeting and stated my objection to being excluded. Several people said they had no problem with speaking in my presence, and in fact commenced. The meeting became a trial, as each person in turn basically gave me a thumbs up or thumbs down. It was frightening, but it turned out OK, as almost everyone was supportive. Later on, James grew concerned that Arrasmith might report something other than what had transpired and publicly asked Arrasmith what he had reported to Rittenhouse. Arrasmith stated he hadn't reported any specifics to Rittenhouse, but I noticed his nose was a skosh longer.

Later that day, Arrasmith presented me with a final copy of the official agency policy on public expression of personal views. He told me that at no time, under any circumstances could I say anything whatsoever about timber supply or unit expansion. I pointed out that this last order wasn't supported by any statement within the official agency policy. He just looked at me grimly.

In an overt attempt to make it apparent that what I had done was wrong, the Forest Service hurriedly scheduled a series of training sessions on ethical conduct. On January 25, Robert called and said the meeting in Thorne Bay had nearly caused a riot when they denied the meeting was in response to my comment letter. A friend from the Craig Ranger District called and told me Ketchikan's personnel officer, Gwen Williams, said I should quit if I disagreed with management. Bingo, another riot. The Ketchikan ethics training was the next day. I directly asked Gwen if it was OK to disagree with management on my own time, and she said it was fine. I pointed out that she had given a different answer the previous day, and she declined comment.

On January 27, the Forest Service received a list of questions that GAO had for them in their investigation of potential illegal activities on the Tongass. Included on the list were specific questions about the logging unit (577-107) that I had laid out on which KPC had changed the boundaries, and ranger Pete Johnson and I had replaced in their original configuration. Gene Eide had sent his employees out to the unit to reduce my fish buffers and to expand the boundaries outside the planned area. KPC came in behind Eide's men and cut outside even this new boundary, almost to the very banks of Logjam Creek. This was likely the work of the KPC forester I warned to never again move one of my boundaries, as the final cutting line was defined by rough hewn axe blazes, instead of the usual flagging and boundary cards. Then the few remaining trees along Logjam Creek blew down, and Alaska Fish & Game spotted the damage. Rather than allow GAO to find out what had really happened on this unit, on January 28, I was removed from the list of attendees at the GAO audit meeting.

Quite specifically, GAO asked:

> "In unit 577-107, the recommended buffer was not implemented and cutting was done outside the layout boundaries. Why did this occur and what is being done to prevent it from happening again?"

This was the official agency response from ranger Anne Archie:

> "Forest Service monitoring found one stream out of three in this unit did not meet TTRA requirements. The one stream in question did meet TTRA requirements for the majority of the buffer, but failed to meet TTRA requirements in the eastern portion of the buffer on the northern side of the stream. In a letter dated December 31, 1992, Dave Rittenhouse outlined steps for District Rangers to initiate and implement to improve our management of TTRA buffers."

There are many forms of lies. One kind is the deliberate withholding of the truth. To my way of thinking, Anne Archie's statement fit in that category.

On January 29, Arrasmith told us Rittenhouse had been called onto the carpet in D.C. and had been read the riot act to get things straightened up on the Tongass. Indeed, it looked like the powers that be stood poised to smite the wrong-doers on the Tongass.

A couple days later Arrasmith told me that he was bringing in Linn Shipley, the assistant ranger at Thorne Bay, to assume my responsibility for writing the response to public comment section of the CPOW final EIS. I protested because this wasn't consistent with how the other projects were being handled, in that those project leaders retained this responsibility. Arrasmith just grinned. When Linn arrived, he was apologetic and uncertain how to proceed. I told him to get his marching orders from Arrasmith.

The next day, Jack Oien presented me a copy of the book <u>Benedict Arnold, Patriot and Traitor</u> on behalf of the engineering staff. I handed it back to him and suggested his buddies in engineering personally sign it for me. He did.

> "Bill ... Good luck in your new endeavors. John Henry"

"Bill ... Got you in my sights. David Morgan"

"William ... We had fun while it lasted. Ethan Allen"

"Bill ... England is a good place to hide your wife and children. Peggy Skipper Arnold"

"Judas (Bill) ... Hope you enjoy the book. William Randall"

Later that week, Sylvia Geraghty was in town and asked if we could meet for lunch. Carolyn Minor joined us, and we met at the Five Star Cafe. I showed them the Benedict Arnold book and told them that I had accepted it in good humor, but that it hurt. Pretty soon I got a package from some people up in Gustavus, Alaska, who had heard about the crank book. Their package contained a copy of Al Gore's Earth in the Balance to remind me of their respect for me.

During this time, I got a lot of phone calls and letters of support from all over Alaska. Many were from fellow Forest Service employees who said they were glad someone finally had the guts to speak up. I wondered why they hadn't done it themselves. Walt Dortch called and gave me his support, and that made me feel good. Others were from various people from Southeast Alaska, including some guys from a Prince of Wales fishing village that wanted to hold a benefit to raise funds for my legal defense. Another one was from a gillnetter up in Petersburg:

> Dear Mr. Shoaf,
>   As a concerned citizen about the future of the Tongass, I would like to thank you for your action on the recent Central Prince of Wales timber sale. Your action has undoubtedly caused you a great amount of stress and soul searching. There are few people with integrity but I believe you are one of those uncommon people.
>   Good luck -- many people think of you as a hero.
> Sincerely,
> Victoria xxxxxxxx

One weekend, I needed to get off the island, so my wolf and I put my skiff in the water and rode out to Bold Island, a nearby, uninhabited spot where I could let him run free. He started digging in some flotsam along the tideline, and I moved some of the bigger material aside to see what had caught his attention. There in the flotsam, with its eyes bulging wide, was a dead great horned owl. Lord! A few weeks later, I found another dead owl in my yard. I mentioned these incidents to James, in the context, "Hey, what's the deal with all these dead owls?" James went white as a ghost and told me that it was a clear omen of my death. He told me to be careful.

A couple of quiet weeks passed, then I got a call from Jack Oien giving me a head's up that it was rumored that Thorne Bay District was going to be assigned responsibility for developing the preferred alternative for CPOW. I did my best to calm down, then asked James and my writer-editor, Mary Carr, to join me in Arrasmith's office. Basically I told him that the entire team had become dis-empowered in a fashion that was inconsistent with what was happening on the other projects. He said that he reserved the right to manage the projects differently, because CPOW had much more complex issues. I told him that I might file a retaliation lawsuit, and he grinned and said that was fine.

The next week, it was confirmed that my team had indeed been relieved of the responsibility of preparing the preferred alternative for the final EIS. Thorne Bay, as rumored, was given the task. Arrasmith and my whole team flew over to Thorne Bay to assist them in their alternative development process. I was given strict orders that my role was strictly to provide information and not to participate in any of the discussions. Don't speak unless spoken to. IDT leader, indeed!

The meeting was uncomfortable. The district was reluctant to be involved in the process at all, according to Robert, because they were as aware as I was that the logging level was unsustainable. Most of the people expected me to be leading the meeting and were aghast that I was kept in the back of the room in virtual chains. Others, who were aware what was going on, seemed non-plussed by my mere presence, despite my enforced silence. After a few hours, I picked up what was really going down.

When Thorne Bay was field reconning the proposed logging units, some units got a superficial look, while others were completely laid out, including road survey. The district alternative was merely a sweep-up of all the units that were already laid out. There was such a desperate race to get timber to KPC that the Forest Service decided it couldn't wait for the EIS to be finished to start sale preparation. They wanted to make sure that every last unit in which they had invested layout time was incorporated into the final decision. Because this was clearly predecisional and illegal under NEPA, I couldn't be trusted to go along with the program.

The next week, Anne Archie, Thorne Bay district ranger, called and said she wanted to bring Charlie Streuli over to work as co-leader of the CPOW team. I told her I respected Charlie and would value his help, but complained about further usurpation of my duties. Despite my protests, Charlie was brought in, first as "co-leader" and subsequently as "district ranger representative." This was a wholly contrived position without precedence on the Tongass.

The following week, Arrasmith called a meeting to make long-range project assignments. Five minutes prior to the start of the meeting, Arrasmith burst into my office and breathlessly asked me if I still wanted to be an IDT leader. I told him I liked the job, but didn't like my boss. Bill Nightingale, one of the other IDT leaders, was sitting next to me and piped up that he didn't want to be an IDT leader. Arrasmith ignored him and raced out of the room.

At the meeting, all future timber sale projects were divided between Bill Nightingale and Larry Lunde. After CPOW, a project for which I was having rapidly diminishing responsibility, my workload was nil. People in the room were stunned, and I could do nothing but hang my head and be glad agency policy seemed to preclude capital punishment.

Two days later was my mid-year performance rating, and not surprisingly, Arrasmith gave me my first unacceptable rating in 15 years of federal service. He did his level best to make the performance meeting as painful and drawn out as he could. Maybe he thought he could goad me into throwing him through the window. It was nip and tuck, but I kept a lid on it.

Arrasmith said my dealings with the media were unacceptable, even though he acknowledged that I was invariably honest, courteous, and responsive. So what's the problem? My external relations with the public were also unacceptable, even though he said I was particularly good with the Natives, Fish & Game, greenies, fisher-

men, and loggers. Well, who does that leave, Dave? Shoulda guessed
... seems KPC had reservations about me, even though I hadn't had
any direct contact with them during the performance appraisal period. It got worse. My appearance wasn't acceptable. I looked at his
double chin, protruding gut, and shirt tail hanging out and just shook
my head. My communications with the management team were no-
good either. I pointed out that last August he had personally ordered
me not to have any communications with the management team. Oh
well, I knew a set-up when I saw one. I formally documented the
meeting and gave him a copy.

This was such a weird time. My self-esteem was shattered, as
my career with the agency was stripped from me in tatters. I must
have been painful to look at ... like a sorrowful cancer victim in the
throes of chemotherapy. I watched as the agency heaped one environmental violation upon the next, one lie to cover the last one, and
one act of retaliation to reinforce the previous one. I didn't know
what else to do but stand my ground and try to do the best job I was
permitted to do. I could see a future version of myself, shuffling
along the street, pushing a grocery cart, mumbling about MELPs,
notices of intent, purpose and needs, etc. It scared me, and I vowed
never to let myself get that far over the edge.

Larry Lunde told me the contractors were having difficulty with
the Lab Bay project. When they went out on the ground to verify
their comprehensive logging plan, they found that many of the roads
and logging boundaries from the 1989-94 sale where not where they
were supposed to be. Worse, many of the contractor's proposed units
had already been cut.

It turned out Larry had another, even bigger problem. The Area's
unit expansion policy had turned into a swap of acres of relatively
low timber volume for acres which had substantially more timber
volume. And much of the 1989-94 sale's 5,000 acres of logging-
without-disclosure had occurred on the Lab Bay area. So much so,
that now the area was irreparably out of compliance with something
in TTRA called "proportionality."

"High-grading," the clearcutting of the best and deference of the
rest, typified the way the Tongass had been logged. Congress ex-

pressly tried to halt this practice by inserting a "proportionality" requirement into TTRA which insisted that the Forest Service only log the best (high volume) stands in any given management area in proportion to their occurrence. In other words, if 20 percent of the timber base in management area X was high volume, then at the conclusion of each timber sale, at least 20 percent of the remaining timber base within management area X was required to still be high volume. However, the wholesale swap of good acres for bad during unit expansion had so thoroughly buggered proportionality, that there was no way the Lab Bay sale could re-right the applecart, even if it cut exclusively low volume stands. None of the alternatives the contractor had assembled were viable because they all violated TTRA's proportionality clause. Quite simply, they were screwed.

Larry and I, along with Pete Klein, one of Gene Eide's foresters, took a look at this problem and wrote a "white paper" (April 22) which analyzed the situation, considered possible alternatives, and proposed a solution. Arrasmith had 'serious concerns' with our white paper. Eide commented that "it should never see the light of day." They awarded the contractor $270,000 to take another stab at it, and the Lab Bay project was ultimately delayed three years.

As my team worked to analyze the effects of the preferred alternative which had been assembled by the Thorne Bay District, we discovered that the District had made no attempt to keep the created clearcuts under 100 acres, as required by the National Forest Management Act. Jack Oien and I published a white paper (April 29) on the problem, again analyzing the situation, considering alternatives, and recommending a course of action. Arrasmith, apparently not liking our analysis, turned the problem over to Charlie Streuli. After much work, Charlie came up with virtually the same conclusion as Jack and I.

Later, Charlie was coerced into backing a hare-brained scheme to split up these oversized clearcuts by leaving narrow little strips of timber, which everyone agreed looked highly susceptible to blowdown. Jack and I teased him unmercifully about these blowdown strips and called them 'Streuli strips.' Arrasmith praised them as proactive ecosystem management.

Next, Arrasmith removed my responsibility to write the Record of Decision for CPOW, although the other IDT leaders retained this responsibility for their projects. He decided that he and Charlie would write it and got so weird about it that he would whisk it off his desk and hide it in a drawer, if I walked into his office. Charlie got so that he too would cover the ROD draft when I stopped by, but I could tell he was only obeying orders.

This whole thing was getting nutso. In May, the director of timber management from the Washington Office, Dave Hessel, was in Ketchikan. I knew Hessel from D.C. and had even worked on his staff for awhile during a two-month detail to timber. Two of the three Ketchikan Area planning team leaders were placed on his itinerary, and one was forbidden access. Take a guess.

Larry, Bill, and I met to hammer out how we were going to address the timber supply issue. We had to be consistent in our approach. We agreed there was no one correct answer, but that it likely lay somewhere between the lower limit established by our logging plan results (minus falldown) and the upper limit established by the computer models used by the Tongass Forest Plan. We agreed to show both limits in our respective projects and therefore show a range of potential future supplies. We documented our decision and proceeded down that path. I was apprehensive, though. My fear all along was that Arrasmith would receive orders to suppress my team's logging plan and instruct me to use forest plan computer models. I vowed that if that ever came to pass, I would file a whistleblower disclosure. That was my line in the sand, and I hoped I was never pushed across it.

My project was first out of the gate, and I wrote the timber section to include both estimates of future timber supplies, as the three team leaders had agreed. I distributed the draft section to various foresters in Ketchikan, out at the district, and up at the regional office in Juneau. Everyone seemed to be in agreement with our approach.

But I should have known that Murphy's Law was dogging my footsteps. In early June, Tom Somrak, a forester on Bill Nightingale's team, came into my office, deeply concerned with some of my timber supply assumptions. I explained to him that the three team leaders had agreed to that approach and that it had been favorably reviewed by other foresters. Somrak went next door to see Arrasmith.

Arrasmith came in shaking his head. He told me that he was under the impression that he had instructed me to remove any reference to my team's logging plan. I told him he had hinted that he wanted me to take that approach, but that he had never formally made that order. Because I firmly felt it represented a suppression of significant information, I told him I would need his order in writing.

A couple days later (June 14) I got it. Boy, did I get it. This letter had obviously been crafted at the regional level. It did everything but call my dog names. My work on the logging plan was called "gross and professionally unacceptable." This letter left little doubt about what approach the agency insisted I take. I told Arrasmith that I strongly disagreed with the letter, but would implement it post haste. I told myself that post haste I would also file a whistleblower disclosure.

Others within the agency were flabbergasted at Arrasmith's letter. Walt Dortch got a copy and responded:

> "Bullshit, Dave. Flat out bullshit. I can't believe you signed this. The game you play is what has led to ruin down here, all falls before keeping that ASQ up, eh? Your bios and others sound the alarm, you suggest they need counseling, suddenly high performers skid, why is that? Shoaf implemented what the Ketchikan Area Management Team directed, RO staff were briefed in person and asked in writing to respond on numerous occasions to this course. To my knowledge there is nothing in writing to support your incredibly gross conclusion that Shoaf acted unprofessionally by doing what he was directed to do. More importantly, to suggest the TLMP process was more interdisciplinary is ridiculous. TLMP calls for precisely the kind of project level truthing that Shoaf and company have conducted (and his process expressly identified the need for field verification) and now that answer is wrong in terms of supporting an equally ridiculous ASQ you try to challenge him professionally. It stinks. Don't bring the agency down with your folly."

The next few days were an absolute blur, as I rewrote sections of the final EIS to implement Arrasmith's order to remove all mention of my team's logging plan. There were a lot of changes to make. One section, which had appeared in the CPOW draft, had concluded, based upon my team's logging plan:

"Following completion of the long-term contract in 2004, there will not be sufficient volume remaining in the Project Area to sustain employment at current or historic levels. The result may be a significant disruption in local communities and logging camps within the Project Area which depend on timber employment, as timber harvesting shifts to other locations on the Forest. These workers will either be out of work or commute to other areas."

Based upon Arrasmith's direction, I rewrote the section, as follows:

"Following completion of the long-term contract in 2004, according to the TLMP Revision Alt P, there will be sufficient volume remaining in the Project Area to sustain employment at current or historic levels. This indicates local timber dependent communities and logging camps within the Project Area can depend on a steady, sustainable timber supply through the end of the first rotation."

Talk about switch and bait...

14

Horns of a Dilemma

(July 1993 - September 1993)

"And as I watched the act on stage,
My hands were clenched in fists of rage.
No angel born in hell
Could break that Satan's spell."
  -- Don McClean, "American Pie"

"Once in a vision, I came on some woods,
And I stood at a fork in the road.
My choices were clear, yet I froze with the fear
Of not knowing which way to go.
One road was simple -- acceptance of life.
The other road offered sweet relief.
When I made my decision, my vision became my belief."
  -- Dan Fogelberg, "The Netherlands"

There simply wasn't any way around it, as I could not disobey a direct order. It was now decision time for me ... what are you going to do about it? Are you really going to blow the whistle on the agency you love? I saw it as the dilemma a parent must face if they find out their teenager is selling crack to grade-school kids. I finally decided that my vow of abject honesty applied to keeping the bargain I had made with myself. I called AFSEEE and told them I was ready to file a formal whistleblower disclosure, but didn't have a clue how to go about it.

Whoosh! The next thing I knew AFSEEE's organizer, Brian Hunt, and a law school graduate, Doug Heiken, were at my house in Ketchikan. They explained the basic whistleblower process to me, but confessed they didn't know how to make a filing. No problem, they flew in a GAP attorney from the Seattle office who did. The first step was to file a personal affidavit which explained the situation and why I believed it constituted gross mismanagement, violation of law, gross waste of funds, or abuse of authority. GAP would represent me and file the formal whistleblower disclosure on my behalf with the U.S. Office of Special Counsel (OSC). OSC would then make a determination whether there was a significant likelihood that my allegations were correct. If OSC found in my behalf, they would then direct the Secretary of Agriculture to prepare an investigative report responding to my charges within 60 days.

There was one more thing. I could choose to allow OSC to identify me as the whistleblower, or request them to preserve my anonymity. Well, hell's bells, everyone and his dog would know who had filed the disclosure, so why not just be up front about it? AFSEEE and GAP both agreed. They explained the Whistleblower Protection Act, which prohibited an agency from retaliating against a whistleblower. They said my best protection was to walk in the sunlight, and that they would see I stayed there. Besides, they told me, Congressman George Miller had me in a huge bear hug and would protect me. I asked if Mr. Miller was a young, healthy man, and was assured he was indeed.

I leveled with AFSEEE about the mixed messages I was getting. A while back there had been a lot of investigations into mismanagement on the Tongass. The Forest Service had gotten scared and backed off for a bit, then had suddenly intensified its "hog and log" regime. What happened to the investigations? Brian and Doug just looked at me, shrugged, and asked "What's it going to be, Bill?" Oh, what the hell, let's go for it!

Brian and Doug left, and the GAP attorney, Mike Rossotto, stayed to help me prepare my affidavit. Besides explaining all the legal ramifications of what I was getting myself into, Mike mapped out a rough critical path to bring my case to successful conclusion. It included favorable press coverage, as well aid from sympathetic members of

Congress and administration officials. When it was time to go to work, he plugged in his laptop, sorted through my meager collection of music, pulled out all the Led Zeppelin tapes, cranked up the stereo to kill, and started to work.

Using Mike's boilerplate and outline, within the week I completed a draft affidavit. It was 28 pages and contained 200 pages of supporting documentation. According to my copious records, this was also the week at work where I made all the necessary revisions to the CPOW final EIS to cover-up all information from my team's logging plan. In addition I ran 37 miles, lifted weights four times, and went halibut fishing (got skunked). Not sure how many times I went to the bathroom, but it was a busy time, and I was keeping close records.

Mike returned to Seattle but kept in close touch, as did AFSEEE. Mike strongly advised me to make a formal response to Arrasmith's June 14 letter which ordered me to suppress my team's logging plan. He said unless I responded, the agency could argue that I obviously agreed with Arrasmith's orders. OK. Mike and I continued to work back and forth at strengthening my affidavit.

Both Mike and AFSEEE stressed one particular point: I had to be absolutely squeaky clean, both in my professional and personal life. Any deviation from the straight and narrow ... a disobeyed work order, a botched assignment, a paternity suit, a DWII charge ... could render my disclosure null and void. It was beyond my Teutonic reasoning. How was my personal conduct related to the mismanagement of the Tongass? If the fate of the Tongass were tied to my own perfection as a human being, then it was surely doomed. Geez, I wanted people to forget about me and just focus on the charges, all of which were thoroughly documented. But that wasn't the way it worked.

On July 6, 1993, I submitted a notarized copy of my affidavit to GAP. On July 8, as Mike had suggested, I submitted an eight-page timber resource report to the CPOW planning record which contravened Arrasmith's letter. Contravened, hell, it said it was bogus, albeit in a technical and professional manner. I placed a copy in Arrasmith's in-basket and left work that day, off for a three-day weekend. James and I went halibut fishing Friday and Saturday (caught eight).

When James and I returned to the dock on Saturday, Larry Lunde saw me and pulled me aside. He told me that the office had been in an uproar on Friday when Arrasmith discovered my resource report. He said most of the management team came over and were screaming bloody murder that I had essentially written the administrative appeal for CPOW. Larry said there was an enraged discussion to see if they could fire me outright. They pursued the firing attempt all the way to the regional office, where Fred Norbury (regional director of planning) had finally dissuaded the lynch mob. Larry's desk was directly outside Arrasmith's office, and he said there was no way he could have avoided hearing it, as it was pretty darned loud. He told me to watch my butt. Now where have I heard that before?

Arrasmith was pretty subdued the next week. He told me that he wished I could have resolved my professional differences without filing a minority opinion resource report. I told him I had tried, but that the agency had evidently made previous commitments which precluded it from obeying the law and telling the truth, and that, while I would always obey direct orders, I wanted no part of their shenanigans. The CPOW final EIS and ROD went to Juneau for final review and then were to be sent to the printer. The project was over.

Now that it had gone to the printer, I was finally allowed to read the record of decision (ROD), which made it excruciatingly clear that the Forest Service had no intention of listening to some rebel planning team leader, oops, make that ex-planning team leader. It was business as usual on the Tongass. Rittenhouse even insisted upon cutting the unit that had the wolf-denning area nearby.

The next week, Chacon and I took off for a camping trip in the skiff. It was my first complete week off in 2 1/2 years, and we enjoyed it immensely. One nice, sunny day, we were dozing on a beach log. I had just cut off my ponytail with my pocket knife, and was daydreaming about what the future held. My eyes were closed, and I could hear the 'whoosh-whoosh-whoosh' of raven wings directly overhead. The funny thing was the whooshing didn't go away, but continued. Huh? I opened my eyes, but didn't see any raven, although I could still hear the whooshing. Thoroughly confused, I finally spotted the raven, way, way up in the sky and watched as it flew across the bay. It seemed odd that the sound of its wings would carry down so clearly from such a height. I mentioned it to James later, who also thought it strange, and remarked that Tlingits believe Raven to be a notorious trickster.

On July 29, 1993, my attorneys at GAP filed an official whistleblower disclosure on my behalf with the U.S. Office of Special Counsel. There were six specific allegations of violation of law:

1. Over estimation of timber supply
2. Post decisional expansion of harvest units
3. Predecisional layout
4. Discrepancy of CPOW Notice of Intent
5. Clearcut size in excess of limitations
6. Proportionality violations (high-grading)

Also documented were the acts of non-merit retaliation against me because of my public comment letter. The die was cast, but I told no one. Not even James or Robert. It was now a question of waiting for OSC to review my allegations and make an initial determination if they were credible.

The other two IDT leaders, Larry Lunde and Bill Nightingale, as well as my wildlife biologist were selected to go to a prestigious national forestry conference, which was going to be attended by all the movers and shakers in the field of natural resource conservation. I was left behind again. It was another slap in my face.

A couple weeks later, I picked up AFSEEE representatives, including their acting executive director, Buzz Williams, a long, tall drink of water, who was a whitewater river guide from South Carolina. We were awaiting word from OSC whether or not they agreed my charges were significantly valid.

Buzz reviewed my affidavit and told me that the whole Tongass debacle was the worst violation of the public trust he had ever seen. While he praised my coming forward, he told me I had about a 10 percent chance of lasting another year with the Forest Service. He told me they would find out everything I liked and take it all away. I was floored. What about the Whistleblower Protection Act? He snorted and just said to mark his words.

On August 20, OSC determined that there was indeed a significant likelihood that my allegations were correct. They sent a directive to Agriculture Secretary Mike Espy requiring him to prepare an investigative report within 60 days. OSC noted that I had alluded to retaliation on the part of the Forest Service and asked if I also wanted to file a complaint along those lines. I thought about it, consulted with AFSEEE and GAP, and finally decided to keep the two issues separate. What I was seeking was proper management of the Tongass National Forest, and I did not want that diluted by the lesser issue of correcting the personal and professional damage I had suffered. What the heck, I could wait 60 days for that.

So far the whistleblower disclosure had been a complete covert operation, but that was about to end. AFSEEE decided to prepare a press release, as part of their plan to protect me by keeping me in the spotlight. I'm a decided introvert, but they convinced me of the important role the media can play in focusing attention and getting remedial action. Nonetheless, I shuddered as I contemplated entering the limelight.

The next week at work, I found myself with nothing to do. After the intense three-year grind of "leading" the production of the largest timber sale in the nation, it was a welcome respite ... for about 15 minutes. I quickly grew bored. What was next? I talked to Arrasmith and he said to chill out for a bit. He seemed smug and benevolent as he told me I had done a good job. He was amazed I could get so much work done without working overtime, and I told him I liked working hard. Nope, Dave, hard work never killed me. Idle time, that's what I can't stand. Idle time. His eyes glowed.

James and I had found a halibut hole fairly close to town which we dubbed "The Spot." We took people fishing there occasionally but didn't broadcast its location, as that would kinda be like an aging actress telling her true birth date. Anyhow, we were fishing at The Spot one day, when all of a sudden Arrasmith's boat passed, and immediately swung back after recognizing my boat. He started fishing, which didn't please us at all. After a coupla minutes, James told me to get my .357 magnum. Uh-oh. I tried to tell him that it was just a fishing hole and we really shouldn't kill over it, when I caught a twinkle in James' eye.

We drifted so our backs were to Arrasmith's boat, then James had me fire straight down into the water, kinda like we had just shot a big halibut. We feigned some mighty activity, like we were dragging something huge over the side, then started to giggle. Arrasmith's boat pulled close alongside ours, and when we drifted apart, we "shot another halibut." By now, we were roaring with laughter. On Monday, Arrasmith was mystified how we could have caught so many fish, while he got skunked. We told him it was the bait and howled.

As soon as AFSEEE's press release came over the newswires, Nikki Murray Jones, a reporter for the "Ketchikan Daily News" asked me for an interview, which I reluctantly granted. I drew the line at having my picture taken, enough was enough. On the morning of August 31, the front page headline of the "Ketchikan Daily News" proclaimed, "Local Forester Reports Concerns of Over Harvest." The story took up most of the first two pages and laid out my concerns, the information upon which they were based, and the steps I had taken to bring the information up the chain of command.

Walking into work that day was indescribable. Because I hadn't mentioned the disclosure to a soul, the morning headlines caught most people unaware. No one mentioned it to me, not a word. I tried to stay at my desk that day, because I was too embarrassed to have much interaction with others. Every time I did get up, there were little groups of people who fell immediately silent, and stared at me as I approached.

In a follow-up story Arrasmith was quoted, "Although that can't be considered public information, there's been no retaliation against Shoaf." The next day the headlines read "Forester's Disclosure Brings Mixed Reaction." Most visibly quoted was Troy Reinhart, then executive director of the Alaska Forest Association [and soon to become public spokesman for KPC].

" ...doesn't take the charges seriously. OSC doesn't use field information for review. It looks at complaints and determines if they're too outrageous or are credible. It's just a bunch of lawyers sitting around a table saying, 'This could have happened.' Acceptance by the counsel doesn't mean it's valid, and they didn't say it was valid. It's like someone calling the police to report an alleged burglary, and the police responding because they think the person sounds responsible. A person who can write and sound logical could submit a disclosure the counsel would consider."

The next day, the editorial page ran a Point of View editorial by Reinhart under the headlines "False charges do not serve public interest":

"Environmental special interest groups take very complicated issues and simplify them to a point they are not a true representation of the truth in their zeal to warp public perceptions of forest management. This is the case of claims made by AFSEEE and its leader, Bill Shoaf, in bashing sound Forest Service management practices ...

They want to stop all forest management activities which provide jobs and the way of life we enjoy in Alaska ... Don't be mislead by the false and sensationalized claims of preservationist groups. People such as Mr. Shoaf and AFSEEE have a political agenda which can only be met by the distribution of inaccurate information presented in a manner which misleads the public ..."

I felt I had to respond, but the editor, Lew Williams, disallowed my submission, because he said it was too long. It was less than half the length of Reinhart's. I resubmitted an abbreviated version, which the paper finally ran about a week later:

"...Actually, my records show I am not even a member of AFSEEE, much less their leader. I stand on my record as a former logger and professional forester with 15 years experience, during which time I have logged, planned, laid out, cruised, appraised, prepared the contract, or administered the logging on just under a billion board feet of timber. This is hardly the track record of a preservationist who, as Mr. Reinhart alleges, 'wants to stop all forest management activities.' What I do stand for is the long-term health and sustainability for the timber industry, as opposed to how high we can stack the current wood pile before it crashes ..."

The "Daily News" was selling a lot of papers these days, as salvos were fired back and forth. One of the more interesting editorials was written by David Person, a wildlife biologist doing doctoral wolf telemetry research on Prince of Wales island:

> "... Using the Virtual Reality Timber Planner (VRP) is easy: just put on the helmet, adjust the blinders, so that you are completely insulated from the real world, and before you can say 'icky, picky ptang', your pipe dream becomes reality. If you need more trees, make them; if those trees disappear, make more. Mr. Reinhart was obviously under the influence of VRP technology when he imagined, among other things, that Bill Shoaf was the leader of AFSEEE, and with the help of VRP, it became reality in this paper."

I received numerous phone calls from national media groups, but was largely uncertain how to deal with them. I am not at all the "60 Minutes" type and dislike attention, so I was not thrilled about having my name in the news. It seemed they were pressing me to condense the problems on the Tongass to sound bites. "Mr. Shoaf, is part of the problem log thefts?" Uh, I'm sure that has occurred, but I don't have any direct information on it and didn't include it within my disclosure. "Oh ... I see. How about 'phantom forests'? Were phantom forests involved in this?" Uh, not really. "Oh ... I see. Ummm ... what was involved?" Well, it was violation of the Multiple Use Sustained Yield Act, violation of the National ... "Hold on, Mr Shoaf. The Multiple Use what? What's that?"

By then the call would usually digress to my holding a primer in Forestry 101, and the caller's being totally overwhelmed and thinking maybe they'd fall back to their story about recent Elvis sightings. Often the reporter would ask for a copy of my whistleblower disclosure, which I abjectly refused to provide. It may sound weird, but I had no desire to embarrass my agency. What I had seen on the Tongass was so unlike what I had observed in the lower 48 where I had grown to truly love the Forest Service. My affidavit even included a clause forbidding AFSEEE and GAP from releasing my disclosure without my express consent. Quite simply, I wanted the U.S. government to deal with the sordid mess on the Tongass, not the media.

The weeks passed slowly. I was largely idle at work. My planning team employees would come in looking for assignments, and I had to shamefully tell them that I didn't have any work for myself, much less for them. I read a personnel report that my position had been abolished, and that there had been an aborted discussion to sever my federal employment. That idea was scrapped, however, and a decision was made to find me more suitable employment. On Sept. 8, we had a meeting to debrief the planning teams. Right before lunch time, when all the other managers had already left, Gene Eide stood up and red-facedly declared that, "These Forest Plan volume estimates are OUT ... TO ... LUNCH!" It was a grandstand show, as Gene was uncertain which way the winds were blowing. A lot of people were in the same boat.

Later that day, Gene told me that he was looking at a position for me over in timber and would I be interested? Yes, I told him, anything to get away from Arrasmith. I asked him what it involved and he said it would be half computer work and half professional forestry, with real honest-to-goodness field time. It sounded pretty darned good to me.

On Sept. 11, in a show of support, 62 of my fellow employees on the Ketchikan Area signed a petition backing me and presented it to the forest supervisor, Dave Rittenhouse.

Dear Dave,
    As employees of the Ketchikan Area of the Tongass National Forest, we wish to express our support for the efforts of our colleague Bill Shoaf to express his concerns about various resources and legal issues. Although we come from different professional backgrounds, we support Mr. Shoaf's integrity and willingness to speak out for the public trust.
    Like Mr. Shoaf, we take seriously our charge of managing Tongass resources for the American people. We respect Mr. Shoaf's courage in speaking out about his professional concerns. We believe an atmosphere of respect for conscientious questioning of management procedures and policies   can only serve to make the Forest Service a better agency.
    The Forest Service's revised vision statement includes the phrase: "Responsibility and accountability for excellence are shared by employees ..." Among the Forest Services's Guiding Principles are that the agency should "maintain high professional and ethical standards; be responsible and accountable for what we do; follow laws, regulations, executive direction, and congressional intent."
    We believe Mr. Shoaf's actions live up to the renewed Mission, Vision, and Guiding Principles of the agency, and we offer him our support.

While I was aware of the existence of the petition, I had nothing to do with its inception, wording, or circulation. The people who passed the petition around said that circulation was limited because of fear of reprisal from management. Nonetheless, this was a tremendous show of solidarity, especially given that a number of co-workers later approached me and lamented that they had been denied the chance to "sign for me."

On Sept. 29, Rittenhouse sent a letter to all employees:

> "I want to thank those of you who signed the September 11 letter supporting Bill Shoaf's courage in speaking out about his professional concerns ... I feel fortunate to have such a talented and dedicated work force on the Ketchikan Area."

The whole Tongass was glued to the soap-opera-like sequence of events surrounding the nation's largest timber sale. The general consensus was that CPOW's resolution would determine the course of Tongass management for a long time to come. As both its leader and chief protagonist, I felt like I was nailed to a tornado.

15

Purgatory

(September 1993 - March 1994)

"Does anyone know
Where the love of God goes,
When the waves turn the minutes to hours?"
    -- Gordon Lightfoot, "The Wreck of the Edmund
    Fitzgerald"

James and I were getting concerned. It was almost mid-September and the coho salmon hadn't shown up yet. We had a caught a few, but not nearly all we needed for the winter. It had been kinda dry that year by Ketchikan standards, and rumor had it that our local coho were schooled up around Ship Island, waiting for rain to make their natal streams swimmable.

Another concern we had was that the deadline for filing an administrative appeal on CPOW was nearing, and the top-dog greenie group on the Tongass, the South East Alaska Conservation Council (SEACC) had not yet filed an appeal. On Sept. 20, 1993, I called Larry Edwards, a Sitka GreenPeace activist and SEACC board member. I respected Larry, and he and my old adversary, Sylvia Geraghty, were the only two greenies in the whole world that I trusted. I told Larry that the CPOW appeal deadline was that day and asked him where the SEACC appeal was.

He went crazy. Larry said that Arrasmith had told Buck Lindekugel, the SEACC lawyer, that the appeal period deadline was

Sept. 22. There was no way they'd make it before then. I suggested Larry hang up, call me back, formally ask me when the appeal period expired, and file a complaint that Arrasmith had given him the wrong date. He did so, and I wrote it up and filed my notes in the planning record, which would be sealed that day when the appeal period closed. Larry hurriedly rung off and caught a plane to SEACC headquarters in Juneau.

Arrasmith paced that day like a father awaiting his firstborn. He called the regional office in Juneau several times to see if SEACC's appeal had been received. Quitting time came and, sure enough, no appeal had come in. The next day he bragged that he'd pulled off a major coup. Because we had sparred so much over the sale, he goaded me with remarks like, "Well, the document couldn't have been that bad, if the major environmental group in all of Southeast Alaska couldn't even find anything ... blah, blah, blah." I received a phone call that day from an aide of Congressman Charlie Rose (D, NC), instructing me to provide him a copy of my whistleblower disclosure. I told him I would indeed obey a directive from a member of Congress, but I did ask for a written confirmation order, strictly for my personal records. I notified AFSEEE and GAP that my disclosure was now in Congress, and they were delighted.

The agency was now forced to make a decision regarding whether or not it would accept SEACC's belated appeal, which was received two days late, on Sept. 22. I kept vigil over the decision, when James burst in, kinda breathless. The coho were in! It was past quitting time, and I stuck my head in Arrasmith's office to tell him James and I would be gone the rest of the week. He seemed incredulous that we would willingly miss the drama of the forthcoming decision on whether or not to accept SEACC's appeal. I told him there was fishing to be had and walked out.

We left pre-dawn the next morning. I hooked the morning's first coho before I even got my downrigger lowered. We each kept limits of six fish and released several others. Despite the thrill of the coho, we were both pretty pissed, as we speculated that our agency would probably be delighted to be given the opportunity to simply dismiss SEACC's appeal on the basis of untimeliness. James and I had often discussed the mismanagement of the Tongass and had more or less agreed that CPOW was a shining example of what was wrong with the Forest Service. In fact, the general consensus throughout the agency was that our EIS had absolutely no chance of surviving a legal challenge. Quite simply, it was dead on arrival.

We fished the next day too. Once again, the fish gods gave us big-time coho. In the brief lulls between 12- to 15-pound salmon's snatching our herring-tipped hoochies off the downrigger and making heart-stopping runs and leaps, we discussed why SEACC's appeal was late. If it was so important to them, why did they wait until the last second before filing it? It didn't make sense. We pulled that thread every way we could, but were simply unable to swallow the obvious conclusion that SEACC's heart really wasn't into the appeal. How could that be?

The last two days we'd each caught a dozen fat coho, enough to see us through the winter. We pulled my dory out of the water the next day, and trailered it out to my place for winter storage under one of my carports. I already had salmon in the smoker, and the heady mixture of salmon and alder smoke filled the air. It was the close of another season, another of life's cycles complete.

That night there was a SEACC potluck dinner at the Five Star Cafe, and I was invited. While I was basically distrustful of the greenies, it was hard to pass up a potluck. In truth, I probably would have attended a potluck to support anything.

I shoved some freshly smoked salmon into a bag and stopped at the grocery store enroute to the potluck. There a friend waylaid me and quizzed me about being a whistleblower. We talked for quite a while, and I noted the passage of time with some ambivalence. I hate to be late to anything ... least of all potlucks. Yet I had a vague sense of unease, as if I were going into the enemy's camp. I finally broke away from my friend and walked into the cafe. Everyone was already sitting at tables, eating. At a glance, I didn't recognize anyone, so I figured what the heck, and headed for the food table; I came to eat anyway.

Jackie Canterbury, a Forest Service wildlife biologist and ex-SEACC president, came up and greeted me while I helped myself to even more potato salad or whatever. The next thing I knew, there were people all around, shouting congratulations, pounding me on the back, and ushering me over to the table with the SEACC leaders. I was skeptical, but eventually the genuine appreciation shown by this roomful of people made me feel pretty good. It was certainly a darned sight better than how I was treated at work. Plus the food was great, especially the smoked salmon!

Two gals came over and introduced themselves. They didn't look like they were there to steal my food, so I relaxed. It turned out they were both commercial gillnetters. I was on my feet in a flash. Lady gillnetters! One gal had on a wedding ring, but the other gal had a naked left ring finger, and when I shook her hand, I didn't let it go. She said her name was Victoria something-or-other and she had written me a letter a while back.

Just then, SEACC decided to start the evening's entertainment, a slide show on the Tongass. As chairs were being rearranged, I asked this Victoria-something to sit with me. She refused, and next thing I knew the lights were doused. Oh well. But, lady gillnetters, eh? What a concept! That night I looked up Victoria's letter and wrote her back.

Time stalled. The Secretary of Agriculture had less than 30 days left to file his investigative report. There weren't even any good rumors about what was happening. The local managers said they knew absolutely nothing and had never even seen my disclosure. I certainly didn't have a clue what was going on. People got nervous. Virtually everyone on the Tongass knew my charges were right, and moreover knew that I undoubtedly had access to official government documents that more than substantiated my charges. There was no question of innocence or guilt. The question was what was going to be done about it. What indeed? People seemed entirely focused on being aligned with the winning side and with going on record as opposing the losing side. But which side was which?

Things were pretty slow at work. Make that real slow. My daily calendar read, September 30 ... "Nothing," October 4 ... "Nothing," October 7 ... "Absolutely nothing," October 8 ... "Annual leave (Couldn't take another day of nothing)." Nothing, nothing, nothing. I talked to the personnel officer, Gwen Williams, about the new position in Eide's shop. She told me she had a real problem with the viability of the job and had only reluctantly approved the position description. She told me it was non-funded and insisted that it be reviewed in 12 months to determine it were truly viable. Oh what the heck, it had to be better than working for Arrasmith.

I signed the acceptance papers and was officially placed on Gene Eide's staff. I moved from my fancy office back to the "Pleasure Palace," coincidentally to the same room I had left three years before. There were two guys already in the office ... the forest silviculturist ("silviculture" is the study of growing and caring for trees) and the fire control officer. A silviculturist on a forest that exclusively clearcuts is only slightly more gainfully employed than someone responsible for wildfire control on a forest with 160 inches of rain annually. As it turned out, they were both much more gainfully employed than the Tongass National Forest's first ever "special projects forester." There were some snickers about the caliber of the three employees in Room 306 ... about three peas in a pod. It hurt.

On my birthday, I attended an evening presentation on karst. Jackie Canterbury came over and sat beside me. She spotted KPC's new spokesman, Troy Reinhart, standing in the back flanked by a coupla goon-types with hardhats and suspenders. Jackie said they were there to intimidate people and encouraged me to go over and punch out Troy for the untrue remarks about me he had published in the newspaper. I had never seen the guy before, and he did look kinda soft and pudgy, so I went over and shook hands with him and introduced myself. When he recognized the name, he sputtered, "You're just another environmentalist trying to shut down the forest." I squeezed his hand a little harder and said, "No, Troy, I want to shut YOU down." His bodyguards thought this was kinda funny, and without them, there wasn't much Troy could do about it.

Later that night, a few of us went over to the Potlatch Bar for a few beers. I proposed a toast to myself, "I'm 45 years old, and my significant other is a wolf. Hurray for the wolf!"

I called AFSEEE and GAP. They told me that OSC had offered no information and that things were pretty quiet in Congress. Geez, the 60 days were almost up, and something in my gut told me that if this were to drag out for an inordinately long while, the simple passage of time would work against me. I began to realize that, while I had many supporters, it was me and me alone who lived in Ketchikan and had to go to work every day at the agency I had blown the whistle on. It felt lonely, and I began to consider the real possibility that I would simply be abandoned, and in the darkness of remote Alaska, the local managers would devour me. Because I had a tendency to fight back, I made a poor victim, but that didn't mean I could single-handedly prevail. I needed to come up with a back-up plan if things went increasingly downhill at work and no respite were forthcoming.

I was determined to stay with the Forest Service at least until my whistleblower case was resolved. If I were vindicated, I should be able to keep my job, although my career was beyond salvage. If the agency prevailed (how could they?) things could get tough indeed. I distinctly remembered Buzz Williams' prediction that I only had a 10-percent chance of lasting a year. He was certainly no fool, so maybe he was right.

As I regarded Ketchikan as my forever home, my local employment options were pretty limited. The local economy had three sectors -- timber, tourism, and fishing. If the Forest Service and I split the sheets, there was little chance I could get, or would want, a job in the timber industry. I didn't especially like tourists and had no desire to open a T-shirt shop, sell plastic totem poles, or whatever. That left fishing. I started forming a loose plan about becoming a fisherman.

And then Victoria, the gal I had met at the potluck, wrote back. It turned out she had moved and was now living in Juneau. The agency had been wanting me to fly up to Juneau to do some database analysis, so I let them buy my ticket and even acceded to staying over a few days. Victoria and I hit it off pretty well, and we continued to visit during subsequent trips to Juneau. We were both in tight situations. It turned out she wasn't a fisherman anymore. She had just gotten divorced, and her ex-husband got the boat while she got the house. He also had custody of their two teen-aged sons, which upset her greatly. She had lost her teaching job because she filed an appeal on a timber sale, and the school board caved into pressure from the local timber industry. They certainly didn't want a teacher who might say the word E-N-V-I-R-O-N-M-E-N-T, right there aloud in the classroom.

I explained my own situation ... that I might be forced out of my job with the government, and that I too might need a new job. Hey, suppose we team up and go fishing together? Humph, she wasn't sure about that, so I threw in the kicker. OK, move into my house in Ketchikan, fish with me, and petition the judge for a re-hearing about your kids.

She quickly agreed, but I could sense she would be a reluctant fisherman. I impressed upon her that I would not allow someone else's kids to come into my home and make a nuisance of themselves or drag me into any form of family rivalry. This would only work if everyone kept their end of the bargain. Somewhere inside me, something screamed, but I ignored it.

Victoria had a set of runes and asked me if I wanted to throw them. She explained they were little rocks painted with ancient symbols, and worked much like tarot or pigeon entrails. She said she found them particularly useful for obtaining sage advice when she was on the cusp of a critical decision. I wasn't a big believer in that kind of mumbo-jumbo, but decided to give it a go. I cast the runes and when we looked up the meaning in the accompanying book, we got this response:

"Just do your task and don't worry about the outcome."

That made a believer out of me. Though I had a virtual fleet of lawyers in and out of my life since the CPOW mess started, this has remained the best advice of all, and I treasured it.

One of my trips to Juneau was a result of my random selection to participate in a nationwide survey conducted by the University of Washington. The survey was to be the guts of a research report they were preparing for the chief of the Forest Service, entitled "Policies and Mythologies of the U.S. Forest Service -- A Conversation with Employees." One specific question which the survey asked was, "Can we sustain our National Forest's current level of resource use for 100 years?" Nationwide, only 35 percent of Forest Service employees said "yes," with Alaska's having the lowest affirmative response (22 percent) of all the regions. It quantified what everybody knew, but more importantly, it established the fact that everyone knew it. So why was I the only one speaking up about it?

Around Veteran's Day, the regional forester denied all the administrative appeals to CPOW. The Forest Service appeal system was amazing. Quite simply, it resembled a divorce where one of the parties got to be the judge. "Let's see, I get the house, the mutual funds, the BMW, the kids ... and you get to pay me, oh, $3000/month." Yeah, the Forest Service appeal system is a lot like that. After spending millions of dollars of taxpayers' money in order to write an environmental impact statement about the effects of cutting timber, does the Forest Service conclude that they are right and proceed with the timber sale? Or do they decide that their mortal enemies, the greenies, are right, cancel the sale, and have to return the millions of dollars they just spent, because they have now failed to meet their timber targets, and the Senate appropriations committee (incidentally chairmanned by Alaska Senator Ted Stevens) takes a pretty dim view of that? Last time I heard, the Forest Service had concluded they were right in something like 202 out of the last 205 timber sale appeals.

In an unusual move, the greenies asked the newly appointed chief of the Forest Service, Jack Ward Thomas, to review the regional forester's decision. The newly elected Clinton administration, led by Vice President Al Gore, had given the boot to the old timber beast chief Dale Robertson and had replaced him with Thomas, a wildlife biologist who had led the spotted owl team. Under intense pressure, the Forest Service took the bait and agreed to have the chief review CPOW. The higher level review of the CPOW appeal represented a significant litmus test for the new administration, and it was watched closely.

It was a critical and contentious time. The two pulp corporations in Southeast Alaska were on the rocks. A new state-of-the-art pulp mill in South Africa was delivering dissolvable pulp to the Pacific Rim at a price that was several hundred dollars a ton less than it could be produced in Alaska, even exclusive of transportation costs. After a long stretch of unprofitability, the Alaska Pulp Corporation closed its pulp mill in Sitka, although it continued to run its saw mill in Wrangell.

This put the Forest Service in a bad place. The basic intent of the long-term contracts was that the Forest Service would feed the pulp corporations Tongass timber in return for their constructing and operating a pulp mill. The decision by APC to close their pulp mill was an obvious major breach of contract, and the regional forester was faced with the decision of whether or not to place APC in breach. This was a heavy-duty decision, as it could lead to the ultimate cancellation of one of the two long-term pulp contracts, which had driven activities on the Tongass for so long. I remembered what I had heard in D.C. almost five years ago ... that the Tongass could only support one pulp contract, and the APC contract would be the one to go.

I don't believe Hunter S. Thompson ever faced as much fear and loathing on the campaign trail as existed in Ketchikan in late 1993. The local press was relentless about keeping timber issues plastered on the front page of the only newspaper in town. Each story wasn't just spun, it was torqued so far to the conservative right that it was hard to tell where editorials left off and the news began. The editorial page seemed a reincarnation of McCarthyism ... death to the greenies, to the Forest Service, and to anyone else who made the good ol' boys turn off their saws. The Alaska congressional delegation went absolutely ballistic. The mood in this mill town grew foul and ugly.

In my copious free time at "work," I sent a happy holidays e-mail down to Mike Lunn, the former Tongass forest supervisor, and the guy who had hired me. He wrote back on Dec. 16:

> "Bill, good to hear from you. I've thought several times back to my selection of you for that job, and each time I feel a sense of pride in my choice. In some ways, I created the climate, and hired most of the people who cared enough to raise the issues. R-10 [Alaska] has a history of beating down dissent ... I think that chapter is about to be concluded. Took a lot of guts to do what you did, and I know how much you've loved the FS. I don't know all the issues you raised, nor the details, but I do know you've done it because you believed it was the right thing to do."

Interspersed between such inspiring letters telling me to hang in there, was a sea of idle time. God, it was awful. Most people who are gainfully employed count a good weekend one where they don't start thinking about their job until Sunday night. By breakfast on Monday, they have their workday well planned. I would arrive at work Monday morning and not have a clue what I was going to do. Not a clue. I had no responsibilities. I wasn't allowed near any part of the timber workload for fear I might uncover some wrong-doing. Every now and then someone would want a small computer project. So I sat and waited for the Secretary of Agriculture's investigative report, which was now two months late.

On Jan. 12, 1994, I received a call from Steve Stine, a Forest Service employee from the Washington office. He was an environmental coordination specialist, working with quality assurance and document management, and had been assigned the responsibility of looking into my whistleblower disclosure. I asked Steve how he ended up with the assignment.

Stine told me that USDA originally assigned the investigation to the Office of Inspector General, but the subject matter was too complex for them to deal with. Rather than enlist an independent forester, OIG referred my case to the Forest Service law enforcement staff in the Washington office, who summarily routed it to their counterparts in Alaska. The Alaska law enforcement staff refused to proceed because the issues were complex, and likely involved their boss, then regional forester Mike Barton. Oops, conflict of interest. So, the investigation was returned to Washington office law enforcement. This time they referred it to the Washington office environmental coordination staff, who began studying it, then returned it when they saw that some of the allegations involved retaliation against a whistleblower. Law enforcement really didn't want any part of this investigation, so they returned it to environmental coordination overtop of some deputy chief's signature, with the instructions to focus on the resource issues only, and to ignore the retaliation allegations.

Stine said he would be coming to Ketchikan the following week to conduct interviews pursuant to producing the investigative report. I was ecstatic, and yet at the same time trying to brace myself for what was likely to become a protracted ordeal. I asked the Ketchikan law enforcement officer, Rich Glodowski, to come see me. I told him what Stine had told me about the way the investigation had been passed around like a hot potato, and Rich confirmed it. I told Rich that I was disappointed that the Forest Service was being allowed to investigate itself, and asked if that were common practice. Rich said that my whole disclosure was a particularly queer duck. First, it was a lot more complex than the typical smash-and-grab with which law enforcement usually dealt. Second, the whole whistleblower disclosure was an anomaly, and NO ONE had ever dealt with one before.

Rich left, and during my run that night, I thought about what he had said. Seemingly, no one had previously filed a whistleblower disclosure against the Forest Service and summoned the U.S. Office of Special Counsel. Attorney General Janet Reno summoned OSC, not some hick forester living on a remote island. What had I gotten myself into?

Stine called back and said he would be flying to the regional office in Juneau on Jan. 18, 1994, and then down to Ketchikan the next morning. He scheduled me for 8:30 a.m. He asked me for a list of people whom I wanted him to interview, and I told him my entire planning team and the other team leaders, as well as Walt Dortch, Mark Voight, and Carolyn Minor. He agreed.

Just prior to Stine's arrival, regional forester Mike Barton placed the Alaska Pulp Corporation in breach of contract for closing their pulp mill. He told them to open the mill and start producing pulp, or he would cancel their contract. He gave them 30 days. APC said they wanted to keep the pulp mill closed, but continue to run their sawmill in Wrangell, which was still profitable. APC had the Alaska congressional delegation, the local media, and timber workers throughout SE Alaska on their side. Barton was backed by contractual law and reiterated his 30-day ultimatum.

As usual the plane from Juneau was delayed because of bad weather, and Stine showed up late in the day Jan. 19, along with Ruth Vein, who was going to conduct interviews regarding my retaliation allegations. Ruth Vein was a budget analyst for Gene Chelstad, the regional director for timber management. Huh? Steve and I rescheduled for the next morning. While we talked for a long time that day, our interview was somewhat rushed because the plane delay had cost him a full day from his schedule.

Stine proceeded with his other interviews, starting with the managers and staff officers ... basically the people I had accused. While these people were afforded the courtesy of private, leisurely, one-on-one interviews, members of my planning team were herded into a room en masse to say what was on their mind. He told them he was in a hurry and only could spend a few minutes with them. Several, notably James and Mary Carr, told me later that they were rushed and weren't entirely comfortable giving testimony in front of a group. Stine also failed to interview Walt, Mark, and Carolyn. Nonetheless, he was more thorough than Ruth Vein. She not only failed to interview any of my planning team or the other team leaders ... but she also failed to interview me. I never even caught a glimpse of her.

On his way out of Ketchikan on Friday, Stine and I talked. I told him I had waited a long time for this investigation and was disappointed that everything was so rushed. He apologized and explained that he had no slack in his timeline, because he needed to return to D.C. for a Monday morning briefing with William McCleese, who was responsible for the chief's decision on the CPOW appeal. Because of the substantial overlap between the issues in the investigative report and the administrative appeals on CPOW, McCleese had to make sure the investigative report and the chief's appeal decision said the same thing.

I called AFSEEE that night and told them that my whistleblower disclosure had been irrevocably tied to the CPOW appeal. Seemingly, if it failed, so did I. Buzz Williams said that my disclosure covered a lot more issues than the appeal, and that it was unconscionable to dismiss those extra charges just to ensure the decisions were the same. He said I'd gotten screwed, but I knew that.

On Feb. 3, 1994, William McCleese, acting for Chief Jack Ward Thomas, reaffirmed the regional forester's decision to dismiss the CPOW appeal.

In my whole career, I had never contacted the chief of the Forest Service. Oh, a coupla times back in D.C., then-chief Dale Robertson and I had nodded to each other as we passed in the hall, but that was about it. I was a mere peon, and they were ... well, the chief. But here was the new chief, whose initial directive to all employees was to "Obey the law and tell the truth," and he has just ratified the largest timber sale in the nation, which neither obeyed the law nor told the truth. I was pretty pissed, and on Feb. 4 sent him a non-secure e-mail which I knew (and intended) would be widely distributed.

"Chief Thomas. There's a story going around the agency that, prior to your official confirmation as chief, someone had asked you what would be the very first thing you would do upon confirmation. According to the story, you responded that you would hire the three biggest, meanest SOBs you could

find to walk around yelling 'Bullshit!' I don't know if that's true
or not, but it does make a good story. Inarguably, I am not
among the biggest SOBs around. But as the former planning
team leader of the CPOW timber sale which you recently approved, I am unquestionably one of the angriest and meanest
SOBs around. So ... BULLSHIT! BULLSHIT! BULLSHIT!"

Much later, I heard that this note so delighted Chief Thomas that
he used it as an ice-breaker at speeches. He would read my note, then
deliver the punchline, "Bill is now working for the Bureau of Land
Management." Ha, ha, ha! Not too far off, Jack.

I was so upset with Chief Thomas' decision, that two nights later
I wrote a letter to Vice President Al Gore, explaining the situation on
the south Tongass and asking for his oversight. Gore's office responded the following month:

March 11, 1994
Dear Mr. Shoaf:
    Thank you for contacting my office concerning the man-
agement of the Tongass National Forest in southeast Alaska.
I appreciate hearing from you on this important issue.
    As you know, President Clinton and I are committed to
demonstrating that environmental protection and economic
progress can be complementary goals. The promotion of responsible timber harvesting policies for all our forest land,
including the Tongass National Forest, has become a matter
of increasing concern among many involved with the forest
industry and other interested citizens who want to ensure that
forests are preserved in a healthy, productive, and sustainable
manner.
    President Clinton and I are both aware of the ecological
and economic importance of our National Forests. As stewards of the environment, we must learn to better protect all of
our natural resources. Environmental protection can be balanced with the needs of all citizens, and, in turn, provide for
healthy and productive forest land.
    In regard to your specific concern, the U.S. Forest Ser-
vice has notified Alaska Pulp and Paper (ALP) that it is in breach
of its contract with the government. The Administration is currently reviewing ALP's proposed recommendations for future
operations. A final decision will be made prior to April 15.
    Again, thank you for writing.

Sincerely,
Al Gore

Once the boilerplate and platitudes were dismissed, Gore's response struck me as queer. I had asked direct questions about the KPC contract on the south Tongass, and he made direct response about the APC contract on the north Tongass. There wasn't any way there could have been a misunderstanding on either of our parts. I began to get a sick feeling that my specific concerns about CPOW and the Ketchikan Area would be used as leverage to cancel the APC contract. Then I feared, the administration would feel that was as far as they could push the Alaska congressional delegation, especially if they ever wanted to get a budget past Senator Stevens' appropriations committee. But where did that leave my whistleblower disclosure?

On Feb. 14, the regional forester gave APC an additional 60 days to reopen their pulp mill or he would irrevocably cancel their contract.

I waited two weeks, then called my contact at OSC, Alecia Marsch. She told me that on Feb. 18, the Forest Service had attempted to bypass the Secretary of Agriculture's review by submitting Stine's report directly to OSC. She said OSC had refused the report and remanded it to the Agriculture Secretary for his personal signature, because the law did not allow his delegation of this responsibility. While she refused to discuss the contents of Mr. Stine's report, she did inform me that it was dated Feb. 1, which confirmed that it was directly tied to the chief's decision to deny the CPOW appeal, which was dated Feb. 3. Alecia then said the investigative report was now four months late, and she would see what she could do to turn up the heat on the agency.

That weekend, Lew Williams published a particularly scathing editorial which listed the names, addresses, and phone numbers of many of the local greenies and basically told the good local folks where they could find the tar and feathers. Some of my friends' names were listed, and I saw red. I wrote an editorial which the paper published, under the heading, 'Not Serious.'

"Last summer I watched MTV's "Beavis and Butthead" with some teenaged children. I explained to them the term 'black humor' and told them the characters were poor role models. I concluded that the show was marginally OK for them to watch, as long as they promised not to take it seriously.

Last weekend I had a similar conversation with a friend about some of Lew Williams' recent editorials. I explained the terms 'yellow journalism' and 'McCarthyism' and told my friend the editor was getting dangerously close to libel. I concluded that the editorials were polarizing the community and did not deserve to be taken seriously. Mr. Williams, if you are really sincere about wanting to inform the public, instead of just selling hype, I suggest you and I participate in a public debate on local timber supply issues. I, of course, would present my own, personal viewpoints. Until then, you are strictly 'Beavis and Butthead.' Heh, heh!"

Rather than accept my challenge, Williams called the Forest Service to find out for what organization I was really working. The public affairs officer said he didn't know.

The Forest Service refused to get in the middle of the argument. The following day, Vaught got me out of a meeting and personally handed me a document stating that my editorial was legal, and that the public affairs officer should have said 'no comment.' Needless to say, Lew Williams never responded to my request for a public debate, but continued to use his newspaper as a soap box, where he could spout forth without challenge.

Fifteen days after the chief had upheld the regional forester's decision to dismiss the appeal, the first CPOW timber offering was given to KPC, and the ink was barely dry before the trees were on the ground. The sale was called "The Magnificent Seven," and it was awarded to KPC as an 'add-back' offering, i.e., replacement volume for underrun on the 1989-94 sale. According to the heavily doctored CPOW FEIS, there was no such thing as underrun. Go figure.

Robert was in town on business and was staying at my house. He told me that, while the appeal had been pending, KPC loggers had been frothing to get at the Magnificent Seven. When the appeal was denied, anyone on Prince of Wales island who could even start a chain saw was cutting timber. In their haste to get the trees on the ground, where no litigation could ever put them back on the stump, the timber was unceremoniously dumped in a jack-strawed mess. He said that the cutting had all the professional dignity of a pie-eating contest.

On March 2, the "Daily News" ran a headline front page story that the Office of Inspector General was investigating whether the environmentalists were exerting undue influence on government decisions to reduce logging levels in the Pacific Northwest. The contention was that the Clinton administration was only listening to the greenies and not to the timber industry. The investigation against the greenies was proceeding rapidly. My whistleblower case had been filed six months ago and not a peep as yet.

On March 5, another 16 units from CPOW were given to KPC. Once again, they were logged as fast as possible to prevent their being halted by an injunction. But SEACC hadn't filed litigation yet. What was going on? I thought they wanted to stop the sale. I felt like I was the only person in the world who gave a damn or who had the courage to stand up to the bad guys. Where was the cavalry everyone had assured me was riding to my rescue? Where indeed?

16

Blind Faith

(March 1994 - June 1994)

"Mother, mother ocean, I have heard you call.
I've wanted to sail upon your waters,
Since I was three feet tall."
    -- Jimmy Buffet, "A Pirate Looks at Forty"

It was hard to maintain a personal life that was apart from the Tongass struggle. I had tugged on Superman's cape real hard, and instead of fleeing for my life, I had squared off in front of him. It was neither a fair fight nor a pretty sight. OSC had turned my whistleblower disclosure over to the Forest Service, who found themselves in the convenient position of investigating themselves. Moreover, OSC was allowing the investigation to stall, which gave the impression it wasn't being taken seriously. Seemingly, Congress and the administration had signed off on canceling the APC contract in lieu of taking a hard look at my concerns. Even the greenies were showing little interest in preventing the logging of CPOW.

I felt like everyone had abandoned me. My chief supporter, AFSEEE, had hired Andy Stahl as their new executive director. This was bitter news. Andy had been the National Wildlife Federation forester who had shut down my district at Mapleton. I had once vied for the privilege of dragging his effigy behind my pickup truck, and still harbored a distrust of him. I needed to maintain contact with AFSEEE, but chose to deal with others within the organization whom

I already knew and trusted.

Fellow employees, who had so demonstrably signed a petition for me last fall, now avoided me, as it became apparent that nothing would come of my charges. No one wanted to be on the losing side. With no one in my corner, the Forest Service felt emboldened to flay me alive. They had me cubby-holed in a non-viable, non-funded position with absolutely no responsibilities. Workload, which had previously been a trickle, became a dry stream bed. This torture is called "enforced idling," and it's the professional version of Chinese water torture. Drip, drip, drip. Nothing, nothing, nothing.

On weekends, I would try to reclaim my life. Victoria and I would roam the docks looking for gillnetter boats with For Sale signs. There was firewood to be cut, a garden to be prepared, a wolf to be enjoyed, and, of course, miles to be run. I would return to work Monday with the resolve to stick it out and force the Forest Service to fix the mess on the Tongass. By 10 AM, I would be so bored and demoralized that I was ready to hang myself.

Shortly after I got Gore's letter, Victoria and I loaded my pickup onto an Alaska state ferry and went north to move her personal goods to Ketchikan. The next week I came in from my evening run, and Victoria was weeping on the phone. When she hung up, I found out she had a lump on her breast that her doctor said looked suspicious. The next day she was scheduled for a biopsy at the hospital.

Even before the biopsy test was run, the doctor said the lump was malignant, and recommended an immediate radical mastectomy. Victoria said to do it, and she was scheduled for surgery in a few hours. It was shockingly abrupt. One second she was fine, the next second she had cancer, and in a few hours she would have a breast removed. The good news was that she had caught it early and had an improved chance of arresting the spread of the cancer. Too soon I was chased out of the room, as the hospital staff prepped her for surgery.

For hours I waited and alternated reading with pacing. Finally, I needed air, and walked down to the boat harbor, which was right below the hospital. Though it seemed like I was somehow being disrespectful to Victoria, I found myself looking at gillnet boats, just for some necessary distraction. Almost immediately I spotted a Sunnfjord gillnetter with a For Sale sign on her, and a reasonable price tag. I balanced the two simultaneous thoughts, "Where did that come from?" vs. "Not now, damnit."

It was many hours before I was allowed to briefly see Victoria, still groggy from the anesthetic. The next day, I visited her, and we learned that her lymph nodes had shown no trace of cancer. There was optimism that removal of her breast and lymphatic tissue under her arm had gotten it all. As she recovered in the hospital, she asked me what I'd been doing. I told her I'd found a Sunnfjord gillnetter. She brightened and asked me about it. When I told her the price, she said to go buy it. A few days later, I brought her home. I didn't have a lot of experience in dealing with the infirm, but did the best I could.

The doctor recommended, and she agreed to chemotherapy, which made her a basket case. She got her shots every other week. The first day usually knocked her off her feet so hard that she just slept. The next two days were brutal, as she suffered extreme depression and was largely dysfunctional. I was afraid to let her cross the street alone. She insisted on continuing to drive and wrecked my Subaru and my pickup.

It was a tough time for both of us. Cancer brings its victims such enormous distress that I felt it was somehow wrong to have my own feelings, as they seemed trivial compared to Victoria's much larger concerns. My home abruptly ceased to be much of a respite from the numbing isolation at work. Her surgery had only been one week after we'd brought her stuff down and moved her into the house, and we hardly got a chance to know one another. While it wasn't her fault she got cancer, it wasn't my fault either. Still, I stood by her.

On March 30, I met the owner of the Sunnfjord, and he showed me the boat. For all my years of running a small sport boat, I knew nothing about diesel engines, hydraulic reels, and 32,000-pound hulls. Still the boat looked pretty darned good. On April 3, Victoria and I bought the *F/V Camilla*, and on April 23, we somehow took the boat out of her slip and had it hauled into dry dock at the local boat yard. I remember opening the hatch to the engine room, shaking my head and vowing to never go down there. Victoria told me I'd learn, but it didn't seem possible. The next week I sold my beloved C-Dory, named *Old Growth*, and put the money toward our gillnetter.

The Tongass bru-haha hurtled onward, and I was frequently contacted by reporters from various media sources. The Center for Public Integrity, a non-profit citizens watchdog group, published a report entitled, "Sleeping with the Industry -- the U.S. Forest Service and Timber Interests."

> "In examining, the Forest Service's activity in the Tongass, observers find blatant disregard for the law, overcutting of protected old-growth stands, political and financial chicanery, suppression of information, and abusive treatment of the agency's employees.
>
> The Tongass National Forest is perhaps the most damning example of the Forest Service at its worst, and of collusion between the agency and the state's congressional delegation."

Naturally, the "Daily News" ran the story as the lead on page one. They quoted Senator Ted Stevens as saying, "It is difficult to comment because of its sheer idiocy. They can't be serious." Alaska's other senator, Frank Murkowski claimed, "The fact is the Tongass has been the leader nationally in promoting development of sound forest management practices."

The Tongass continued to receive bad press from "High Country News," "Fly Rod and Reel," "Wildlife Conservation," and almost every major newspaper in the country. The "London Globe" wrote:

> "The Forest Service is an agency that loses money cutting down trees that almost everybody would rather be left standing for owls to live in."

Because they seemed to be the only organization that truly cared about my plight or about forest management on the Tongass, I authorized AFSEEE to use me as its poster boy for fund-raising activities. My name even appeared on the front of an envelope they sent out to prospective donors:

> "I love the Forest Service, and it breaks my heart to observe local managers not abiding by environmental laws passed by Congress to govern forest management.
> -- Bill Shoaf, 15-year Forest Service employee who spoke out about Forest Service mismanagement"

Yes they did, no they didn't ... the back and forth warfare! All presented by the "Ketchikan Daily News," with a biased twist for the sole purpose of inciting public unrest ... and selling newspapers. God damn that hateful publication! I canceled my subscription and refused to ever let it in my household again.

On April 14, 1994, regional forester Mike Barton canceled the Forest Service's long-term contract with APC. There was now only one long-term contract remaining. Timber offerings which had been previously reserved for APC were summarily awarded to KPC. CPOW offerings, which been assembled before the ink was dry on the Record of Decision, were tossed to KPC, who devoured them like a shark would a herring. APC might be down the tubes, but the rallying cry of the "Ketchikan Daily News" was "'Long live KPC!" and "Jobs!" Two weeks later, Barton retired and was immediately hired by the state of Alaska as director of transportation. Talk about a den of thieves.

Eide took pity on me and gave me a rare assignment to lead an unannounced log accountability audit on the Ketchikan Ranger District. This was usually a small formality, required by regional regulation. I enlisted a team of accountants, timber sale administrators, and law enforcement officers. We found poor log accountability practices, some timber sales that hadn't been inspected in four months (I reflected how on the Boise Forest, I used to drive my own personal rig to inspect my timber sales), and outrageous examples of unit expansions. Gene shook his head at the report, and said it was just supposed to be a formality and that I wasn't expected to actually find anything.

It was becoming increasingly apparent to me that my whistleblower disclosure was never going to be given a hard look. It had simply been used as a bargaining chip to cancel the APC contract on the north Tongass. When the deal was struck, it was tossed aside and ignored. I felt like I had been hung out to dry, and after the log accountability audit, Eide refused to give me further assignments. At my mid-year performance rating, he gave me high praise, but I cut him short. I told him I wasn't doing a damned thing and wanted him to assign me some responsibility. He said he was working on it, but I didn't believe him.

I believe that it is OK to feel down in the dumps for awhile, but that eventually you have to do something about it. OK, Shoaf, what's it going to be? You might not have a job much longer, and you've got a boat sitting out in dry dock. There's a 24-hour halibut opening coming up June 6-7. Go get 'em.

I started spending every spare moment at the boat yard. At first all I knew how to do with the boat was clean it and wax it, so I did that. Then I dragged myself up the steep learning curve of commercial fishing. The boat, as she was currently rigged, was incapable of longlining halibut. I struggled to design a system that might work, but I had no point of reference, as I had never even seen a longline, much less watched anyone else fish one, much less ever fished one myself. I could tell a halibut from a salmon, and that was about it.

I tracked down the history of the boat. She had been built in 1981 by Sunnfjord (the BMW of the commercial boat world) as a 32-foot demonstration boat, rigged as a shrimper and a pocket seiner. Everything on her was oversize ... the boom looked like it belonged on a 58-foot limit seiner, her rudder was enormous, the fish hold looked like a racquetball court, she had a full displacement hull and a monstrous 13 feet of beam. Sunnfjord sold her to a coupla dentists who rigged her as a gillnetter, but primarily used her as a tax write-off. When they had fully depreciated their investment, they leased her to some working fisherman. Then they had trouble getting their lease money, and put her up for sale. And that's where Victoria and I stepped in.

Victoria had some money from the sale of her house, which she had owned outright. We bought the boat 50/50, established a business account, and a fishing partnership. We broke one of the most inviolate laws of the sea and renamed the boat. I suggested *Blind Faith*, and Victoria liked it immediately. Yeah, *Blind Faith*, indeed.

We left the boat yard May 23. I was such a greenhorn that I made pulling the boat into her slip at the dock look like "Best of Demolition Derby." I was absolutely terrified of the boat. Next was buying all the necessary line and other equipment for halibut fishing, dragging it down to the boat and rigging it. I couldn't believe how much there was to learn and do.

Halibut are bottom dwellers that prefer depths of 60 to 250 fathoms. As a fathom is 6 feet, we're talking about serious water here. Halibut are pretty serious fish too, as 200 pounders aren't rare and 100-pound halibut are common. The basic setup is to tie several big, round, inflatable buoys to enough floating buoy line to reach the sea bottom, then a 35-pound anchor, followed by the sinking ground line, which is laid along the ocean floor for a mile or more, then another anchor at the far end, then another buoy line and buoy. The buoy and ground lines are 5/16 inch in diameter. Baited hooks are then snapped onto the ground line. The hooks are rigged with a 6-inch stainless steel snap tied at one end of a gangion (gan-yun'), which resembles stiff, strong parachute cord, and a huge, C-shaped circle hook maybe 3 feet away at the other end.

The lines are generally stored on a huge hydraulic drum on the back deck. To make a set, the buoys are tied to the buoy line and thrown behind the boat, which goes ahead slowly. As the hydraulic reel (also called a drum) turns, the buoy line is spooled off the reel and behind the boat until the connection with the ground line is reached. At this point, the first anchor is attached and everything starts sinking except the buoy. Once the ground line starts spooling out, hooks are snapped on every 12-15 feet. This is where it gets dicey. Circle hooks are wicked and will grab onto anything and never, ever let go. Consequently, the fisherman grabs the snap, throws the hook end overboard, then snaps it to the ground line. If the snap is made to the spooling ground line while the hook is still on deck, the hook could catch on the fisherman and drag him overboard to his death. Many fisherman have perished this way, and traditionally fisherman cut the sleeves off their shirts, so there's less for the hooks to catch on.

Victoria and I rigged up maybe a thousand snap/circle-hook/gangion combinations, and then drummed our new buoy and ground lines onto the hydraulic reel. It was a lot of work, and we barely got done before the opening. We picked out one of the local cold storage plants, "Silver Lining" and walked in and introduced ourselves. We told the "fish pimp" that we were just starting out in the business and would be fishing halibut and shrimp that season, and then gillnet the next. After some spitting and whittling, we were added to their fishing fleet.

We planned to buy bait on Friday, take on ice Saturday, and leave for the fishing grounds Sunday morning. The opening started Monday, June 6, at noon and lasted 24 hours. Bait 'em up, snap 'em on, and haul em' in. Over and over again, until 24 hours were up.

On June 1, SEACC finally litigated CPOW. So much had already been released to KPC and been logged that I wondered why they bothered. I was told that my whistleblower disclosure had caused so much uproar within the greenie community that SEACC was under pressure to follow up on my charges. To do otherwise would have forced them to relinquish their spot as the top-dog greenie group in SE Alaska. But it seemed that they were just going through the motions. This was the largest timber sale in the nation, and the leader of the sale had just blown the whistle on it, basically doing all their work for them. And all this was occurring in their back yard. I didn't understand their reticence.

When I read the SEACC lawsuit, it was compelling. I wondered how the Forest Service would manage to wiggle out of this one. Unlike the administrative appeal process where the Forest Service simply insisted they were right and the appellant is wrong, they had to face a judge. Encouraged, I called OSC for an update on my case. I was told that my contact Alecia Marsch no longer worked there, and that no one knew anything about my case.

Victoria's oldest son, Aaron, came down to fish with us, and it was a pretty motley crew taking to sea in the *Blind Faith*. A total greenhorn, a woman on chemotherapy, and a kid. They say the gods take pity on fools and fishermen (seemed I fit both categories.) Well, they might have taken pity on us, but they seemed intent on jerking us around a little first.

We had about 3,000 pounds of ice in the hold, several hundred pounds of bait, enough gear to make two sets, and enough food to feed an army ... even if one of the members was a teenager. At noon on Monday, we tossed in our buoy and started dumping in the first set. I was snapping on the hooks, Victoria was watching me, and Aaron was running the boat. Somehow, everybody lived through making the first set, so we raced to make our second set. That went OK, too. Hey, nothing to this halibut fishing.

Yeah, right. Traditionally, halibut gear should sit on the bottom through a tide, or around six hours. The weather was good, so we drifted until about 5 PM, when we decided to haul our first set. Everything that could possibly screw up, did. The hooks came in so tangled that I had to shut off the hydraulic block to unsnap each one. The line didn't go back on the drum straight, but rather in a horrible snarl. Sharks, skate, rockfish, and then voila ... a few halibut. It was almost dark by the time, we got the first set aboard, and the entire boat was a mess. Everyone had been yelling at each other, Victoria was in the ozone, and I was exhausted.

We started to run over to our other set, when the engine gauges started acting weird. Victoria was convinced it resulted from a defective plug-in cigarette lighter on the dash, so I worked on that while she ran the boat. Finally, I got concerned it was something beyond the cigarette lighter and raised the hatch to the engine room. Water started splashing onto the roof of the cabin! The engine room was rapidly filling with water! Omigod!

Victoria wanted to abandon ship, Aaron wanted to run the boat on the rocks, but instead I took over and brought the boat over close to shore and anchored. I jumped down in the engine room and, because I wasn't yet skookum enough to know how to run the big engine-driven pumps down there, started handing up buckets of sea water to Aaron. Water kept pouring in. Finally, I shut off all the thru-hull valves and the boat stopped taking on water. The small, float-valve bilge pump started taking down the water level, and Aaron and I kept up the bucket brigade.

Victoria called the Coast Guard on the VHF and gave them a heads-up on our situation ... concern, but nothing life-threatening. The Coast Guard came back to us on the radio, as did another boat that was close by. While the Coast Guard kept monitor, the other boat came over and lent us a pump. These guys were weird. They had on cowboy boots and were using hot dogs or something like that for bait. They hadn't caught any fish, and admired the few halibut we had that were still lying on the deck. Nonetheless, their boat wasn't taking on water, and they had come to our aid. I thanked them, and when they were assured we wouldn't sink, they took off into the dark.

The whole boat was carnage. Uncleaned fish were lying in snarled tangles of gangions. The line on the reel was a huge bird's nest. The engine room had water up above the engine mounts. We started cleaning up, and by midnight, had the fish iced in the hold, the engine room dried, and the gangions thrown in tubs. We ate and then lay in our bunks, awaiting daylight. No one slept.

The next morning, we bravely went out and hauled our other set. With the thru-hull valves closed, we had no way to wash the decks, or clean the fish. When I opened the valves, the boat took on water. So the choice was clean the decks and sink vs. stay afloat and let the decks stay a mess. When we finally hauled the last buoy, we all gave a shout of relief, and took off for town. No one had been killed or seriously maimed, although I had knocked myself unconscious on three separate occasions when I ran into the hydraulic block with my head. I felt like I had gone 12 rounds with Mike Tyson. Aaron and Victoria cleaned and iced the fish, while I ran the boat back to town, ahead of a huge following sea.

We unloaded just under 800 pounds of halibut, which was amazing given the fiasco we had undergone. The Coast Guard met us there to inspect the boat, and the fish cops made sure we hadn't violated any laws. We were absolutely giggly in our joy at just surviving the trip, and people looked at us like we were nuts. All in all, it was quite an inauspicious beginning to my fishing career.

Now that I had a vague idea about the business of halibut fishing, I set about making changes in the way the boat was rigged, and in our technique. I learned how to run all the pumps in the engine room, and, safely tied to the dock, I tried to recreate the flooding incident. But no matter how I turned the thru-hull fittings, I couldn't get the boat to take on a drop of water. Weird. I kept studying the mechanics, listening to other fishermen, reading manuals, thinking, and learning.

I wanted to participate in the winter shrimp fishery, so we bought a bunch of used shrimp pots and tried to figure out how to re-rig the boat for shrimping. Geez, there was a lot to learn. It's said that the most important secret in fishing is to choose your parents wisely. My parents were thousands of miles away and didn't know beans about fishing.

17

The Black Hole

(June 1994 - March 1995)

"Take this job and shove it!
I ain't working here no more."
-- Johnny Paycheck, "Take This Job and Shove It"

The office was a depressing, demeaning ordeal. Basically I sat and stared at the wall. I was involved with an aerial photography project that was largely dysfunctional. It was exclusively make-do, hit-and-miss work.

I continually badgered OSC, but they wouldn't or couldn't tell me anything. I pressed them to commit to a date when they would demand USDA produce the required investigative report. The law said 60 days, with another 60 days if requested in writing. It was going on a year. I wondered if the law had any teeth, or if OSC had any balls?

Finally, on July 18, OSC told me to expect the investigative report that week or the next. When I still hadn't received it by the following Friday, I wrote letters to Attorney General Janet Reno and Chief Jack Ward Thomas pleading for action. I tried to explain to them that I had been promised that it was a good thing to be a whistleblower, that I would be protected, and have a prompt disposition of my case, and that the whole government had abdicated their end of the bargain and walked off, leaving me hold the bag. I may as well have tried to explain calculus to my wolf.

On August 5, Victoria and I drummed a shackle of gillnet onto our reel, and took off on a subsistence fishing trip for sockeye salmon. We caught about 50 sockeye, which was more than we could ever use, so we headed back to town, planning with whom we could share our bounty. When we got back to the house, the long overdue USDA investigative report was in the mail. I showered, then took the report in the sunroom, bracing myself for what I knew it would say.

The report for which I had sacrificed my career and waited a year, was a three-page letter signed by Agriculture Secretary Mike Espy, dated July 25, 1994. It concluded, and I summarize:

> "Corrective action is already being taken in several areas related to improving the decision-making process of timber management activities on the Tongass National Forest. The improvement will result in stronger documentation of management decisions.
>
> I see no evidence of gross mismanagement or gross waste of funds, as alleged in the complaint. No additional corrective action is necessary.
>
> The reprisal allegations were not substantiated."

Attached to Espy's report was a 16-page report from Steve Stine, dated February 1, 1994. Stine concluded none of it happened. There was no mention of any report from Ruth Vein on whistleblower retaliation.

That was it. Poof! There was no socially approved or legally condonable means to express my rage, so I took a run and another shower. I was still pissed and felt like running again, but it wasn't practicable. So what's it going to be, Shoaf, let it be and lick your wounds or declare war? Humph, three guesses.

The next day I notified OSC that I intended to challenge Espy's report. Whistleblowers are guaranteed the last word, according to 5 U.S.C. Section 1213(e)(1), and I intended to avail myself of that right. By the next weekend, I had already drafted a response, and I sent a copy down to AFSEEE and GAP for review. Unfortunately, Michael Rossotto had left GAP, and his counterparts in D.C. had already moved on to other cases.

AFSEEE was still solidly in my corner, and I needed to let go of my past differences with their new executive director, Andy Stahl, who was unquestionably a brilliant litigation strategist. After leaving the National Wildlife Federation, where his lawsuit had shut down my former district at Mapleton, Oregon, he joined the Sierra Club Legal Defense Fund and became the brainchild behind the spotted owl lawsuit. When I called Andy, he pooh-poohed our old feud and outlined a game plan.

First, Andy enlisted the aid of Dr. K. Norman Johnson, arguably the most respected forester in the nation. Dr. Johnson was a professor of forest resources at Oregon State University, primary author of FORPLAN (a linear programming model the Forest Service used to estimate timber supplies), senior author of the 'Gang-of-Four' report on the PNW spotted owl, and a member of President Clinton's FEMAT. He was also a close professional associate of Chief Jack Ward Thomas. Andy asked Dr. Johnson to review my whistleblower disclosure, and he graciously sent me a personal letter dated September 17, 1994, and I summarize:

> "Mr. Shoaf's findings are consistent with my experience with federal forests of the Pacific Northwest. Forest Service use of forest planning models like FORPLAN, which I personally developed, have consistently resulted in overestimates of sustainable harvest ... The Tongass National Forest would be wise to consider a similar adjustment, such as Mr. Shoaf recommends ... Eventually, the effects of unrealistic timber targets become visible. When they do, the harvest level drops precipitously as the land is given time to recover. Then, as in the Pacific Northwest, we all wonder why we did not realize this problem when there was time to correct it. According to Mr. Shoaf's analysis, the Tongass National Forest has an opportunity to make a needed course correction. It seems doubtful that this change will start with the CPOW timber sale. Only one thing is sure, the longer the Forest Service waits, the farther will be the drop in harvest and the more unstablizing will be its impact."

Andy offered his personal services as an arbitrator between the new regional forester, Phil Janik, and me, with the intent to make me whole from past retaliations. Andy knew I was close to leaving the agency, and had no desire for AFSEEE to lose their number one whistleblower. I had no desire to lose a $57,000/year job, so I gave Andy the go-ahead to proceed.

AFSEEE started a campaign to have people send me personal

letters of support, and I received over 300. Some enclosed donations, which I counter-signed over to AFSEEE. These letters were emotionally buoying, but at the same time they were almost embarrassing because they seemed to imply I was some kind of hero. This continued assertion was far removed from the truth. I saw myself as an ordinary guy caught in an extraordinary situation, and wanted the focus on the agency and on honest, responsible forest management, not on me. I didn't want the responsibility of being a folk hero.

If the truth be known, I wanted to become invisible, to return to the womb, to once again be a productive forester for an agency I respected and loved. But it seemed that was no longer possible. If I wanted to do well for the Tongass, it seemed I had to wrap myself into this Che-type persona which was fundamentally inconsistent with my nature. It was like the proverbial python trying to swallow a Volkswagen, once started, there was no way to stop, even though success was impossible.

Andy also had some ideas about how to respond to Espy's report. He noted that Espy's report said the retaliation allegations were not substantiated, but didn't include any corroborating evidence. So why not make a request under the Freedom of Information Act (FOIA)? On Sept. 1, 1994, I submitted a FOIA request to Espy for all documents that supported his statement that I wasn't retaliated against. By law, he had 10 days to reply. When Espy didn't reply by Oct. 6, I sent another letter asking for an explanation of his delay.

On Oct. 21, I received an agency reply from Milton Sloan that said the documents were with another agency. On Nov. 7, I received a letter from Lamar Beasley which said the documents didn't exist and advised me of my appeal rights. On Nov. 9, I sent Espy a letter, and I summarize:

> "O.K. I formally appeal the FOIA decision. I know for a fact that the records exist. At least part of the requested information consists of employee interviews conducted by Forest Service employee Ruth Vein at the Ketchikan Area forest supervisors office during the week of Jan. 18-21, 1994. Secretary Espy himself states 'statements given for the reprisal section of the investigation were sworn.' There are likely other documents as well, because your denial of the existence of any supporting documentation would imply that Secretary Espy simply rubber-stamped a 'no retaliation' decision on a

whistleblower case. This may well be so, but at least support-ing/contradictory information was available as basis for his de-cision.

I do not appreciate the delay and run-around I am getting on this FOIA request. First USDA said another agency had the documents, then it countermanded itself and said the docu-ments don't exist. What's next ... my dog ate them? "

I was pissed! On Jan. 23, 1994, USDA sent a letter stating that:

"Due to the complexity of the issues raised in your re-quest, it has taken us longer to respond...The response and documents must be reviewed by WO personnel staff and re-search and operations division of OGC for legal sufficiency ..."

On Jan. 23, 1995, I asked Attorney General Janet Reno to look into the matter of the USDA's deliberately suppressing information in conjunction with an OSC investigation and willfully refusing to comply with the FOIA. In mid-March, the requested documents ar-rived, six months late, and heavily blacked out, to the point of being unusable.

While this little drama was playing out, I discovered that FOIA's could be a lot of fun and started requesting information from the agency about falldown on the CPOW and North Revilla logging units.

Almost every week, I requested information from the Forest Ser-vice and analyzed it for them. It was said on the Tongass, that if a needle fell in the forest, an eagle saw it, a deer heard it, a bear smelled it, and Shoaf FOIAed it. If the agency managers were too stupid, too scared, too lazy, or too criminal to take a hard look at their own actions, I did it for them, and distributed the results widely. Finally the Forest Service simply stopped responding to the FOIAs. They were already breaking every major environmental law that existed ... and getting away with it ... why not simply break the law regarding the FOIA too.

That fall there was a series of brown bag lunches at work, with speakers presenting programs on natural resource issues. One of the speakers was Dave Person, the wolf researcher who had written the rebuttal editorial to Troy Reinhart about the "virtual reality timber planner." Dave had radio-collared two members of the wolf pack that used the denning area I had tried to protect near Trumpter Lake and sadly noted that they had vacated the area after it had been logged. It took all my waning self-control to keep from thrashing Rittenhouse for his insistence that that area be logged.

My respite was fishing. There was another halibut opening scheduled for Sept. 12, this one for 48 hours. We were a lot better prepared this time, but the weather outlook was brutal, with storm force winds forecast. We left town two days early, while the getting was good. The area we fished was fairly well protected, and the whole operation went 110 percent better than our first opening. But we were largely out of the fish.

On the way home, we got in some heavy weather, and the *Blind Faith* started getting slammed around pretty badly. Just then, a mayday call came over the VHF radio, and we listened as the *F/V Westerly* capsized and went down. Victoria knew the boat well, and listened in horror as the story unfolded that a girl friend of hers had been drowned in the accident. All in all, seven boats in SE Alaska went down in what turned out to be the last-ever halibut derby. We showed up at the dock at our cold storage plant to unload our few fish. When I started to apologize for the poor catch, the dock workers told me they were just thrilled to see a boat at all ... most guys never even got their gear in the water.

On Sept. 28, I filed my challenge to Espy's investigative report. My challenge was 16 pages and included an additional 60 pages of supporting evidence. I concluded by saying:

> "This has been a very frustrating process for me. Since moving to Alaska over four years ago, I have seen the agency on the same road to destruction that led to so much suffering in the Pacific Northwest. I have urged local forest managers to follow the laws, wisely conserve our resources, and be honest with the public as well as with ourselves. Totally failing in that endeavor, I went over their heads and filed a whistleblower disclosure, which I was assured would put things right. Instead what I got was discriminatory retaliation, a year's delay, and an IR which was a complete whitewash.
>
> I don't know the reason -- maybe there are too many political deals to cover-up. Maybe cancellation of the long-term APC contract on the Chatham/Stikine Areas of the Tongass carried with it a deal for continued hog and log "management"

of the South Tongass. If this is so, then the Tongass should not be permitted to continue being called a National Forest. Perhaps a new name would be more appropriate, e.g., "Ted's [Stevens] Place." I don't know.

I do know that attempting to prop up a local timber economy which isn't sustainable puts local communities at considerable risk. The Forest Service can't singlehandedly guarantee community stability or insulate them from larger forces which may affect their future by simply harvesting timber in excess of long-term sustainability. Rather, it is the Forest Service's responsibility to assure a reliable timber supply (based on the capability of the land to sustain this level of harvest in concert with other resources) which can contribute to a more stable economic future for timber-dependent communities. Failure to assure the supply is sustainable has proven fatal to many Down South towns.

I do know that the Whistleblower program doesn't work. There is a widely held policy of shooting the messenger, and it is faithfully followed. Most people who break the code of silence do so at the expense of their career. For many, it is a career-ending decision. Agencies have means of breaking an employee's will, as I documented in both of my affidavits, that work just as surely as firing them. Moreover, by parading the heads of whistleblowers on pikepoles, managers keep a tight rein on the rest of the work force. It will be a sunny January day at Pt. Barrow before another Tongass whistleblower comes forward. So much for the Whistleblower Protection Act, but maybe that was just designed for Beltway hype.

Chief Thomas wants the agency to regain its credibility with the public by telling the truth. Yet he is condoning Forest Service managers who willfully break every major environmental law in the book, cover up information, lie to the public and the Congress, and illegally retaliate against whistleblowers. I maintain that, if the Forest Service is indeed to regain its credibility, these managers should be removed from their jobs, banished from ever working again in Alaska, and tried in a court of law for their crimes. Yes, their crimes ...

I find I can no longer support this caricature of what was once the Forest Service. While there are thousands of good, honest, hard-working people in its ranks, some of its m a n - agers are so corrupt that the only hope for the Forest S e r - vice is that it be completely dismantled. We have indeed lost the public trust, and when it goes, it's gone, gone, gone (Bruce Springsteen). I will respectfully submit my resignation w h e n my whistleblower disclosure/complaints are resolved, and I can work out satisfactory terms for my departure."

To my knowledge, this 16-page report and 60 pages of accompanying documentation went unread. The agency made no response, because there was nothing they could say. All they could do was cover it up, and hope it went away. OSC just wanted the case closed. Oh well, I had my say.

Two days after I filed my challenge with OSC, Victoria and I left on our first shrimp opening. Shrimping involved baited pots tied onto a groundline, much as in halibut fishing, except the groundline is coiled on top of the pots, instead of drummed onto the reel. Also instead of a mile long, the sets are only 200 yards long. It was a laid back fishery with a five-month-long season, without the anxiety of having to catch all you possibly could in 24 or 48 hours. I loved shrimping, and it became by far my favorite fishery.

No words can approximate the beauties that I saw and the joy that my soul knew on the shrimping trips. I think that one of the reasons that I was able to endure the Forest Service retaliations for so long was that I had things that so delighted me ... fishing, running, gardening ... that the evil forces were never able to completely overcome them. The black could darken that joy, but it could never destroy it, and when the darkness faded, the seed of joy grew again.

I grew to know the boat better, and gained confidence in *Blind Faith*'s ability to get us there and back again, as well as confidence in my own ability to handle her. But I never grew over-confident, as the weather was frightful, and seldom forgiving. That first winter, the bay around us froze solid one bitterly cold night, as we lay anchored. Another night at the same anchorage, we rode out storm-force winds that blew galvanized wash tubs all over the back deck. Once we got caught in a bad blow while hauling gear, and had to run into the storm to find shelter. It was blowing so hard, we could only make 4 knots headway against the wind. *Blind Faith,* indeed.

On Oct. 20, 1994, the Forest Service announced they had authorized a buyout, in an attempt to downsize the work force. The deal was $25,000 to walk out the door and not return, with a window of opportunity from Jan. 1 through March 31, 1995. I wanted nothing more to do with an agency that broke the law, lied about it, covered it up, and retaliated against whistleblowers. And for their part, the agency wanted nothing to do with an employee who was accusing them of illegal actions. The buyout sounded like the best deal I had. If I had to leave anyhow, why not take $25,000 out the door with me? The one kicker in this was Andy's negotiations with the agency. Maybe he could get them to mend their ways and correct the damage done to my professional career. It seemed doubtful, but Andy Stahl was the persuasive leader of an increasingly powerful organization. He had scheduled a meeting with regional forester Phil Janik on Dec. 9. Maybe he could pull it off.

I didn't want simply a paycheck. When I hired on with the agency in 1978, I was paid $3.83/hour to plant trees. Now I was making $28/hour to do absolutely nothing. I was ashamed to accept the money. If all I cared about was money, I would probably still be screwing around with computers at an insurance company. I wanted to be allowed to again participate fully in the management of the Tongass.

One of the problems facing all natural resource agencies was that the science of forestry had made a radical renaissance in the early 1980s. I graduated in 1978 and felt remarkably like someone who had earned a degree in geography in 1491. Pre-1980s forestry was based on the singular premise that forest management was equated with conversion of old-growth forest to young-growth tree farms. New ecologic studies showed that the young-growth tree farms were remarkably dissimilar from the former forest, and significant, extremely complex environmental degradation was occurring.

However this new thinking didn't jibe with how the old-school Forest Service managers wanted to run National Forests. They had some heavy, cut-it-or-else political commitments to meet, both with their superiors within the agency and the local elected officials. National Forests are fiefdoms, and the Forest Service gets to keep their budget and their jobs only as long as they please the local political honchos. Consequently, the old-school managers felt obliged to continue the status quo. If the new thinking showed the same-old-same-old was the wrong thing to do, then it was necessary to stop the new thinking. It was endemic throughout the agency, and particularly widespread on the Tongass.

On Nov. 14, Department of Justice attorneys advised the Forest Service that the litigation SEACC had against them on CPOW was bulletproof, and that the agency was in an untenable situation. DOJ recommended an out-of-court settlement. It was rumored that Chief Thomas had been unsettled by Dr. K. Norman Johnson's letter to me. Reportedly Chief Thomas didn't mind representing an agency that was illegal, unwise, or dishonest, but damned if he'd allow it to be unscientific. He was having second thoughts about having allowed CPOW to go forward.

SEACC's mission was not to get proper forest management on the Tongass ... that was secondary. SEACC's main mission was to protect their membership's favorite places. Because SEACC was largely a Juneau-based group, most of their favorite places were on the northern Tongass.

But they did have a favorite spot on the southern Tongass ... Honker-Divide, which was the name loosely given to the corridor of the Thorne River on Prince of Wales island. This was a proposed wild and scenic river and a favored canoe route. SEACC had gotten roped into litigating CPOW, because it was so controversial, but really didn't care about CPOW. When DOJ proposed an out-of-court settlement, SEACC seized the moment to cut a deal whereby they'd drop their CPOW litigation in return for the Forest Service's promise to refrain from logging Honker Divide. The Forest Service would get to log every stick of CPOW, and SEACC would get out of a lawsuit they really didn't want in the first place. Plus they got to protect one of their favorite places.

Andy was deeply plugged into the greenie pipeline, and he told me all about this pending deal on our flight up to Juneau to see Janik. Aside from AFSEEE and academic types, it seemed no one cared about responsible forest management. The Forest Service cared about maintaining their bureaucracy. The Alaska congressional delegation cared about staying in office. Residents of Ketchikan and other SE Alaska communities cared about jobs and economic growth. The timber industry cared about corporate profits. The Alaska Native corporations, given how wantonly they clearcut their ANCSA-given lands, seemed to care only for quick income. The greenies cared about preserving some picnic spots and hobnobbing around D.C. It was pretty apparent and depressing.

The meeting with Janik went so-so. He gave me the impression he hadn't invested the time to get truly up to speed on my situation, and that I was strictly a pain-in-the-neck that he had inherited, but had not created. He listened, but made no promises, other than his solemn word I could expect a resolution by Jan. 15.

On Dec. 21, Chief Thomas decided that, deal with the greenies be damned, he wasn't comfortable proceeding with CPOW. He ordered the Record of Decision remanded, the project halted (other than 150 mmbf of timber that had already been released to KPC), and a supplemental EIS written to address the issues of falldown and timber sustainability. The chief didn't necessarily care what the supplemental EIS said, he just wanted it written. The local officials, an iron-clad deal with the greenies in pocket, decided to simply go through the motions of producing a supplement to CPOW. They didn't even form an interdisciplinary team, but instead assigned Anne Archie, Dave Arrasmith, and Pete Griffin to write an esoteric, non-scientific document.

To celebrate even this temporary victory, I gave up alcohol for the New Year. Although I loved my ritualistic two beers after my run each night, I saw it as an austerity move for the lean times ahead. I thought it was going to be a relatively short-term abeyance, kinda like Lent, but I was never to touch alcohol again.

On Jan. 12, 1995, Phil Janik called. He said he was removing himself from further negotiations with me and placing the whole responsibility with Dave Rittenhouse, the guy who started the retaliations against me in the first place. He expected the matter resolved completely within two weeks. I could almost hear the klink of his ring as it hit the side of his silver wash basin.

On Jan. 18, I had a long, frank talk with Gene Eide. Gene said Rittenhouse wasn't happy about Janik's orders for him to handle my case. I told him I wasn't either. Gene noted there was bad blood between Rittenhouse and me going back to that August 1991 management team meeting, where Rittenhouse yelled at me so hatefully. Gene said "he sank down in his chair that day because he knew it was very poor conduct for a forest supervisor."

Gene said he agreed with many of the issues that I had brought up in my whistleblower disclosure, but strongly disagreed with my methods. He also said he disagreed with many of the actions taken against me, especially some of the documents written to discredit me. Then he told me Rittenhouse had handed him the task of negotiating with me. Unfortunately, he had to leave town and might not get back to me for a couple of weeks.

I thought about all this, and sent off a note to Chief Thomas and regional forester Janik. I chastised them for passing resolution of my case back to Rittenhouse. I also pointed out that the agency was avoiding responding to me in a timely fashion. Janik called me at home and said maybe he was naive about what had transpired in Ketchikan.

On Feb. 13, Gene and I met again. He gave me a letter signed by Rittenhouse which was merely an offer to keep me gainfully employed. I told Gene that it didn't meet my needs and had made absolutely no attempt to make me whole. He said Rittenhouse would be willing to meet with me one-on-one, and I agreed.

Gene said if he were in my situation, he would probably resign. He said he had absolutely no assignments for a GS-12 forester of my caliber. I told him I was considering taking the buyout. When I left Gene's office, my head was pounding so hard, I had to take sick leave and go home and lie down.

My former CPOW wildlife biologist, Norm Matson, had assumed the role of planning team leader for the Chasina timber sale. He was in need of some logging systems help and asked if I'd be willing to help. I said sure. In a little bit, he came back agitated. He said he'd asked Gene if it was OK for me to help him. Norm said Gene screamed at him not to mention a word of work to me, because they were trying to force me into taking the buyout. I just shook my head.

On Feb. 16, I had my meeting with Rittenhouse. He mentioned work assignments in a couple of contrived positions ... one involved part-time duties which had previously been held by a non-professional GS-7 employee out at Thorne Bay. At that point, I just shut down, it was hopeless. I made up my mind that second to quit.

It had been my goal to have my whistleblower disclosure case settled before I left, but trying to get anywhere with OSC was like trying to push a rope. On Feb. 8, I called OSC and talked to Joyce Carnell. She said she was aware of my case but had never read it, because she had a backlog of over 100 cases. She said she had no knowledge of natural resource issues, and I noted she couldn't pronounce the word "Tongass." She asked me to call back in a week.

On Feb. 15, I again called Ms. Carnell. She said my response to Espy's investigative report didn't seem to contain the same issues as my original whistleblower disclosure. I explained to her that my initial whistleblower disclosure had addressed six separate issues, and referred her to the page where they were listed. She was not aware of that. I then walked her through my challenge to Espy's report and showed her section headings where each of these issues was addressed. She was not aware these sections existed and vowed to review the document in light of this startling new information. It occurred to me that in 18 months, OSC had never even looked at my disclosure, much less read it.

On Feb. 22, I called OSC for the last time as a Forest Service employee. Ms. Carnell said that USDA would not be issuing a new investigative report because Mike Espy didn't even work there anymore (he resigned when he was under investigation for abuse of authority). I asked her what would be forthcoming, and she said she didn't know. Ms. Carnell and I started to discuss my case, but she stopped me early on and asked what 'EIS' meant. I thanked her for her time and hung up. I wrote the following in my diary:

> "Honestly, I am very frustrated. Joyce Carnell has no knowledge of natural resource issues and has not even taken the time to read my materials, much less understand them. OSC allowed the Forest Service the convenience of investigating themselves, then simply rubber-stamped the denial of wrongdoing. How is the whistleblower program intended to work? Although law states that cases will be resolved within 60 days, years go by, then an uninformed decision is finally rendered by some bureaucrat whose obvious agenda is to clear the backlog. Resolution by attrition, I guess. At what level is an agency held accountable for its actions and how is that accomplished?"

On Feb. 28, I signed my resignation papers, which were approved March 16. Around this time I got word that Rittenhouse was awarded a transfer back to his beloved cowboy country as the forest supervisor on my old forest, the Boise. I had once vowed to get so drunk at his going-away party that I'd puke. Now it didn't look like I'd make it, but then again I didn't drink anymore anyhow.

On March 24 the "Ketchikan Daily News" ran the front-page headline, "Whistleblower Resigns from Forest Service," and on March 31, 1995, I walked out the door and never, ever looked back.

18

Life Outside the Forest Service

(April 1995 - September 1995)

"Now I don't mind choppin' wood,
And I don't care if the money's no good.
Just take what you need and leave the rest,
But they never should have taken the very best.
-- J. Robbie Robertson, "The Night They Drove Old
Dixie Down"

Not wanting to sit around and mope, the very day I quit the Forest Service, I unslipped *Blind Faith* and took her up to the boat yard, where she was hauled out of the water and placed in dry dock for maintenance and repairs. Facing a future with no salary, no pension, and no health insurance was one thing. Facing it with nothing to do was quite another. I'd been through that once and was not looking forward to a repeat.

I worked in the boat yard from dawn til dusk, seven days a week. I installed an autopilot, replaced the insulation around the diesel stack, tore out and replaced some rotten plywood along a bulkhead in the engine room, plus a host of piddly chores. In addition, most of the shrimp pots needed mending. The *Blind Faith* was starting to shape up nicely, and I was getting to know the boat.

One cold rainy afternoon in late April, I got home early from the boat yard and was lifting weights. The phone rang, and this guy told me I had won something or other that was worth $10,000. I wanted to get back to my workout and didn't want to fool around listening to some Ed McMahon wannabe's sales pitch. While trying to hang up tactfully, this guy mentioned the words "foundation," "board of directors," "AFSEEE," and "Andy Stahl." Whoa, wait a second here, are you trying to tell me you're on the level? It turned out he was. "He" was Michael Cavallo, a Massachusetts philanthropist who had set up a foundation to recognize integrity in the federal work force. His foundation selected three winners each year, each of whom received $10,000 during a presentation held on Capitol Hill in D.C. AFSEEE had nominated me, and the Cavallo Foundation board of directors had selected me. I would be flown to D.C., wined and dined, and set up with media interviews so the Tongass would get some exposure. By now, I was sitting down, and Michael suggested I call AFSEEE for verification. I did and they did. This was the first (and only) good thing that had happened to me as a result of being a whistleblower.

Being a commercial fisherman required more than having a boat, some gear, and a nearby ocean. Most fisheries required licenses, which were issued in a fixed, limited number by the state of Alaska. However, their sale was handled on the open market and followed the law of supply and demand. Gillnet permits were trading for around $75,000, and we couldn't even find one for sale. We ended up leasing a permit for the season from one of Victoria's girl friends, who had recently lost her husband to Agent Orange-induced cancer. Halibut had changed over from the derby style all-you-can-catch-in-24-hour affairs to allotted quotas, which were based on previous years' catches. Because we had no long-time history in the fishery, we had to buy quota shares, which were trading for about $8 per pound. We bought a little over 5,000 pounds, which ate up my $25,000 severance pay buyout from the Forest Service. Shrimp was still an open fishery, i.e., it didn't require a limited entry permit, thank god!

In mid-May, Victoria and I set off for the first halibut trip of 1995. We had 5,000 pounds of halibut to catch and wanted to have it out of the way before gillnet season began. That spring, I had bought some used longline gear, and we were now fishing 2-mile sets. One of the local superstitions was to hang a devil's club (*Oplopanax horridus*) leaf in the wheel house for good luck. We had done so when we first got the boat, and had picked a new leaf for 1995, figuring that the old leaf's magic may have dissipated. I discussed this with James, and he suggested respectfully tying the old leaf onto the first circle hook of the new season. I did as my friend suggested, and we dumped in a set that first night, then got up pre-dawn and dumped in our second set. We hauled the first set, and sure enough there was a halibut on the devil's club hook, which I carefully released unharmed. All in all we were pretty pleased with the first set, as there were several big fish. The weather was good, so we just drifted while we cleaned and iced our fish and baited a coupla more tubs of hooks.

In late morning I grabbed the buoy and started hauling our second set. Motherlode! Almost every hook had a halibut and some were huge. I'm pretty strong and am capable of gaffing a 100-pound fish aboard by myself, but generally appreciate help with anything over 75 pounds. The fish kept coming aboard, until the decks were awash in halibut. I needed help with a big one, oh say 175 pounds, and as I backed up to drag the fish's tail over the gunwale (top railing), I tripped and fell on my back in a huge pile of halibut. I lay there unhurt, amid the slime and the blood, and Victoria's face, big and round as the moon, was scant inches above mine. She had an impossibly wide grin and said we had a deckload of money.

As I got up, I looked back to admire the fish, and she clobbered me. She screamed not to ever look back at the fish in admiration. Gaff 'em, drag 'em up, and turn the hydraulic block back on. This is work and there's fishing to be had. She was right, and that incident marked the transition between fishing-for-fun vs. fishing-for-money. Nonetheless, I was determined to enjoy this job.

The weather forecast wasn't too skookum for our second halibut trip. There was a nasty beam swell crossing the strait, but we went ahead and dumped in a set that night. The next morning it was positively snotty. Rather than dump in our second set, we just hauled the first one and called it a day, as there weren't many fish and we'd gotten slammed around pretty bad. The forecast for the next day was horrible, so we decided to sleep in and not fish. That's the nice thing about the quota share system in relation to the old derbies, if it's rough out, you don't have to fish.

I awoke the next morning and turned on the VHF to catch the updated marine forecast. The first words I heard were "storm warning has been upgraded to a hurricane." We spent the rest of the day trying to find a better anchorage, but the other places we tried had steep hills behind them, which caused such horrendous "williwaws" (winds which roll over the top of a hill and increase speed down the other side) that we simply dragged anchor. We finally returned to our first anchorage, where I rowed our skiff to the beach and attached a shore line to farther secure the *Blind Faith*. As it turned out, we were fine. Initially I was concerned about our food supplies, until I remembered we had fresh fish in the hold. It turned out pretty darned pleasant, being anchored securely in a big blow, and baking fresh halibut.

It took two days for the seas to lay down, and it was getting time to get our catch back to town. We dumped in our two sets, gave them a short soak, then jerked them back in. The sets yielded only four halibut, but they were huge. One weighed 234 pounds. This fish was wildly thrashing on the surface, and when I gaffed it, the halibut slammed the back of my gaff hand against the side of the boat, breaking most of the bones. I held the gaff, while Victoria put a line through the fish's gills, then we ran that line through the power block and hoisted it aboard mechanically. I ran in the wheel house, swallowed eight aspirins, wrapped my hand in black tape, and finished hauling the set. What are you going to do, that was a $500 fish and there might be more to be had.

Without health insurance and with little money reserves, there wasn't much I could do about the hand as far as seeking medical aid. Besides I didn't like doctors much. The next week, we were tied alongside the net float rerigging the boat from halibut to gillnetting, when the net bar slipped and caught my wrist against the side of the boat. This was probably the worst pain I've ever experienced, and I confess I screamed bloody murder. Some people on shore called an ambulance, and two paramedics arrived by skiff. I refused to get in because I didn't feel I could afford treatment. I now had a broken wrist to go with my broken hand.

Thank god, Michael Cavallo flew us back to D.C. sparing me any farther physical abuse. Michael had generously purchased not only my ticket and one for Victoria, but had also sent an invitation for the presentation to my parents. It was a magical time. My sister drove up from North Carolina, and it marked the first time my family had all been together since my short-lived marriage to Yvonne. We toured museums and went to the zoo. I found D.C. was actually enjoyable when a guy didn't have to live or work there.

The arranged press interviews were largely a bust. Talking to East Coast reporters about Alaskan forestry issues was the penultimate frustration. It was like we were speaking two different languages and didn't have an interpreter. It seemed once more I had blown my chance to speak up for the Tongass, and I semi-mourned the loss.

The award presentation was held at the Capitol in one of the Senate hearings rooms. I got to meet Michael Cavallo himself, and was delighted to find him a modest, thoroughly unpretentious man. He told me that Congressman George Miller would present my award. The two other winners that year were a woman who had tackled the government over a hazardous waste disposal site, whose contamination had killed her husband, and an U.S. Army lawyer responsible for resolving civil rights violations, who had been sexually harassed by her supervisor.

Suddenly the room became hushed, and in rushed George Miller, flanked by a virtual bevy (or whatever the proper collective term) of beautiful women in black mini-dresses. He sought me out, shook my hand in congratulations, and almost immediately proceeded to the podium. It was one of the proudest moments of my life ... to be presented $10,000 and a prestigious national award by a prominent congressman. I made a short, carefully rehearsed speech, and in a moment, it was over. It was wonderful my parents were able to witness it, as it was probably the only thing I ever did right in my life. Don't blink, Mom and Dad, cause it isn't likely to happen again.

We got back to Ketchikan late Wednesday night, and Saturday left on our first gillnetting opening. Quite a switch, eh? From gorgeous women dressed-to-the-nines to totes of slimy salmon. From sweltering in oppressive heat and humidity in D.C. to standing on deck in tall rubber boots, polar fleece pants, wool shirt, knit cap, rollerblader's knee pads, rubber gloves, and full rain-gear. Welcome to gillnetting.

Aside from our brief, light-hearted subsistence trip of the previous year, I had never even seen gillnetting, much less had an inkling of an idea how to do it. Gillnets are 1,200 feet long and 30 feet deep. The net hangs between a corkline at the top that keeps it afloat and a weighted line at the bottom that keeps the web hanging vertically in the water. A big inflatable pink buoy is tied to each end of the net, so that it's readily visible to other boats.

The net is set perpendicular to the beach. To set the net, the fisherman tosses the buoy over, puts the reel in free spool, and slowly heads the boat away from the beach. When the net is completely out, the other buoy is attached, and the net is then free to drift, wherever it will, according to the tide and the current. Sometimes it stays straight, other times it bunches up and needs to be tugged into shape. Hopefully, the net drifts up or down the beach, but often it remains in one spot. The net can do a lot of weird, unexpected things, and sometimes it actually catches fish. And those times are the best.

The net is usually hauled every 1 1/2 hours, but again, there is a large variation here. Sometimes the current will pull the outside buoy around so it is even with the inside buoy, and the net ends up parallel to the beach. This is no-good, and is called "end-oh." On calm, windless days, a boat can grab onto the end of the net and hang onto it like a big sea anchor ... for hours and hours at a time. This is referred to as "drifting and dreaming."

When the net is hauled, the buoy is grabbed and unsnapped, and the net is made to the reel, which then hydraulically winches it back onto the reel. Seaweed and other flotsam, including jellyfish, are picked out in sometimes mind-boggling quantities. Salmon are untangled from the web, as it is drummed aboard, and thrown into a huge fishbox. When the net is fully in, it is immediately reset, often in a different spot. Then the salmon are thrown into the fish hold, where tanks contain a slurry of ice and sea water. Fish are delivered daily to large tender boats, which remain anchored to accept the fisherman's catch.

Salmon like to be as close to the beach as they can get and prefer the earliest hours on the stormiest days. To me, it seemed prudent to keep my boat away from the rocks, sleep in a little later, and only fish the nice weather. There was an inarguable conflict, and to learn to become a gillnetter, a fisherman needed to learn to follow the salmon, as well as the rest of the fleet.

Gillnetters didn't like free-thinkers. Their world revolved around doing the same thing over and over again. You had to keep your net at least 1/4 mile away from a stretch of beach being fished by another boat. Anyone still in the anchorage after 3 a.m. was slovenly, and the better fisherman were up at 2 a.m. Keep your net in the water, take care of your boat, and watch your attitude. That was the credo, and they were the crankiest bunch of guys around.

In SE Alaska, only a few carefully regulated areas were open to gillnetting, and it was here that the license-holders crowded together to compete for sets. Basically, gillnetting was a war, not between man and fish or between man and ocean, but rather between man and man. Certain boats had been fishing the same stretches of beach for a quarter of a century, and they were not about to let anyone else enter their turf. Furthermore, they had other boats that would come to their aid to help them chase off usurpers. Shots were fired occasionally.

Enter a total greenhorn who didn't understand any of this and who didn't like to get pushed around. Omigod! The first set we made encroached on someone's territory and a horrible screaming match ensued. Four years later, if I walked past this guy's boat, it was a good chance we were going to get in yet another brawl.

The gillnet area we fished was about six hours south of Ketchikan, almost on the international border between the U.S. and Canada. The season consisted of weekly openings starting at noon, the first of which was traditionally on Father's Day. Durations varied, with the anticipated strength of the salmon run, but typically lasted from noon Sunday through noon Thursday. The season lasted 14-15 weeks, again depending upon the run strength.

Victoria and I fished hard that first season. We didn't get as close to the beach as we might have, and mostly settled for second set out. We also weren't among the 2 a.m. crowd, but we finally found our own stretch of water which we called home. Gradually we settled into a routine. Despite making virtually every rookie mistake that could be made, getting into brawls with many of the better fisherman, and using a crummy net that came with the boat, we caught in the neighborhood of 75,000 pounds of salmon that first season. Of course, the price per pound was abysmal, so it only translated into about $25,000. A quarter of that went to the lease agreement for the gillnet permit, a quarter went to boat upkeep, and Victoria and I split the rest. It didn't figure out to a very high hourly wage.

As the end of September approached, we drummed the net off the reel and prepared for the start of shrimp season. It looked like we each stood to net (pardon the expression) about $10,000 apiece from halibut and gillnetting seasons. As my house payments were about $1,200 per month, and I had grown remarkably fond of eating, it seemed like I was going to have to come up with something else to help make ends meet. Victoria thought she just might have an idea.

19

Stabbed in the Back

(October 1995 - March 1996)

"And ain't it just like a friend of mine
To come and hit me from behind."
-- James Taylor, "Carolina on my Mind"

Victoria was a member of the board of directors for the local greenie group, Tongass Conservation Society, or TCS, who prided themselves on being a group of rebels, opposed to the KPC mill and industrial-scale logging on the Tongass. But so far they had never really done much but stamp their foot and annoy the Forest Service and the local newspaper. With Victoria's encouragement, I went to a board meeting and asked them to hire me on as a conservation forester. My proposal was to write hardcore comments, administrative appeals, and litigation for every timber sale on the Ketchikan Area of the Tongass.

I explained to the board members that this would be a radical departure from the way they had been operating. I proposed a seek-and-destroy mission against every timber sale on the south Tongass. From my perspective, the best way to stop the travesty of the Tongass was simply to turn off the timber tap. When the Forest Service turned on the faucet to pour KPC another overflowing draught of Tongass timber, nothing would come out of the spigot, because TCS would have every sale tied up in court. And no deals! I told TCS that if I even heard the d-word, I was gone.

This would mean TCS would face increased notoriety and a protracted fight that could get more than a little hot. They all nodded grimly and said they were up for it. We shook hands on it. There was no need to sign anything, this was a blood oath. They held their breath when they asked how much an ex-$57,000 a year professional forester charged for his services. I wanted $500/month, and they hired me on the spot.

It felt weird to be working for the greenies, but alone I would stand a poor chance opposing a powerful timber industry employing several hundred workers. But an environmental organization with many members has "standing," whose sheer weight can often tip the scales of justice the other way.

Although I didn't consider myself a greenie, I believed the only hope for the local timber industry was to dismantle what was currently in place, force a hiatus, and rebuild an industry based upon a sustainable level of logging. If to effect this change meant that I had to link arms with the greenies and walk side by side with them for awhile, well, then so be it.

There was no way the Forest Service was going to voluntarily change the way they logged the Tongass. For each timber sale, they had to go to areas that the forest plan indicated were zoned for logging and then use the forest plan's estimate of how much timber was available. When the foresters and engineers did the logging plan, they always found less timber than the forest plan indicated. And a lot of what they did find was uneconomical to log. As the logging plan was laid out on the ground, more acres fell out ... caves, salmon streams, steep slopes, fragile soils, substandard timber, etc. It was a lot like packing ice across the desert. You ended up with a heckuva lot less than you started with.

Obviously, the Forest Service couldn't bring this information forward, so they hid it. Not only didn't they provide the answers, they didn't even ask the questions. This wasn't nuclear physics. How much timber did the forest plan say was available? How much did the logging plan and subsequent field work indicate was really there? Pretty darned simple. As a matter of fact, it was an agency regulation known as Forest Plan Validation Monitoring.

And because they were usually under the gun to get even more wood to KPC, they would hurriedly wrap up the EIS before all the proposed units were reconned in the field. This meant that the units would shrink when they were laid out, so they'd just kinda borrow some timber from a unit that was supposed to be logged way in the future. Hell, no one would miss it, and just to be sure, they wouldn't tell anyone about it.

This wasn't simply bureaucratic chicanery. The oh-so-what if the agency violated some meaningless little bit of red tape that nobody really cared about. It wasn't an accident, a miscalculation, or an oopsie. It was the willful, deliberate decision to allow wildly unsustainable logging of the world's largest temperate rainforest.

At Congressman George Miller's request, the Government Accounting Office (GAO) investigated the Ketchikan Area's unit expansion policy and printed a report which stated:

> "We examined 41 instances in which boundary changes had occurred in areas logged by KPC and found that in 39 instances the documentation was not adequate ... we recommend that the Secretary of Agriculture direct the Chief of the Forest Service to require Alaska Regional Office officials to periodically check to ensure that forest supervisors are properly documenting the environmental significance of boundary changes made after EISs have been issued in the Tongass National Forest."

But there were other problems too that needed swept under the carpet. What the hell, the Forest Service had a big broom. The Tongass was a uniquely different old-growth ecosystem than existed in other areas of the Pacific Northwest. Elsewhere, individual trees, largely Douglas-fir and western redcedar, might reach 600-1000 years of age, but the surrounding forest was ravaged by fire on a 200- to 500-year cycle. This meant these ecosystems were composed of ancient trees in old forests.

Because the Tongass's 160 inches of annual rainfall precluded cataclysmic fire, this ecosystem was composed of ancient trees in a virtually primeval forest. There was constant blowdown, but it tended to be fairly small patches scattered throughout the forested landscape. Consequently, there hadn't been any significant breaks in the old growth since the last ice age, and second growth was largely unheard of until the Forest Service started logging. No plant or animal species had evolved to fill the second-growth niche, because there never had been any second growth. When the old growth was logged, all the old-growth-dependent species went with it because Mother Nature hadn't made a back-up plan.

This meant the more acreage was logged, the greater the drop in wildlife populations and biodiversity. The whole ecosystem crashed ... everything that hopped, slithered, crawled, flew, or swam ... from eagles to deer to salmon.

But the biggest loser in the unsustainable logging of the old-growth was, surprisingly, the Alaskan logger and the future Alaskan timber industry. There was an increasing demand for quality old-growth Sitka spruce, yellow-cedar, and redcedar. It had virtually no competition on the global market, because it didn't exist in any appreciable quantities elsewhere. These species grew only in the Pacific Northwest, where old growth was largely a thing of the past, as stands had been converted to shorter-aged rotations or placed in reserves where the Forest Service and the timber industry could only drool at them.

There is no similarity between old-growth forest products and young-growth forest products. A rose may be a rose, but a Sitka spruce is not a Sitka spruce. Old-growth wood tends to be clear and tight-grained, which makes it superb for dimensional lumber, furniture, molding, veneer, and so on. Young-growth's suitability is virtually limited to low-grade stud production or chips. If the Tongass's old-growth could be sustainably logged, the industry could assume a huge market advantage as time passed, because it would be the only source for old-growth forest products. To be blunt, the Alaska logger is more dependent on old growth than is the spotted owl.

But the timber industry was here now, and it was infinitely more profitable to just cut as much as they could as fast as they could, and then get out. It was expected to take a minimum of 250 years before the forests would even BEGIN to return to old-growth conditions, but the historic pattern of the American timber industry is cut and run.

The Forest Service managers didn't seem to give a damn about the future either, so they made the decision to "manage" the Tongass forest on a 100-year rotation. This simply allowed it to be cut more quickly ... higher logging levels equal bigger budgets plus more staff plus more kudos plus more political favor. This kind of mathematics they understood.

The facts were that at 100 years, Tongass second-growth had no means of competing on the world market. It was slower growing, more expensive to log, and more costly to transport to end users than young-growth products Down South. According to the Forest Service's own data, the average tree in the average Tongass stand at 100 years of age is only expected to reach 10.8 inches in diameter. This is smaller than the average tree in the average stand in a Down South Doug-fir stand at 30 years of age, where the logging and transportation costs are much less. No builder is going to go into a lumberyard and choose an Alaskan 2x4 for $20, when a locally produced one is available for $1.99.

That was the great lie. Not only did the conversion of Tongass old-growth forests to second-growth create a dysfunctional landscape for wildlife and salmon, but it also put the Alaska logger out of work for another 150 years. Pretending it was going to be cut again at age 100 was like opening the refrigerator and lifting the lid on a container of last week's leftovers, and vowing to eat it tomorrow. It simply wasn't going to happen.

Also, it was a huge loss of taxpayer dollars to log the Tongass, notwithstanding the creative bookkeeping practices invented by the agency to hide these losses, such as ignoring the cost of building logging roads and the cost of writing the EISs. Everything was exorbitantly expensive, because the remoteness necessitated everything's (fuel, equipment, people, logs, and so on) being barged in and out. Plus the Forest Service didn't intend for KPC to actually pay for the logs. Not really. For the price of a Big Mac, the Forest Service handed over 500-year-old spruce. The more acreage that was logged, the more taxpayer money was lost.

Now here's the rub. The National Environmental Policy Act of 1969 required agencies that prepare EISs to consider a broad range of alternatives, which, in the case of the Tongass timber sales, equates to a range of logging levels for each sale. I quote from the law:

> "This section is the heart of the EIS ... present the environmental impacts of the proposal and the alternatives in comparative form, thus sharply defining the issues and providing a clear basis for choice... (40 CFR Section 2.14)"
> "Rigorously explore and objectively evaluate all reasonable alternatives ..." (40 CFR Section 1502.14(a))

"Include reasonable alternatives not within the jurisdiction of the lead agency. (40 CFR Section 1502.14(c))

So if the Forest Service developed a range of alternatives and analyzed the information truthfully, it would show that the more they logged, the more money they lost, the greater the dip in wildlife populations, and the sooner they put the Alaska logger out of work. Managers would have a hard time selecting alternatives which provided enough wood to keep the KPC contract afloat. I could just see Rittenhouse saying, "This alternative is going to kill the most deer, salmon, and eagles, lose the most money, and hasten the demise of the local economy. Sounds good to me."

So here's what they did ... they made all the alternatives have the same logging level, like quintuplets dressed alike, except with different colored booties. This kept the decision-maker from looking like a fool when he selected the alternative with the highest logging level. They rationalized it was OK, as long as all the alternatives had terrible consequences. The agency said the forest plan made them do it. The long-term contract made them do it. It wasn't their fault.

What was behind this strategy was that if it succeeded, fine, they had won. If greenies successfully challenged it in court and shut down the sales and buggered the long-term contract, the local managers could wash their hands of the whole affair and blame the contract's demise on the greenies. Not their fault. I thought back to the conversation I had with then-Alaska regional timber director Gene Chelstad when he said he "... intended to let NEPA break the long-term contract." I thought back to the comment my CPOW wildlife biologist kept making, "Bill, I think they're trying to throw it. I think they want the sale successfully litigated."

All these timber sales would be dead meat in front of the U.S. Ninth Circuit Court of Appeals, although the path to that hallowed court was tedious indeed. Litigators had to establish a track record of involvement with a timber sale. They had to submit scoping comments, which the Forest Service would ignore. Then they had to submit comments on the draft EIS, again which the agency would ignore. Then file an administrative appeal, at which time the agency would pull on their reading glasses, mightily shuffle papers, before pushing their spectacles down to the tip of their nose and mumbling ... "appeal denied." Then litigation filed in front of the conservative,

Republican-appointed Alaskan judges, who would try to tie up the case as long as possible before dismissing it. Then finally the case would get its first fair hearing in front of the Ninth Circuit Appellate Court, which had shown an amazing tendency to slam-dunk Forest Service timber sales. I suspect the appellate judges' decision had something to do with the fact that these sales clearly broke the law.

In mid-September, I sent another letter to OSC seeking resolution of my whistleblower disclosure. On Oct. 12, Catherine McMullen of the Disclosure Unit called to let me know that OSC had forwarded my challenge of the investigative report back to USDA for an agency response. USDA had filed a response Sept. 11, but OSC had misfiled it. She said U.S. Special Counsel Leonard Grabinsky would review USDA's response to my challenge (if he could find it) and make a determination if the agency response was acceptable. She expected Grabinsky's decision within three weeks.

Ms. McMullen also noted that I had resigned my position under duress. She said in reviewing my case they just noted I had alleged retaliation against me by the agency. Six months after I was forced to leave the agency, OSC finally figured out there may have been some retaliation involved. And OSC was the agency empowered to ensure I came to no professional harm under the umbrella of the Whistleblower Protection Act? Ms. McMullen asked if I wanted her to refer my case to their complaints unit. Sure I said, thanked her for her efforts, and hung up. The next week I received an official letter saying OSC had established a complaint case file for me and were ready to receive my affidavit. Yeah, take a number and wait 10 years.

Meanwhile, the Forest Service had finally published the Draft Supplement to CPOW, as directed by Chief Thomas. The agency thought nobody cared what this document said, as SEACC badly wanted out of their lawsuit and had already cut a deal with the Forest Service in that regard. So, virtually assured that no one would challenge the CPOW supplement, the agency published a document that was relatively thin in the number of pages it contained, but thinner yet in defensible facts. Lewis Carroll's <u>Alice in Wonderland</u> was more firmly grounded in reality. They finally acknowledged that there was such a thing as falldown, but that it was only 15 percent ... instead of the 50+ percent that other studies had shown. I decided to read the CPOW supplement and on Sept. 21, 1995, I once again entered my comments into the planning record for the timber sale I personally started almost five years previously. I concluded by saying:

"For years I listened to Bob Vaught's analogy to explain the narrow purpose and need for the CPOW project. Remember the one, 'if the purpose and need was to build a hospital on Gravina Island, why would I consider an alternative that builds a firehall on Prince of Wales?' Please allow me to make my own analogy. Suppose instead of selling timber, the Forest Service was an egg distributor, with a huge inventory of eggs in cartons. Now suppose that you knew you had a number of cartons that didn't have any eggs at all (planning falldown), there were more cartons that had eggs that were rotten and that nobody wanted to buy (economic falldown), and that all the rest of the cartons contained an average of three broken eggs (recon and layout falldown). Now further suppose that you had to calculate how fast you could sell your eggs (sustained yield) before it was necessary to replenish your inventory of eggs (rotation age). Now stretch your imagination and suppose you calculate your selling rate as if you didn't have any problems at all with your eggs (CPOW FEIS and ROD, TLMP, etc.). When it's time to actually sell a carton of eggs, you find one of the cartons that has some fresh ones in it (NEPA). Then you open that carton, find that there are three broken ones in it, so you raid three eggs from one of the other cartons (unit expansion). Obviously, you may be able to fill the first few egg orders, but will become less able to do so in the future as you run into empty, rotten, and raided egg cartons.

Mr. Powell, this analogy is the reason the Chief required you to do the CPOW supplement. But you still haven't counted the eggs right. Go back and do it again.

I believe that the Forest Service has many hard-working intelligent people, capable of producing the highest level of natural resource science. It is my personal opinion that the CPOW Draft Supplement to the FEIS is not a product of that high level of science, but rather has been intentionally bastardized by individual officials to rationalize arbitrary actions of a purely political considerations, with little if any foundation in science. It is my personal opinion that the actions of these individual officials are a clear violation of 18 U.S.C Sections 2073 and 1001 of the U.S Criminal Code, and that the Nation, as well as the Forest Service, could benefit from a hard look. Obey the law and tell the truth indeed!"

I couldn't help but compare my 1995 comments to the ones I had gotten in so much trouble for in 1992, which by now seemed rather innocuous. It was the same timber sale and the same issues, but my tone had gotten ... well, a tad bit more hostile, as demonstrated by the small fact that I wanted the bastards put in prison. The difference was that I no longer had respect for the agency I had loved and faithfully served for so many years. I felt like the Tongass managers had stolen the Forest Service, as surely as the Grinch stole Christmas, and I wanted them to give it back.

The fall of 1995 was a nice mixture for me of shrimping and reviewing Forest Service EISs. Each provided a relief from the other, and I was kept busy. Plus the extra $500/month from TCS went a long way to making ends meet. It was touch and go whether I would be able to hold onto my beloved house, and this extra cash gave me some increased hope.

Forest Service EISs arrived in a daunting box containing a foot-thick stack of documents, weighing 20 pounds. I picked them apart, found the weak spots, drafted a scathing comment letter, and ran it by my board of directors, who seemed delighted with their increased notoriety. They had rapidly become a player in timber politics on the south Tongass and enjoyed the attention. Yeah, go get 'em, Bill!

Robert and James told me that some of the Tongass managers went bonkers when they became aware my new vocation. James said he overhead a conversation in the hallways where it was suggested that they cut a deal with me to get me off their backs, but quickly concluded that, "I was a hard case and too moral to cut deals."

A plethora of new timber sales were under proposal. The draft EIS for Lab Bay was finally released, which called for the logging of 85 mmbf in the area directly north of CPOW. This area was the most logged-over portion of SE Alaska, and I say that from personally having done the logging plan for the sale. Here's a sample of what TCS had to say about Lab Bay :

> "...this project began four years ago (August 1991). TCS has heard that the government assigned this project to an independent professional services contractor and has spent over $4 million in its preparation, administration, and execution. This

would imply that the NEPA evaluation alone would cost approximately $50/mbf, which exceeds the indicated net stumpage rates for any of the alternatives. The most 'profitable' alternative has a projected present net value of NEGATIVE 10 million dollars."

Next was the Chasina timber sale which supposed to log 40 mmbf over in the area where Victoria and I fished halibut. As a matter of fact, the Forest Service was proposing to log the timber in the little anchorage where we had found shelter from the hurricane that spring. Without the timber, there would be no lee from the winds. Therefore, TCS was ... ah, concerned. Here were a few of their thoughts:

"...am commenting on behalf of Tongass Conservation Society (TCS), a local non-profit, conservation organization concerned about the welfare of the Tongass National Forest. TCS represents a diverse constituency including Alaska Natives, local residents, property owners, subsistence users,environmentalists, recreationists, cavers, sport hunters/fishermen, professional guides, and commercial fishermen. Many of our members use the project area, so your proposed action has the potential to affect the welfare of our organization.

TCS wants the Chasina EIS to analyze in detail a full range of alternative levels of harvest and not just 101 ways to harvest 40 mmbf. It's about time the Forest Service walks its talk about listening to the public -- please abandon the policy of forcing all alternatives to meet the purpose and need volume constraint. We DON'T LIKE IT -- and have been telling you that for years."

Barely a month had gone by, and I felt I had earned my first paycheck. The TCS board did too. It's hard to know what the Forest Service thought, as they had operated without oversight for so long maybe they thought bullets couldn't hurt them. Or maybe they had another deal cooked up. Who knows?

In early December, I received a letter from OSC, dated Nov. 28, 1995. In the words of Leonard Grabinsky, deputy associate special counsel for prosecution:

"I have determined that the [agency's] findings appear reasonable..."

"... we have sent copies of the report and your comments to the President, the Senate and House of Representatives Committees on Agriculture, and the Comptroller General of the U.S. We have also filed a copy of the report and your comments in our public file and closed the matter."

I pictured the final scene from the movie "Raiders of the Lost Ark," where a forklift places a box containing the Ark of the Covenant atop a stack of identical boxes amid a huge warehouse filled with identical stacks. I lost my career, job, pension, health insurance, and damned near everything else for a filing a whistleblower disclosure that no one ever read, much less took seriously.

The law had stipulated my case would be resolved within 60 days, yet two years and four months passed between my filing in July 1993 and OSC's "resolution" in November 1995. Whistleblower Protection Act, indeed!

I shopped around for funds to secure legal counsel to represent TCS in timber sale litigation on the south Tongass. I spoke to the Sierra Club Legal Defense Fund (SCLDF), but they wouldn't make a move without SEACC's blessing. So I spoke to the Natural Resources Defense Council (NRDC), and they didn't want to make a move in SE Alaska without SCLDF's blessing. It seemed like the greenies had as much red tape as the government and SEACC held the tape dispenser. I had observed their lumbering, half-hearted deal-making and wanted no part in it. Without litigation money or legal counsel, TCS had no chance to accomplish anything.

The next proposed timber sale was Control Lake, which was a 187 mmbf extravaganza just to the southwest of CPOW. I knew this area well, as it originally had been part of the CPOW project, and I had done all the logging plans for this sale too. It was particularly controversial because it contained the popular canoe route Honker Divide, which was the only one of SEACC's 'favorite places' on the south Tongass. SEACC had spent some time organizing a citizen's group which had produced a "citizen's alternative," which proposed much lower logging levels.

I worked quite a long time on preparing TCS's comments for the Control Lake timber sale, and when I was done, I posted them in the TCS office for review by the board. I did not support SEACC's citizen's alternative, but rather the no-logging alternative. I phoned all the board members, and they all said they were in agreement with what I had written. I mailed my Control Lake timber sale comments to the Forest Service and sent a courtesy comment to SEACC. A few nights later, Victoria and I went to the regularly scheduled board meeting. One of the board members, Jackie Canterbury, was acting weird. She wouldn't look at me, and said she had changed her mind about appealing and litigating timber sales. She now felt that the best way to fight KPC was by harassing them for pollution from their pulp mill. The board president said he had gotten an angry call from SEACC about my comment letter and suggested the board take another vote on my it. The board's new vote reaffirmed the previous decision, with Jackie being the lone dissenter.

That night I asked Victoria what she thought of the meeting, and she too thought Jackie had behaved strangely. Victoria noted that Jackie was also on the board of directors for SEACC and speculated they were uncomfortable with my stealing their thunder on the lower Tongass. Victoria said SEACC's fund-raising was way down, while TCS's was way up. She wondered if SEACC had lobbied Jackie to get TCS to turn down the heat.

The next night, the board president called and said he had re-polled the TCS board and they now wanted to rescind their approval of my comments and incorporate some changes recommended by SEACC. Among the changes was support of the citizen's alternative. I told him that the comments had already been received by the Forest Service and that I resented making changes just to please SEACC. He insisted, so I again obeyed a direct order with which I disagreed. I also handed in my resignation, effective Dec. 31, 1995. I had lasted three months.

Omigod! I had become too radical even for the greenies!

I had a lot of supporters throughout SE Alaska, and when news of my resignation made it around the grapevine, several people called to ask what had happened. I told them it looked like my working for TCS constituted a threat to SEACC's omnipotence on the Tongass, and that they had lobbied Jackie and others to more or less force me out of my job. Some people looked into it for me and confirmed my suspicions.

Andy Stahl called and told me straight-off that he wasn't going to get involved with the politics of greenie organizations within SE Alaska. Small wonder, as Jackie Canterbury was also a member of his board of directors! But he did want my help in a timber theft lawsuit against KPC. The case was going to be handled by the Seattle law firm, Schroeter, Goldmark, and Bender. I told Andy I would help as best I could.

I confided to my buddy Robert that maybe I just had to face the fact that my approach was either universally unpopular or wholly wrong. I told him that I was bowing out of involvement in the Tongass ... hanging up my guns, so to speak. Robert shook his head sadly and said that he was sorry to hear that, as he "thought there was hope for the Tongass, but that there was much less so without your efforts."

Robert's words stuck with me throughout the next few weeks. The Forest Service had published the final EIS for the CPOW Supplement. I read the document with as much professional objectivity and dispassion as I could summon. I found it to be the single most dishonest, unprofessional document I had ever seen.

Maybe numbers will help explain what they did. The old Tongass Forest Plan, written in 1979, said there were 71,000 acres of forest available for logging within the CPOW project area. The new Tongass Forest Plan reduced wildlife protection and increased the timber base to 114,000 acres. My team's logging plan looked at these 114,000 and found only 50,000 acres that could be made into viable logging units. The Forest Service spent approximately a million dollars to hire an independent contractor to re-examine the 114,000 acres, plus an additional 5,000 acres that were slated to be transferred to the Native corporations. The contractor found 70,000 loggable acres.

The Forest Service decided that the REAL answer was a bastard child logging plan based on any area which was deemed to be loggable by either my team's plan or the contractor's plan. They concluded there were 91,000 loggable acres. But even that wasn't enough, so they decided to compare the results to the 71,000 acres that the old 1979 Tongass Forest Plan said existed. Their conclusion: there were more loggable acres than acres of forest. I'm not kidding!

I asked others for feedback. James said that it was an embarrassment. Robert said that no one in Thorne Bay would even read it, and that people just trudged along with their heads down, like robots obeying the beckoning of their masters. Pete Griffith, the leader of the CPOW supplement, said that the document so angered him that he felt like "slugging the guy that made him write it like that." We both knew he meant Arrasmith.

On Feb. 9, 1996, I filed an administrative appeal of the decision to implement the CPOW supplement. Here are a few quotes:

> "I like metaphors. Suppose there are two jars of marbles, each containing black ones (unharvestable acres) and white ones (acres of loggable units). The object here is to calculate the percentage of white marbles in the first jar. The Forest Service spends eight months counting all the marbles in the first jar and says there are 50 white marbles and 64 black ones, for a total of 114 marbles. Not liking the answer, the Forest Service spends about a million dollars to have the marbles counted again. This time 70 white ones are counted within the jar and another 5 white ones on the counter (encumbered lands). Any reasonable person would conclude that, although the counts were different, there were somewhere between 50 and 70 white marbles in the jar. The supplemental ROD, however,concludes there are 91 white marbles. The kindest word that I can use for this logic is 'whopper.'
>
> Remember the object was to determine the percentage of white marbles in the first jar, and the Forest Service has already averaged the separate and distinct counts of 50 and 70 and gotten 91. But instead of dividing 50, 70, or (what the hell) even 91 by the total number of marbles in the first jar (114), the Forest Service divides by the number of marbles in the second jar, which someone counted 17 years ago, leaving a note saying there were 71 marbles in this jar. So the Forest Service compares the 91 white marbles it maintains are in jar one to the 71 total marbles in jar two and concludes there are more white marbles in jar one than total marbles.
>
> This metaphor, of course, is totally preposterous, but that is EXACTLY the logic that has been followed in the CPOW supplement. If it is important to determine the percentage of planning falldown which can be expected to occur within the TLMP 1979 timber base, then do a MELP on the TLMP 1979 timber base. I would expect that planning falldown would be somewhere between the 38 percent found in the contractor LSTA and the 56 percent found in the CPOW MELP.
>
> Mr. Janik, I will address my closing remarks to you personally. First, don't you think that it's just a little bit weird that a dyed-in-the-wool timber beast and IDT leader files a whistleblower disclosure and now an administrative appeal

against his own sale? What do you think would make that happen? I'll tell you -- since timber supply became a significant issue, CPOW became a cesspool.

"Toady" planners, with virtually no field experience, whispered hypothetical logging levels in the ears of Forest S e r - vice managers. And willingly they believed. Because even managers have bosses, and the number one directive in the Alaska Region is "consummate the KPC contract at all costs or Ketchikan will fall into the ocean." Well, that's bullshit!

It's time to put away the mind games of this absurd, out-of-control project. Do you realize that in successive documents the Forest Service has estimated timber supply forthe CPOW project as (1) the CPOW MELP, (2) TLMP Rev Altn P suitable-available acres (all of 'em, no falldown), (3) TLMP 1979 suitable-available acres, and (4) summation of the CPOWMELP and contractor LSTA.

Frankly, Mr. Janik, I don't really care if you log CPOW. I also don't care about consummation of the KPC contract, the Forest Service's budget, or what the Alaska congressional delegation thinks. What I DO care about is the people whose forever homes are in SE Alaska, and I think they deserve to be told the true future implications of today's unsustainable logging levels. And this project has missed the mark.

Please consider what is at risk here. This isn't an environmentalist's appeal about how many goshawks should be roosting on the head of a pin -- it's about whether there will be ANY future timber industry in SE Alaska. Those are high stakes indeed -- consider them well."

The new Ketchikan forest supervisor, Brad Powell, met with me on March 11, 1996 regarding my appeal. New agency regulations required him to attempt to negotiate a settlement with me, much as I had done with Sylvia Geraghty many years before.. We met at a local coffee shop, because I refused to enter the Forest Service office. We were polite and cordial, but no deal was offered, thank god.

I knew there was absolutely no chance of winning my administrative appeal, so I called Andy Stahl and asked him if he knew of any competent attorney who might be willing to litigate the timber sale, with fees on a contingency basis.

A few days later, Andy called me back. He put me in touch with Liam Sherlock, a lawyer out of Eugene, Ore., who was quite willing to accept the case pro bono. AFSEEE agreed to pay Liam's filing fees and office expenses. Working strictly via mail, FAX, and phone, Liam and I assembled a case and had it ready to go shortly after the

Forest Service denied my appeal. Our case focused exclusively on the failure of the document to consider a range of alternative harvest levels, which was a violation of law that could be argued rather succinctly. The timber supply issue, although my strongest concern, was more general and would require a succession of expert witnesses, who would greatly add to the expense and complexity of the case. Andy and Liam felt we had a solid chance to prevail.

Liam felt the case would be strengthened if several other people were added as co-litigants. Although I had little trust in others by now, I acceded to Liam's counsel and asked several people to join me as co-litigants. I explained to one and all that our attorney was operating pro bono, and that there was little chance of their having any exposure to countersuits. They all submitted signed, notarized affidavits. On April 19, 1996, our lawsuit was filed in the U.S. District Court for Alaska.

We had a pretty narrow window of opportunity to obtain a preliminary injunction, and failing that, to get it immediately docketed for the U.S. Ninth Circuit Court of Appeals. Unfortunately, the window got slammed on our fingers. SEACC was furious about the lawsuit, as it queered the deal they had cut with the Forest Service whereby SEACC would drop their own CPOW litigation in return for the Forest Service's promise not to log Honker Divide. So they were up in arms, and unfortunately one of my co-litigants was a SEACC board member.

The "Ketchikan Daily News" printed the story of the lawsuit on page one under a banner headline, and named all the co-litigants. One, Becky Knight, a SEACC board member, called and demanded to be removed from the lawsuit. She said I had never told her that she was a co-litigant, but was just providing a letter of support. One by one, most of the other co-litigants bailed out.

Becky Knight then called the SEACC staff attorney, Buck Lindekugel, who called the U.S. Attorney for the CPOW case and actually blew the whistle on me for trying to get his "client" in trouble. What a mess! I called Liam, who was clearly unimpressed with this turn of events. He was now in big trouble, as the Alaska judge, looking for any excuse to avoid making a ruling on the merits of the case, threw the book at Liam for attempting to represent an unwilling client. The judge was talking admonishment, suspension, disbarment, and castration.

It seemed totally unacceptable to me that Liam, who was kindly taking on this case out of the goodness of his heart, would have to endure any hardship. So I wrote Liam an affidavit in which I personally accepted all blame for any misinformation given to the "co-litigants." Liam said I could potentially face contempt of court charges, but that seemed almost like small potatoes by now.

The offshoot of the whole affair was that Liam had to re-file the entire lawsuit with the abbreviated list of litigants, and we missed our window of opportunity. The Alaska judge issued a preliminary decision that the Forest Service said it had obeyed the law and that was good enough for him, and who were these three litigants anyhow?

Later Victoria said she distinctly remembered my original phone calls asking people to join me as co-litigants. As a matter of fact, we had even written down notes for the phone calls, because she was going to make some of the calls for me. So there was little doubt about it. I was weary of fighting the bad guys who were in front of me, and now my backside didn't seem so safe either.

20

Downward Spiral

(March 1996 - November 1996)

"I had a job, I had a girl.
I had something going, mister, in this world.
I got laid off down at the lumber yard.
Our love went bad, times got hard.
Now I work down at the carwash,
Where all it ever does is rain.
Sometimes I feel just like a rider
On a downbound train."
-- Bruce Springsteen, "Downbound Train"

I went to Seattle to participate in preliminary discussions about the timber theft lawsuit. To summarize this case, AFSEEE had filed a false claims or qui temp suit that said that KPC had stolen National Forest System timber and that such actions had defrauded the government from receiving rightful remuneration. Moreover, the Forest Service had either abetted the timber theft or at least allowed it to occur. Under false claims, AFSEEE was entitled to a third of the foregone payments. Because this was an alleged crime against the government, the Department of Justice was reviewing the case to see if they wanted to intervene as co-plaintiff.

Representing AFSEEE was the powerful Seattle firm Schroeter, Goldmark, and Bender. Chief counsel in the case was Corrie Yackulic, a former Sierra Club Legal Defense Fund attorney. Corrie was fresh-faced and wholesome, a dead ringer for Ali McGraw, and a highly skilled attorney. She also agreed to take on my whistleblower complaint case which alleged the Forest Service had retaliated against me.

Andy and Corrie had become interested in the log theft case as a result of personal statements issued by former Ketchikan forest supervisor Mike Lunn and former Thorne Bay district ranger Pete Johnson. Both these officials questioned irregularities in the Tongass log accountability practices and maintained that it looked like KPC had been stealing National Forest System timber for some time. John Click, the former Forest Service check scaler from Thorne Bay also provided testimony that log theft had occurred. What was lacking was evidence, because the logs were definitely gone.

While I had no direct knowledge of any specific timber theft, I provided testimony about discrepancies between accepted log accountability practices on Down South National Forests versus what had occurred on the Tongass. On other National Forests, the Forest Service laid out the logging units, then carefully cruised the timber to get a definitive estimate of volume and log grade. The sales were then sold either lump sum or scale ("scale" means to measure the volume in the logs). In lump sum sales, it was strictly caveat emptor. The purchaser accepted the Forest Service cruised estimate and maybe got a little extra or sometimes a little less. If for any reason trees were either added to or deleted from the sale during logging, these trees were cruised and paid/credited at contractual rates. When the purchaser hauled the logs from the sale area, they were individually branded, and the truckload was assigned a unique ticket number, so that its transport could be monitored. The purchaser then scaled the logs and reported back to the Forest Service how much timber was logged and removed. It was an effective system with weighty checks and balances.

In scaled sales, the Forest Service also cruised the timber, but treated their cruise strictly as an estimate. Timber was paid for by multiplying the contract rate by the amount of timber actually removed. Once again, before removing the logs from the sale area, each individual log was branded, and each truckload was assigned a unique ticket number. But now the log truck had to pass through a scale shack where the load was tallied by Forest Service scalers or by independent bureau scalers, who were continually check scaled by the Forest Service. Usually not every load was actually scaled, but rather was subject to sample scaling using random number generators, white-or-black marbles, sealed cards, or other techniques to ensure non-biased sampling. Sometimes every load was weighed, and a relationship was established between weight and scale. Sometimes the logs on every truckload were counted, and a relationship was developed between piece count and scale. Each truckload and ticket was accounted for, and in the end, the Forest Service matched its scale reports with its cruised estimate.

In the early days of the Tongass, the Forest Service didn't even layout the logging units, much less cruise them. Forest Service inspectors were seldom even on the ground, so they had little idea how much or even WHERE timber was being removed. Logs were loaded onto trucks and bundled, so that the entire load could be removed as one composite piece. The logs were then trucked to a transfer site where they were removed by huge cranes and dumped into the saltwater in an area ringed with floating logs ("boom sticks") chained together to form a raft. A tug boat would then tow the entire raft to Thorne Bay where periodically some of the individual log bundles would be selected for scale. Sometimes the logs were sorted in Thorne Bay prior to shipping to their destination point. Sometimes they were towed directly to the pulp mill in Ketchikan.

This was a loose system. Ownership of the logs was not passed between the government and the purchaser until the logs were actually scaled, so if something happened to the logs before they were scaled, it was the government's loss. This something happening could be the log raft's breaking up in a storm, bundles' being stolen, or simply the raft's disappearing in its entirety. And because the Forest Service had no cruised estimate of how much timber had been logged, they had no idea how much timber could be expected to show up at the scale shack. They took KPC's word for it.

If Stephen King had my knowledge of forestry and were given the assignment to develop a log accountability system that would PROMOTE log theft, it is unlikely even his fertile mind could design something more conducive. Uncruised, unscaled logs floating in rafts in remote bays, being loaded onto Japanese log barges under the cover of darkness during stormy periods when there was no way the

Forest Service would be able to float plane out for inspections. It was analogous to a bank advertising that it was going to send all its employees out for a long lunch at noon, leave the doors open, the vault unlocked, and the money uncounted so they wouldn't know if some were missing. Seriously, it was that bad.

The rumors about log theft on the Tongass were legion. While I had no direct knowledge of its having occurred, if it didn't occur here on the Tongass, then it never occurred anywhere. It is true that accountability practices did get somewhat better over time. The Forest Service started to layout logging unit boundaries and make more of a presence on the ground, but they had no real cruising program until the mid-1990s. They made half-hearted attempts to enforce individual log branding, bundle tickets, and raft numbers, but there were lots of documented inconsistencies. Only the gods know how many inconsistencies and outright violations were ignored.

The previous Ketchikan check scaler, Tom Clothier, maintained that he was afraid of flying, and he refused to go out to Thorne Bay to oversee the independent bureau scalers, who potentially could have been in collusion with KPC. It was common knowledge that the Forest Service employee responsible for selecting bundles to be sample-scaled always went on the same days, at the same times, and always selected bundles from the same position in the raft. It was pretty easy for KPC to ensure that substandard-sized bundles were in those locations at those times, which would then be statistically extrapolated as representative of many more bundles. It was almost as if the Forest Service WANTED KPC to steal timber.

John Click, who replaced Clothier as Forest Service check scaler during the early 1990s, was an honest man and wouldn't go along with games. He tried to bring integrity to the log accountability program, and told horror stories about his observations on the Tongass. He explained that much of the potential log theft was not the actual physical stealing of logs, i.e., covertly moving them from one location to another, but rather more a white collar crime of unethical scaling practices and manipulating the numbers. Of course, KPC complained about John, so he was run out of the agency.

The Department of Justice lawyers listened to all this impassively. Where was the evidence that logs had been stolen, where was the evidence that KPC had done it, where were the missing logs? No evidence, no crime. I explained that before leaving the agency I had established a database of all the logs scaled on the Tongass, and there might be some merit in examining that data. They looked glassy-eyed, until I volunteered to help process the data. Then they loaned me a micro-computer and demanded the data from the Forest Service. The Forest Service never delivered the data in a usable format, and Department of Justice apparently didn't care. They wanted a way out, as well as their computer back.

A timber theft task force of law enforcement agents was assigned to focus on the Tongass, then mysteriously demobilized. There was something different about the Tongass. Something that made it beyond laws that applied to other National Forests. Something that was better left undisturbed. Department of Justice backed out of the case, and the lawsuit fizzled.

Perhaps it was just as well for me, as I had other fish to fry. Or in this case, other fish to catch and ice. Once again I had *Blind Faith* hauled into the boat yard for annual maintenance and some repairs. After a month's work, I plopped her back into the water mid-April and headed out halibut fishing the next week. I was pretty well broke and didn't have the money for the May house payment.

Fortunately, we were able to scare up about 1,600 pounds of halibut before the weather went to hell on us. It was a welcome cash infusion and kept me financially solvent for another month. By now, I was starting to get the hang of fishing halibut. I had done it enough that I had an idea of how to do it and where to go, and also had the '*Faith* rigged so that she handled the fishery pretty well.

The next trip netted about 1,500 pounds, and the final trip about 2,500. As a matter of fact, I cut loose the final seven halibut from the last set, because our running tally showed we were just over our annual quota. After the long, lean winter, it felt mighty good to have some money in the bank once again.

Offsetting this mildly prosperous feeling was growing concern over my beloved Newfoundland x Rhodesian ridgeback, Max, who at age 16, was starting to fail badly. Although a stern look from him could still send my young wolf cowering, Max's once muscular body was now wraithlike, and he was having difficulty making it up the steps into the house to be fed at night. One night as I pet him, I realized that I hadn't seen him smile in ages. I had vowed that I would never let my own weakness cause that wonderful animal to suffer. It was time. The next day I said my goodbye to him at the vet's and wept inconsolably. God, I loved my dogs! They say that when you die, you go down a long dark tunnel toward light and loved ones. When I walk that path, there may not be any human well-wishers there for me, but my dogs will be there, no doubt!

Gillnet season was two weeks away, which left ample time to get the boat rerigged. As the fleet started to assemble in Ketchikan, I talked to some of the guys I knew from the previous year. With a year under my belt, I was no longer the rookie, although hardly a veteran. It was nice to be accepted by the fleet. The rumor on the docks foretold of horribly low fish prices. At our pre-season meeting, my cold storage plant confirmed the low prices and commiserated that they realized we couldn't make it on $.25/pound chum salmon. Two days later, they cut the price to $.20. Pink salmon were $.05/pound. How could salmon be worth five cents a pound? Dog food cost more than that. So did potting soil ... dirt, for Hell's sake!

Using humor to bolster a sagging attitude, the guy I ran with on the *F/V Lady Elizabeth* developed the concept of "humpy math," whereby the price we paid ashore for any commodities or services was converted to pounds of "humpies" (pink salmon). Gasoline was 35 pounds per gallon, bread was 40 pounds per loaf, and machine shop services were an amazing 1,200 pounds per hour.

On the first gillnet set of the season, I was freespooling the last of the net off the reel, turning the drum with my hand. For some unknown reason, Victoria jammed the boat in gear and gunned it. The sudden acceleration spun the drum and a spoke revolved and broke my right thumb.

A few weeks later, I had a sack of groceries sitting on the front seat of my truck. Chacon and I were going for our run, and I had him on his leash. When I opened the door for him to leap in the truck, the groceries panicked the skittish wolf. He bolted back out and ran underneath the truck door, dragging my hand, still attached to his leash through the crack in the door. When he felt himself caught, he pulled, trying to flee the deadly groceries. When a 120-pound terrified wolf tries to pull a man's hand through a crack, guess what happens? All the bones in the heel of my right hand broke, and the rest of the summer I couldn't use it much. A couple times I forgot and shook hands with people, who'd look on in amazement as I crumbled to my knees and screamed as the bones rebroke.

But there were fish in 1996. Oh, Lord there were fish. I remember several times having to stop fishing and go anchor up while we waited for our tender to arrive, simply because we didn't have any more room for fish. But the glut of fish merely exasperated the price problem by flooding the market with cheap fish. The price fell even farther, rather than increasing as it normally did during the course of the season. My cold storage didn't even want the pink salmon and would only accept bright chum salmon. So over the side went the pinks and dark chums. It made no sense to go fishing, only to discard your catch because no one wanted it. This brought back some unpleasant memories of my former employer. It was a grim financial year for gillnetters.

With the price of salmon in the toilet, I brought them home to feed to my wolf. Every week I cooked up big kettles of salmon for Chacon and also canned countless quart jars for the winter. After one particularly gruelling opening, I was just starting to lug a 100-pound cooler up the ramp when a guy coming down the ramp bumped into me. He was drunk and in the company of a couple Native guys. The drunk started cussing me out for getting in his way, and I just lost it. In seconds, he was lying on the dock amid a bunch of slimy fish. The Natives were definitely trying to avoid eye contact with me and decided there was something more interesting a little further down the dock. I scooped up Chacon's fish and met Victoria at the top of the ramp. She thought it was pretty funny.

The next day I was in Murray-Pacific, our local marine goods supplier. In walked the drunk from the day before and laid this slimy jacket on the counter. He went and selected a new coat off the rack, paid for it, then asked the clerk where the trash can was. He didn't seem to recognize me (lord, he must have been drunk!), so I asked him if he were going to throw out his old coat. He kinda sneered at me and asked if I wanted it. I said sure, took it home, threw it in the washer, and have been wearing it ever since.

In early September, Victoria and I were tied up at the net float, taking off the summer net and drumming on the fall net. Summer nets have 5 1/8-inch meshes for catching sockeye, while fall nets traditionally have 6-inch meshes for catching much larger chum and coho salmon. Out of the clear blue, Victoria told me she had accepted a full-time, permanent teaching job (I didn't know she had even applied) and wouldn't be fishing anymore, not even next week's opening.

My whole world spun. I had just barely scraped by last winter, and that was supplemented with a few months salary from TCS. This year's salmon earnings were much less, and now I had lost my fishing partner. I called Robert and asked him to come fishing with me the next week. He was thrilled.

Robert is a better friend than any man deserves though he lives 10,000 lifetimes. Tough and competent, he also has a gentle soul. We fished a coupla days, then got socked in by a 50-mph storm that drove the whole gillnet fleet into our tiny, ill-suited anchorage. For two days we took turns at anchor watch, as the storm raged. Robert provided both an ear for my complaints, as well as a second mind to formulate solutions.

It seemed pretty certain that my fishing partnership with Victoria was over. Perhaps it was just as well, as she had been a reluctant participant. I had to come up with cash to buy out her share of the business, and the only place I had any money at all was the equity in my house.

Oh no, not my house! I had always wanted to die in that house. Now I simply wanted to die. Robert kept me from bottoming out by asking me where else I had money. I told him that obviously my whistleblower retaliation complaint against the Forest Service was a potential source of funds, if I were to prevail. My complaint had been filed Oct. 1995 with OSC, and I had been told retaliation cases tended to drag on even longer than disclosure cases, which for me had been two years and four months. Corrie had told me she was going to wrest the case from OSC and appeal it to the Merit Systems Protection Board that fall, when I would be ashore more regularly. Cases before the MSPB were legally required to be decided within 120 days, which meant I should know by March 1997. It wasn't soon enough to save my house.

Robert sympathized that it wasn't fair for the government to establish a Whistleblower Protection Act and then fail to perform its obligations. He suggested renaming it the Whistleblower Prosecution Act. We joked about it, but it's true. I had lost my job, my career, my health insurance, my pension, and now, apparently, my house. All the while there are laws to ensure retaliation and hardship don't occur. It made the whole deal even more unpalatable that the bad guys kept their cushy jobs or moved on to something better.

When the storm abated, Robert and I returned to Ketchikan. I started looking for tiny houses that I could cash out with my home equity and still leave enough money to pay off Victoria. Even the low end of the Ketchikan housing market was more than I could afford. And virtually all the places at the low end of the market were trashed-out junkers that would require a lot of repair to make habitable. I had enough self-awareness to know that living in a dung-heap would not help my already depleted self-esteem. I needed to find something small and cheap, yet half-way livable.

The next week I hired a kid from Hydaburg to fish with me. He showed up drunk and couldn't sober up by morning. I threw him off my boat and stayed tied to the dock that week. The next week, I took a kid who was seasick the whole time. It was foggy, and we weren't catching anything except dark chum. He wanted to get back to town, and so did I. We left early, and I spun the net off for the season.

Finally a real estate agent showed me a place that wasn't quite completed, i.e., it hadn't made it past the plywood sheathing stage and was in disrepair. But it was solid and had a good foundation. It was 20 feet x 14 feet, with a loft. The entirety of the downstairs was considerably smaller than the kitchen of my house, exclusive of the pantry. But it was cheap and vacant. In Alaska, there are three types of dwellings that can truly be called cabins. One is the bona fide log structures, which are often lovely and costly. Second, is anything built in the backcountry or bush. Third, is anything too small or sub-standard to be legitimately called a house. This place satisfied the latter criteria That night I asked Victoria if she wanted to buy my house. She said yes. I swung both real estate deals and negotiated buying Victoria's half of the fishing partnership, while I prepared for shrimp season. I hired a young kid on the dock, Dan Funk, to shrimp with me, as well as to help me with some two-man chores I had planned for the cabin. Dan was an ex-Forest Service employee, who was living on a small, decrepit sailboat down next to the '*Faith*. He had quit the Forest Service when he drew a chance to buy a homestead site way up north in the Alaska lottery.

On calm days, Dan and I went shrimping. The fishery had undergone a tremendous change since I started in 1994. It was originally a sleepy, Mom-and-Pop type fishery designed to keep some of the locals employed in the winter and provide fresh seafood to the town folk. The season lasted from Oct. 1 through the end of February, and allowed us to make some off-season money. In 1995, the fishery changed, as big catcher-processor ships moved in and really started hammering the shrimp. They fished huge pots that would barely fit on the back deck of *Blind Faith* and they fished round the clock. There was absolutely no way I could compete with that type of operation.

Alaska Fish & Game was concerned about the change in the fishery and placed an emergency early closure on the 1996 shrimp season, which lasted precisely five weeks, instead of the scheduled five months. I had just lost my winter job.

I was able to pay off Victoria, buy the cabin, and make it livable. When the wolf came in and did the canine circling routine before lying down, he would brush up against all the walls. I bought big bags of rice, beans, and pasta from the co-op. I had a freezer full of fish. No TV, no newspaper, no beer, no mortgage, no women, no vacation, no medical ... yeah, I might be able to hold on until halibut season. Including my Alaska Permanent Fund check, my net income for 1996 was near $4,000.

My first wife, Diane, had remarried but became incensed that the loss of my federal job meant that I couldn't continue providing health insurance for the one child who remained at home. She asked the Oregon Department of Human Resources to modify my child support payments. The agency asked me to provide my federal tax returns, which I did. However, instead of using this information, they arbitrarily levied my income at $38,000 and escalated my monthly child support payments to a level higher than my total net income. When I challenged this in court, the Oregon Assistant Attorney General, acting as Diane's counsel, argued that I never should have become a fisherman in the first place. He claimed that I really should have invested my life savings in the booming stock market, and then convinced the judge to levy my annual income on fictitious stock market earnings. After 14 years of never once being late on a monthly child support payment, I continued to pay what I could, but joined the ranks of the "deadbeat dads."

The world despises a whiner, so I felt it best to kinda withdraw from the world for a bit, because there was definitely some whining coming on. How far I had fallen from when I arrived in Alaska six years before, with a successful career in D.C. behind me, a gorgeous wife, a fabulous house, and a good salary. How much further would I have to fall? Was this the wages of honesty and professional ethics? Or was it just an incredibly unfortunate chain of events? Or had I brought it on myself? It was hard to know where one possibility left off and the other began. Was there a fine, black-and-white line, or did it blur and grow fuzzy in shades of grey? Alaska winters provide an opportunity for introspection, and I did my share.

In early November, Corrie filed an individual right of action on my behalf with the Merit Systems Protection Board. Shoaf v. USDA, as it were. Discovery, depositions, and a trial. Lord, what were these words? The only times I had ever faced a judge before were when I'd gotten divorced or the recent child support debacle. I remembered how those cases had turned out and hoped this would be different. I should have known better.

21

The Trial

(November 1996 - March 1997)

"I'm not a crook."
-- **Richard Nixon**

*"All lies in jest, still a man hears what he wants to hear
And disregards the rest."*
-- **Paul Simon, "The Boxer"**

*"He's as blind as he can be
Just sees what he wants to see.
Nowhere man can you see me at all?"*
-- **John Lennon and Paul McCartney, "Nowhere Man"**

In September 1995, my whistleblower case had changed from a disclosure of Forest Service violations to a complaint of Forest Service retaliations against me for my having been a whistleblower. These words "disclosure" and "complaint" are formal, legal terms, and OSC has separate organizational units to deal with each. It was only when the disclosure case was closed that I was willing to proceed with the complaint. This was because the former was professional and involved the agency's dishonesty and mismanagement of the Tongass. The latter was personal and involved the agency's wrongful treatment of an honest man who blew the whistle on them. For obvious reasons, I didn't want the two cases mixed.

The Whistleblower Protection Act (Public Law 101-12 -- Apr. 10, 1989) states that an agency may not initiate any form of retaliatory adverse personnel action against a whistleblower. To prevail in the case, the complainant must show three things:

1. he made a protected disclosure;
2. the agency was aware of the disclosure;
3. adverse personnel actions were initiated against the complainant and that retaliation was a contributing reason behind these adverse actions.

It's not necessary to prove that retaliation was the whole reason or even the main reason, just that it contributed toward the adverse actions. The law farther provides that the whistleblower may wrest the complaint from the U.S. Office of Special Counsel, if no action has been taken on the case. The case may then be heard before an administrative law judge on the Merit Systems Protection Board, who then has 120 days from the time the case was filed to render a decision. The complainant may then file a timely appeal with the full panel of the Merit Systems Protection Board. Beyond that there is the appropriate Circuit Court and, of course, ultimately the U.S. Supreme Court.

On Dec. 22, 1995, OSC stated that its initial review indicated that a further investigation was warranted into my charges of unlawful reprisal for whistleblowing. As OSC was the same agency that allowed my disclosure case to drag on for two years and four months, instead of the 60-day response time required by law, Corrie Yackulic informed OSC that she intended to pursue an individual right of action on my behalf with the MSPB. On May 8, 1996, OSC washed its hands of the whole affair and terminated its investigation, advising me that I had 65 days to file with the MSPB.

On July 10, 1996, Corrie filed an individual right of action on my behalf with MSPB. Because her client was out gillnetting in the hinterlands of Alaska, she immediately moved for a three-month continuance, which she was granted. On Oct. 31, 1996, she refiled a modified individual right of action with MSPB.

This set a peculiar clock ticking. By law, MSPB cases must be resolved within 120 days. This meant that discovery, depositions, case preparation, trial, summary briefs, and decision had to be jammed into a four-month period ending March 2, 1997. As the judge reserved the final 30 days for writing his decision, there were really only three months available.

Lawyers hate clocks. Because Corrie's firm Schroeter, Goldmark, and Bender didn't necessarily specialize in personnel cases, they hired a firm which did. Enter Marty Garfinkel from the firm Frank and Rosen. These firms and these lawyers were amazing. Their client was a stone-broke fisherman/forester from Alaska, who had a ponytail and wore rubber boots and wool shirts. Moreover, he was uncomfortable in the city and absolutely terrified of tall buildings. They did everything possible to make me feel comfortable, welcome, and valued. They paid my expenses to come to Seattle, they gave me lunch money, ... they even ran with me at noon. But probably most importantly, they were absolute tigers. Make that tigers-from-hell!

For its part, the Forest Service wanted to make a war out of it. They were conceding nothing. The agency had never lost a whistleblower complaint, indeed few had ever even reached the trial stage. But for whatever reason, both sides readily concurred that this was a potentially precedent-setting, landmark case that would be bitterly fought and appealed to the full MSPB, no matter which side prevailed in front of the administrative law judge. So against these tigers-from-hell the Forest Service matched Chris LeMasters, a giggly, young gal who had been a personnel clerk at Ketchikan, but who had since been promoted to personnel specialist in the regional office in Juneau. It was like matching PeeWee Herman against Mike Tyson, and made no sense. But none of this had ever made any sense.

Don King couldn't have created a more ballyhooed boxing extravaganza. Here was David, managed by the tigers-from-hell, moving up 16 weight divisions to slug it out with Goliath, managed by PeeWee Herman. And to make it more interesting, David insisted on 110-percent honesty, while Goliath was determined to win at all costs. It was quite a match-up. And the referee ... oh my.

Corrie and Marty were pretty concerned about the administrative law judge we had drawn, James H. Freet, who throughout his career had shown a distinct tendency to favor Goliath. Moreover, Corrie and Marty were absolutely buried in the reams and reams of paper I had provided ... whistleblower disclosures and complaints, timber sale appeals, FOIAs, EISs, Forest Service documents ... all babbling about logging plans, falldown, unit expansion, rotation ages, environmental laws. What was all this stuff?

Corrie had been raised in Eugene, Ore., and had spent time as a lawyer for SCLDF. She knew the terminology and environmental law dead. Marty was from the Bronx and only knew of one tree and that was growing in Brooklyn. But he was a quick study, and had more determination than Helen Keller. Their assessment of our case was guardedly optimistic, at best. Our biggest stumbling block seemed to be my constructive discharge, i.e., I quit voluntarily rather than being fired. I told them that their client didn't give up or back down easily. I told them about my adopted kids who had watched their dad kill and dismember their mom, and how difficult it was to try to be a father to them. Yeah, I quit that one. And I told them about the marathon I quit at mile 24 after my leg kept buckling from cramps induced by fish poisoning. Then I told them that those situations were nothing compared to what I had put up with from the Forest Service before finally quitting.

They never mentioned it again.

Corrie and Marty also explained that our payoff from the case, even if we did prevail, was relatively small ... back pay, reinstatement, and legal fees. If I were anything other than a federal employee, they could demand compensation for emotional suffering, and the stakes would be way higher. Moreover, I told them flat out that I didn't want to be reinstated with the Forest Service, as it would be like a spouse returning to an abusive home situation. They knew that could decidedly bias our case and finally convinced me that it wouldn't violate my 110-percent honesty rule to testify that I would consider an offer of reinstatement. So I did, because I would, but not very much, if you know what I mean. These lawyers were patient!

The 13-page individual right of action which they filed with Judge Freet on Halloween eve 1996 focused on the three things they had to prove: I was a whistleblower, the agency knew I was a whistleblower, and the agency willfully and maliciously retaliated against me because I was a whistleblower.

And the Forest Service said ... nope didn't happen. Bill was a valued employee, who had some professional disagreements with management, and unexpectedly quit. If my finger prints weren't irrevocably on file, I wonder if they wouldn't have denied ever having heard of me. "We never heard of the plaintiff, your Honor, and if we had, we wouldn't have done any of the things that he mentioned, because they are clearly illegal, and we never do anything illegal, sir." And the judge, nodding sagely, "Well, that certainly clears up that matter."

How do they sleep at night? And more importantly, what gods allow them to awaken in the morning?

Oh well, here was the lineup. Witnesses for the plaintiff: Shoaf, the other two IDT leaders (Lunde and Nightingale), James, Robert, Norm Matson, ex-forest supervisor Mike Lunn, and Andy Stahl. Witnesses for the defense: Rittenhouse, Vaught, Archie, Eide, Arrasmith.

Fighters take your corner, come out fighting at the bell. Ding! Oops, forgot we have to do depositions first. I didn't have a clue what depositions were. Corrie and Marty explained that they were pre-trial interrogations, taken under oath in the presence of a court recorder, which allowed counsel to have an idea what these witnesses would say during trial testimony. And woe be unto any witness who contradicted himself between deposition and trial testimony.

On Dec. 9, I flew to Seattle to attend the first round of depositions, which were to be held telephonically. The Forest Service employees were ensconced with Chris LeMasters in a quiet room in Alaska, while my lawyers, the court recorder, and I were on the other end of the phone in Seattle. My job was to keep quiet and pass notes furiously. Unfortunately, the first round of "deps" was held in Marty's 12th-floor office, which was seven floors above my panic level. The elevator rides were horrible, and we had to keep the blinds drawn so I didn't hyperventilate. It was awful.

The first witness was Bill Nightingale, a Forest Service planning team leader. He corroborated the facts of Rittenhouse yelling at me at the management team meeting, saying on-lookers were stunned and shocked at the vehemence of Rittenhouse's onslaught. Nightingale said that my presentation hadn't been antagonistic or confrontational, and that I just quietly stood my ground during the tirade. He also said that the gag order was definitely a removal of my duties, as were the response to public comments, alternative development, and record of decision. He stated he had never before heard of a project where the IDT leader didn't retain those responsibilities.

Nightingale further said that my stock had fallen fairly rapidly because I had violated a hallowed tradition by taking my concerns outside the quiet halls of the agency. He commiserated that the local managers were notoriously poor listeners and decision-makers, and were put out that I had brought them bad news about dwindling timber supplies.

Next was Larry Lunde, the other planning team leader. Larry also corroborated that the gag order, response to public comments, alternative development, and record of decision all constituted an unparalleled removal of responsibilities for any planning team leader.

Larry said management was definitely treating me differently than the other kids on the block, largely because I had brought up issues that they wanted to keep quiet. He said the agency spent a lot of energy in doing damage control. When asked about overhearing the meeting outside his office where the management team tried to fire me, Larry said he couldn't remember it. Marty reminded him that he was under oath, and although Larry couldn't quite bring himself to remember all the particulars of that incident, he said that he didn't doubt that they wanted to fire me because they were very upset. As a matter of fact, my stock had fallen just about out of sight. When asked if my professional performance ever justified this fall in my stock, he said that my work was always at a high level of quality.

Bob Vaught was the first agency witness and said that he came up and personally apologized to me after Rittenhouse verbally blasted me. But he didn't agree that Rittenhouse was angry or hostile. He denied that he told me that he believed Rittenhouse was setting me up for something, because "it's my opinion that that's something we do not do." He also stated that "we think that we have been legal in all the things that we have done."

When the issue of normal responsibilities for planning team leaders came up, Vaught provided a clinic in the fine art of changing your story under oath. He correctly stated that response to media, public comments, preferred alternatives, and records of decisions were normal duties for planning team leaders. There was a lunch break, and Chris must have clued him in on the party line, because after lunch he denied that it was common practice for planning team leaders to talk to the media, categorically denied there was any attempt to minimize my responsibility to respond to public comments, and changed his story to say the forest supervisor, not the IDT leader, had complete dominion over every phase of the development of the preferred alternative and the record of decision.

Vaught also denied "... that we did predecisional work on the [CPOW] units and then we brought in someone to ensure that those units were made part of the record of decision ..." He also asserted "... employees should not only be allowed, but encouraged to present their viewpoints ..." and that submission of my public comment letter "didn't cause any conflict or controversy within the forest supervisor's office."

That was all the depositions we managed to get in that week. On my way out, I asked Corrie if she thought it would be a good idea for me to get a haircut. Her 'yes' was so immediate and enthusiastic that I couldn't do otherwise.

On Jan. 5, I returned to Seattle with a self-inflicted haircut, much to Corrie's delight. Kicking off this batch of depositions was Anne Archie, who the previous year had been a awarded a prize transfer to the White Mountain National Forest in New Hampshire. She stated that I was not a technically adept forester ... "of being an on-the-ground resource-based forester, I think the technical skills were not there." She also felt I should have spent more time on the ground, and that I didn't incorporate recon information submitted by her foresters. But beyond that she couldn't remember much, as she had 66 "I don't recall responses." Poor Anne.

Rittenhouse provided the next testimony. He denied that he gave me a tongue-lashing, but rather "... sternly expressed his concern." He couldn't recall if he raised his voice. Rittenhouse admitted that he had told my supervisor, Walt Dortch, that I was the one who had referred him to the Concern Program. When Marty asked why he ratted me out, given Concern Program referrals were strictly confidential, especially when involving one's supervisor, Rittenhouse said Walt had asked him directly who had done it, and he didn't want to lie.

He said that my public comment letter had placed an additional burden on the agency, and he called the Office of General Counsel to see if "we could continue with Bill as IDT leader." Under some pretty intense questioning by Marty, Rittenhouse also acknowledged that my comment letter was one of the contributing reasons why I was given a gag order. He further conceded that he had Arrasmith poll the other staff officers and hold the IDT "trial" to see if my comment letter had adversely affected morale. I could visualize Chris passing him notes that Vaught had testified that my comment letter was encouraged and didn't cause any concern at all.

He denied that Linn Shipley had been brought in to handle public comments, but rather had brought in to get up to speed on Alaska issues. Marty pointed out that Linn had been a longtime Alaska employee. He was evasive in response to the question about removal of my responsibility to develop the preferred alternative and the record of decision, as well as his motivation for bringing in a co-team leader. He also acknowledged predecisional logging unit layout and road surveys, which again refuted what Vaught said.

If anybody ever has the idea that lawyers don't work for a living, they have never been around Marty Garfinkel. Listening to him trying to coax straight answers out of Rittenhouse was like watching a well-trained blue heeler cut recalcitrant cattle. Marty was relentless, and we'd both roll our eyes as Rittenhouse gave rambling off-the-subject dissertations.Then Marty would slam him with a different version of the question. But Rittenhouse wouldn't budge and refused to divulge information.

As I was scheduled to be deposed next, Corrie and Marty gave me a primer on depositions. They stressed that there was absolutely nothing I could say during deposition that would help our case. My answers would strictly be used to build the Forest Service case. They preferred me to use one-word responses whenever possible. They warned me not to try to be charming, funny, or in any way entertaining. I told them I would follow my personal 110-percent honesty rule, then begged them to move my deposition to Corrie's office, which was on the fifth floor. I had been having horrible nightmares about jumping out of windows and throwing puppies off bridges. What could they do?

This was the first and only deposition that was held in person, as opposed to telephonically. To give Chris LeMasters a boost, the Forest Service brought in another personnel specialist, Linda Goldman, who was from San Francisco. They questioned me tag team style. I wondered if they would play "good cop/bad cop."

Chris and Linda were polite, but were most definitely looking for chinks in my armor. They probed my previous qualifications to be an IDT leader, but dropped that in a hurry when I told them I had been an IDT leader for a timber project on the Boise, had been on numerous IDTs on the Mapleton District, and had been a member of the Forest Service highest level planning team in D.C.

They questioned me extensively about the management team meeting when Rittenhouse chewed me out in front of my employees. They repeatedly asked me about what specific words he used, and I said I remembered few of the specific words, because the unexpectedly abject anger and hostility of his tirade was much more impressionable. They quizzed me about my performance ratings on the Tongass and were particularly interested in establishing that no adverse actions were taken against me because of Arrasmith's giving me an unsatisfactory rating on my 1993 mid-year evaluation. They dropped that line of questioning when I rattled off a long string of adverse actions which followed that evaluation.

They asked me if Tongass managers had ever denied me anything I'd requested. I drew a blank and couldn't answer, and they gleefully moved ahead. Suddenly I went back to their question and told them about requesting managers not strip me of my responsibilities and to give me some meaningful work to do. That was the end of that question. Next they badgered me about my reaction and feelings when I was transferred to the timber staff. I told them I had mixed feelings ... glad to be away from Arrasmith, but frustrated to be banished from my previous job in shame. They kept re-asking this question, and I kept responding that my feelings were mixed. Finally they told me to forget my feelings and to tell them my reaction. I responded, "I think it would be hard for you to discern my feelings, but it would be easy to discern my reaction. Similarly, it would be easy for me to know my feelings, but hard to know my reaction." Metaphysics weren't their bag, so they dropped that too.

Arrasmith's deposition was next, and I briefed Marty that he'd told me that he kept a file on me, documenting my daily actions. Arrasmith flat out denied he had ever done so. Marty showed him an e-mail documenting that he had kept records of my having been observed eating lunch with Sylvia Geraghty and Carolyn Minor. Marty asked if it were normal to keep notes on how employees were spending their off-duty time. Arrasmith then denied that he told me, almost immediately upon his arrival, that he had been told to consider removing me from my position.

Next he denied that my public comment letter had anything at all to do with my gag order. Again, I could visualize Chris passing him a note saying that Rittenhouse admitted that it had. He also denied that media discussions were ever my responsibility, even though the other IDT leaders, Nightingale and Lunde, said they were. He denied that bringing over Linn Shipley to head up the writing of the response to public comments and bringing in Charlie Streuli as co-IDT leader were a usurpation of my duties. According to Arrasmith, removing my responsibility to develop the preferred alternative and the record of decision were done simply because CPOW needed to be managed differently than the other EISs.

Arrasmith said that I would continually look him in the eye and promise to do one thing, then go off and do something else. I guess he was calling me a liar. Then he said I had threatened him, and that he had complained to the personnel officer about fearing for his family's safety. Next he denied the meeting about firing me that Larry Lunde had witnessed. And finally he denied that I had been excluded from attending the forestry conference.

Corrie was going to interview Eide, who had the potential to be a key witness, as he had a shred of decency and liked to think of himself as a truth-teller. But he was such a company man that it was hard to tell what would come out.

Corrie certainly did her best, but Gene was abrasive and mostly barked yup, nope, and I don't recall. He swore and lashed out at Corrie a coupla times, but he may as well have tried to drown a fish.

Eide admitted that Rittenhouse "had climbed all over me" and that he had "sunk down in my chair that day because he knew it was very poor conduct for a forest supervisor." Moreover, he agreed that Rittenhouse and Vaught had told him to "keep Shoaf on a very short leash."

Gene also stated that I was a technically adept forester, physically and professionally capable of doing field work, and had been straightforward and honest. He stated that my being idled wasn't his fault, he just didn't have any work for me to do.

The next day Corrie and Marty had a telephonic pretrial hearing with Judge Freet. I got a call from them later and was told that the judge refused to read the record as a means of bringing himself up to speed on the issues of the case. He demanded my lawyers prechew all the complexities and them spoon feed him something that would effortlessly slide down his gullet. What was worse, Judge Freet insisted the disclosures be rewritten in his own words, even though he had a poor understanding of the applicable environmental laws or the underlying forestry issues. My lawyers were upset and refused to permit such a gross categorization of the issues, because, if they agreed to it, the court record would be forever tainted.

They leveled with me. Neither Marty nor Corrie felt we had a ghost of a chance with Judge Freet, as he was simply too biased on the side of the agency. They felt he would be particularly disinclined to find for a plaintiff who was getting paid to do nothing, because it quite likely would seem like an ideal situation to him. Because of this, our whole focus in the trial would be to build a record which could be appealed to the full MSPB. Apparently, appeals to the MSPB were based strictly on the record and did not consider new information or testimony, hence the necessity of developing a full and accurate record.

The next week Marty took a telephonic deposition from Robert, who provided key perspective as a Thorne Bay District employee. He testified that the CPOW logging units were planned better than any previous logging units, because I had more field experience and spent more time on the ground than had any other planning team leader.

He said the district was upset that they got the assignment to develop the preferred alternative for CPOW and was shocked that I was not permitted to lead the alternative development meeting over in Thorne Bay, and relegated to a don't-speak-unless-you're-spoken-to role. Robert also said Charley Streuli was uncomfortable in his assignment as co-IDT leader.

Finally Robert discussed the petition many people in Thorne Bay had signed in my behalf because they thought I was being retaliated against. He said Anne Archie brought up the topic at a safety meeting and was asked what she would do if she were in my position. According to Robert she said, "Hypothetically, I would quit, but this is a personnel issue, and I don't want to discuss it because drugs or alcohol may be involved."

Ketchikan's total rainfall for 1997 was an amazing 192.8 inches, and I swear half of it fell the week of the trial. I picked up Corrie and Marty at the airport, and they barely unpacked before they got to work preparing their case.

The trial started at 9:00 a.m. Jan. 29 at Ketchikan's Ted Ferry Civic Center, in a huge assembly room that easily could have seated 300 people. Corrie was looking her Ali McGraw best. Marty looked like a lawyerly version of James Wood. I had on my best jeans, a blue shirt, and my only tie and looked like a 48-year-old Green Beret fitness instructor trying to make a fashion statement. Judge James H. Freet was fat, had greasy, long white hair and was a smoker. Corrie leaned over and whispered that the judge probably hated me because I represented everything he disliked. Thus reassured, I was eager to start my long-awaited day in court.

Judge Freet immediately pounced on Corrie and Marty for not having reduced my disclosures to baby talk. He insisted that this was necessary so that he could start writing his decision. I was horrified. The judge couldn't understand the issues and already wanted to start writing his decision, before he heard a single word of testimony? Corrie and Marty proposed that I take the stand and be allowed to explain the nature of my disclosures. Judge Freet assented and I was sworn in as a witness.

I didn't get far before the judge interrupted. My testimony wasn't giving him what he wanted. He wanted to know what part of the falldown report was a disclosure, where it formally said laws were being broken, and what the USC reference was for the allegedly violated law. He refused to allow me to continue testimony, while he and Marty slugged it out. I was totally clueless about what was happening, so I sat on the witness stand dumbfounded.

At one point I was on the stand for an hour and 45 minutes, during which time I said a grand total of one single word. Marty once tried to ask me a question, and the judge refused to allow me to answer. Corrie asked the judge if he was truly disallowing counsel to ask their own client a question when he was duly sworn on the witness stand. After a while, I just walked off the stand and sadly sat by Corrie. I had waited four years to have my say, and now the judge wouldn't even let me talk. It was late afternoon, and the hearing was almost halfway through its scheduled two-day duration. We took a dinner break.

We were still at the foundation stage of the hearing at 7:00 p.m. No direct evidence or testimony had yet been permitted. Initially Judge Freet wanted each disclosure boiled down to a couple sentences and an explicit reference to what law I alleged had been violated. When Marty convinced him that it wasn't necessary for a law to have been broken, just that I reasonably thought a law MIGHT have been broken, he wanted everything redone. Corrie and Marty vehemently opposed the judge's attempt to categorize and redefine the issues. They had their case and they wanted a chance to present it. He refused to hear it, because he didn't want to listen to something that might later to prove to be irrelevant. So they argued, back and forth.

Sometime around 8:00 p.m., Corrie again objected for the record that her client was being denied the opportunity to provide testimony. Finally, the judge called a halt to his foundation inquisition and dismissed several of my disclosures from further consideration in the case, because he didn't understand them.

I was recalled to the stand. It must have been 9:00 p.m. The first 12 hours of a scheduled two-day hearing had been wasted. Marty expected me to be on the stand for three to four hours. We tried to get as much of my testimony into the record as fast as possible before the judge found some reason to stop us. We continued until around 11:00 p.m., when court was adjourned for the night.

We were so wired, we went into the bar for a midnight snack. Never having seen a judge in action before, I asked if this were normal. Both Marty and Corrie said it was the worst display of courtroom ineptitude they had ever seen. They debated filing a formal motion to have Judge Freet recuse himself from the case. The problem, they said, was that the judge was used to cut and dried personnel cases, and my case was too complex for him to absorb. After having consulted with her firm, the next morning Corrie filed a motion for the judge to disqualify himself from the case on the grounds of extreme incompetence and bias. This was pretty serious stuff. The judge was extremely non-plussed, but had to make a ruling on it. He decided he was eminently competent and impartial and ordered the proceedings continued.

I resumed the stand, and Marty led me through the meeting where Rittenhouse climbed all over me. Part way through, the judge halted testimony and said that it "... fell a comfortable margin short of constituting an adverse personnel action." Marty spit some case law back at him that said an oral reprimand is an adverse action under the Whistleblower Protection Act. Chagrinned, the judge let us proceed.

He stopped us again at the testimony concerning Arrasmith's threat, immediately upon his arrival at Ketchikan, to remove me from my job. The judge didn't think that was a personnel action either. Marty and the judge went round and round on this issue too, and we finally were allowed to resume testimony. When we got to the point where my responsibility to respond to public comments was removed, the judge halted us again. He couldn't see the relevance of that either.

Marty successfully argued that it was the totality of events that led to my resignation. The Forest Service had done their homework thoroughly, and on each action put their toes squarely on the line that separated illegal from legal personnel actions. Taken individually, they were somewhat insignificant, but collectively they were daunting.

I got a few more words in, when the judge halted us again. My testimony was taking too long, and he wanted to move on to other witnesses. Marty promised him he would finish quickly with me, and soon I felt like the proverbial dog tied to the rear bumper of an accelerating truck.

We made it to the report I had written which discussed the significant number of CPOW logging units which exceeded the 100-acre maximum size clearcut allowed by law. This was the single disclosure the judge understood on its face value merits during the previous day's foundation hearings. Today it was beyond his grasp. When Marty tried to explain it to him, the judge said it was too late and he should have done it yesterday. Marty pointed out that the judge indicated yesterday that he understood it, and how could he possibly have anticipated the judge's cognizance would disappear overnight.

Marty asked, "Are you saying that because we did not provide to you, by attorney representation prior to Mr. Shoaf's testimony, a concise statement as to what we are alleging is a disclosure in regard to the clearcuts, that on that basis you are going to preclude us from eliciting any testimony on this disclosure?" The judge answered, "That is absolutely what I am saying."

Next the judge balked at the relevance of my disclosing that the Forest Service had clearcut 5,047 acres without analyzing its effects or even informing the public. I guess he thought that was OK. Corrie's courtroom body language failed her, as she writhed in agony. She grabbed Marty firmly and urgently whispered in his ear. Marty then asked, "Judge have you read these exhibits?" The judge replied that he hadn't.

At one point, the judge told Marty that only one person was allowed to interrupt, and that was he. At another juncture, the judge issued Marty a formal admonishment. It sounded like just another 'bad dog' to me, but Corrie told me later that it was bad news. They would have these battles, then when testimony would resume, Marty would turn to me, his eyes still blazing. I knew fear. Geez, I hoped my answers were OK, cause I didn't want to annoy Marty, who was bobbing and weaving like a boxer. At 12:45 p.m., Marty finished with me and court was recessed for lunch.

I recognized a reporter from the local radio station, KRBD, and the "Ketchikan Daily News." They wanted to talk to me, but I declined comment. This was personal and none of their business. I was sick of having my named plastered on the front page. Marty gave them a short statement, and the newspaper published a page one story, "Whistleblower tackles USFS." Terrific!

Chris LeMasters conducted her cross-examination immediately after lunch. I would have been nervous, but looking at my two lawyers made me feel like a guy who suddenly decides to open his wallet and count his cash in Central Park, with his two savage Rottweilers looking on protectively. Chris asked a few questions, the Rottweilers growled a coupla times, snarled once, and Chris couldn't think of anything more to ask. I was dismissed as a witness.

Corrie called James as the next witness. Tlingits have a traditional way of talking that is more descriptive, almost story-telling, as opposed to rote recitation of chronological events. The judge wasn't buying James' story and continually interrupted him, demanding Corrie direct her witness's testimony to the point. In one instance, the judge said, "... that last testimony was so lacking in specificity, and so subjective, that I consider it to be of no probative value on any issue that I see to make a decision on." He was being rude to my friend, and Marty had to push me down in my seat.

Corrie brought in Norm Matson. The judge seemed a little more amenable to Caucasian witnesses, so Corrie was able to establish that Norm thought I was a good planning team leader, that I had been systematically stripped of my responsibilities, had my job abolished when there was continued need for it, and was denied other available work so I would be forced into resigning. Pretty quick and to the point.

We took a short break, and Corrie met with Bill Nightingale and Larry Lunde who were waiting outside the courtroom for their turn to testify. Marty and I were talking, when Corrie ran up, white as a ghost, and took Marty away. Soon Marty came back and said they smelled a rat with Nightingale, that he seemed 'awfully cold.' They asked me about his honesty, and I said he had never lied to me, but by now I didn't trust anyone.

Because the depositions provided by Nightingale and Lunde were so strongly in our favor, Marty and Corrie decided that oral testimony could only diminish them. Consequently, after the break Corrie told the judge that in concession to allowing the agency time for their own witnesses, she would be willing to forego Nightingale and Lunde as witnesses and merely have their depositions read into the record. I think this was the first point our side scored with his honor.

Chris called Arrasmith to the stand, and his testimony was so well rehearsed that he fairly shot his responses out before Chris had a chance to ask the questions. God help her, if she got them out of order. Arrasmith oozed, Chris cooed, the judge beamed, and the Rottweilers howled. Marty handled the cross-examination of Arrasmith, and scored some zingers, though whether any of it made any import on the judge is hard to know.

It was fascinating to observe my lawyers in the courtroom, where their behavior was much different than I had observed in their law offices. Marty was the war horse, the brawler, who didn't mind getting sweaty and bloody. Corrie was cool and calculated. If it were a basketball team, Marty would be the power forward, fighting for rebounds and throwing elbows. Corrie would be the point guard, making the dazzling pass and swishing 3-pointers. Kareem Abdul-Jabbar and Magic Johnson came to mind. I was awestruck.

We took a short break, and the court recorder, who was Native, motioned me over. She made a face, and said that Arrasmith had been extremely arrogant on the stand. Then she looked at me and asked if I had been the fellow with the pony-tail over in Hydaburg who had discussed tree spirits with the elder. I nodded and she smiled.

Anne Archie was the next agency witness. We knew that Anne's song and dance was going to be that the reason I was relieved of many of my responsibilities was because the district didn't feel they had enough involvement in CPOW, and also because I had rebuffed some of their input on field conditions. To dispute that, I had done some research, using my personal records and some information from the EIS.

When it was time for cross-examination, Corrie said "good evening" to Anne, then proceeded to shred her to confetti. Corrie got Anne to testify that my logging plan was poor, then had her read the statement written by her own people, "In general, the recon reports indicate that the units looked at so far can be implemented as planned with little changes only. In talking with some of the district's key recon people, I am getting the same impression ... that the planned units and roads may need a few changes, but in general the planned units and roads can be laid out as planned."

That pissed off Anne, and she yelled at Corrie, "Are you listening to me?" Corrie then referred Anne to a table published in the CPOW final EIS which showed that the district had field reviewed about 200 units and then showed her my researched calculations that her employees had spent 1,230 person days reviewing CPOW, either in the office or in the woods. "Thought you said your district didn't have much involvement, Anne? Sounds like a lot to me. Do you have information which countermands this?" Uh, no.

Corrie then had Anne read a document she had written herself. "People here [Thorne Bay] are adamant that Bill is in bad trouble because he wrote the letter to CPOW. I have explained that he is no way in trouble about the letter and Rittenhouse is not planning any retaliation. I am definitely NOT BELIEVED!!!" Then she had Anne admit that she personally felt it was inappropriate for me to have written the letter, and that if I didn't support the project, maybe I needed to find something else to do.

Then she forced Anne to admit that she had personally asked that I be placed in the "don't-speak-unless-spoken-to" role at the alternative development meeting, then used my silence to castigate me for being an unfit leader. Finally, Corrie got it out of Anne that there was only one single unit where I didn't incorporate her foresters' recon information, and the decision not to do so had been a joint decision between myself and the engineering staff. Moreover, her forester mysteriously received a temporary promotion after he complained that I didn't accept his input.

Rittenhouse took the stand, and Chris lead him through his testimony ... no, nothing wrong at Ketchikan, Shoaf didn't disclose anything, we didn't retaliate at him. Rittenhouse was droning on about how it was perfectly OK to change unit boundaries however he felt like it, when the judge suddenly stopped him and asked if maybe there weren't some limitations on the amount of boundary changes the Forest Service could make.

Suddenly things weren't quite so rosy in River City. Rittenhouse stammered, Chris was clueless, and the Rottweilers, sniffing blood, pulled against their chains, whimpering to be freed. Judge Freet asked, "Mr. Rittenhouse, if you want to make a change in a unit, is there a point at which you have a legal obligation to give public notice before you make that change?" The baying of hounds filled the air, and we frantically passed notes for Marty's cross-examination.

Then suddenly the judge let Rittenhouse off the hook and reverted to his insightful comments, e.g, "NEPA is an environmental law, right?" Chris steered Rittenhouse away from any more resource issues and spent a great deal of time establishing that Rittenhouse had accepted a job on the Boise after I had submitted my resignation but before actually walking out the door. She seemingly wanted to prove that I could have rescinded my resignation after it became apparent one of my chief nemeses was about to leave the Tongass. She finished direct examination on that note, and Corrie unsnapped Marty's leash.

Within seconds, Marty had an admission out of Rittenhouse that it was a legal requirement under NEPA to prepare a supplemental EIS if the agency makes substantial changes in the proposed action. Rittenhouse, however, refused to acknowledge that clearcutting 5,047 acres constituted a substantial change. I fed the Rottweiler fact-bones. The 1989-94 timber sale proposed to log 30,000 acres, but, due to falldown, could only log 21,000 of those acres. So to partially make up for the falldown, Rittenhouse authorized the logging of an additional 5,000 acres without doing any NEPA analysis or public disclosure. Marty got him to admit that one acre out of every five logged was actually outside the boundaries, but Rittenhouse still refused to call it significant.

Marty flew into other topics, windmilling questions, changing directions, confusing Rittenhouse, who appeared dazed. It was like watching a surging challenger pinning the reigning champion on the ropes in the 12th and final round. Isn't true that ...? Yes! Isn't it true that ...? Yes! Isn't it true that ...? Ding! Judge Freet rang the bell ending the end of the fight, I mean hearing. It was over.

We didn't get done with the hearing, it would be continued in Seattle in a few weeks. We packed up quickly and left the courtroom for the bar. It must have been 11:00 p.m. We basked in the afterglow of the adrenaline rush the three of us had ridden. Marty looked at me and said, "Bill, I want you to know it has been a privilege to be your lawyer." What a thing to say. I was deeply moved. Corrie asked, "Bill, I've been wanting to ask you this for a long time. Why did you do it?"

Easy question, eh? I didn't have one answer for her, I had 20, and none of them were right. I don't lie. I don't like to get pushed around. No one else would do it. I love the Tongass and don't like to see it abused. I love Ketchikan and don't like to see its long-term good sacrificed for short-term gain. It was my responsibility as a professional forester. It was my duty as a federal employee. Once I started, I couldn't stop. I don't know why. Maybe I never will.

The hearing was reconvened in Seattle on Feb. 13. It took place on the 28th floor, and I had to go up in the freight elevator. Corrie mentioned my tall-building fear to the judge, without trying to make me sound like a complete whacko. He kept the blinds pulled, but I was terrified, light-headed, and had an alternating floating-sinking sensation in my gut.

Corrie's first witness was Andy Stahl, and watching them was like watching couples' figure skating championships. They had grown up in the same hometown and had worked together at SCLDF for years. Corrie would intone the questions, then busy herself with her notes, not even listening to Andy's response. When she noticed he was through talking, she would read the next question and go back to her notes. Andy was polished and needed no prompting. After all, we were just building a record for an appeal to the MSPB.

At the conclusion of his testimony, Andy said, "... that's the remarkable thing about everything that went on with Mr. Shoaf in Alaska. These problems were common knowledge in the lower 48 on virtually every National Forest. We all knew that the forest plans were overstating the amount of timber that could be cut. But only in Alaska did the Forest Service deny the fact. We [AFSEEE] took. Mr. Shoaf's concerns to the nation's leading expert on sustained yield. Dr. K. Norman Johnson at Oregon State University. He said Shoaf is right. The Tongass National Forest is wrong."

Chris called Gene Eide to the stand, and he immediately went into his "oooooold forester" routine, much to the delight of Judge

Freet. Gene dismissed the idea of unit expansion, saying some units got bigger, some smaller, hey, change is a part of life. But he stayed clear of any discussion of a premeditated policy to make up for falldown by willfully logging outside the boundaries without disclosing its effects or informing the public.

Chris focused on my tenure as special projects forester. Gene painted the picture that he didn't have any work to give me, and when he did, I completed it way too quickly. It wasn't his fault. I should have gotten my own work. "From whom, Gene?" I wanted to scream. "From Rittenhouse? From Arrasmith? From Archie?" Gene did a pretty good job of discrediting me, then his testimony was interrupted to take telephonic testimony from former forest supervisor Mike Lunn.

The agency had strongly objected to allowing Mike Lunn as a witness. Mike was a staunch critic of some of the events on the Tongass, and had initiated the timber theft investigation, which Corrie, Andy, and I had parlayed into a lawsuit. Corrie had previously spoken with Lunn on the phone about his testimony and felt it could potentially cement our case. Unfortunately, Lunn's testimony, while glowing in his praise of my professionalism, said that my disclosures didn't evidence any violation of law, which was a major issue we had to prove. Corrie came back to the bench shaking her head.

She composed herself quickly and cross-examined Eide. She worked hard on Eide, who had said a lot of things to me, which I documented, and which Corrie had brought up during his deposition. Well, Gene didn't want to remember those statements, and when she forced him to read them back to her, he acknowledged that maybe he had said them, but that he hadn't meant them. Corrie nailed him on it. When Gene said that I should have gotten my own work, she asked, "Are you saying that Bill Shoaf, who communicated to you his frustration at not having enough work, whom you describe as someone eager and anxious to get work, did not make an effort to stay occupied?"

When Corrie finished with Eide, we mercifully took a lunch break and I endured another elevator-ride-from-hell and reached terra firma again. We went back to Corrie's office and had wonderful sack lunches sent in. I was starved and ate mine and Corrie's. I never wanted the lunch to end, and would have eaten Marty's and Andy's lunches too, if it could have delayed going back up to the 28th floor. My mean lawyers insisted, so back up we went. I was pretty well panicked and tried my best to look normal. I thought of the old "Saturday Night Live" line of the berserker screaming, " I'M NOT CRAZY!! Are there cobwebs on my face?"

Marty was permitted to continue his cross-examination of Rittenhouse which the judge had interrupted in Ketchikan. There was no 'Good day, Mr. Rittenhouse,' it was right back to the "Isn't it true that ...? Marty kept the questioning focused on the facts that the Forest Service had been directed by the chief to remand the CPOW record of decision and re-issue a supplemental EIS to address falldown and logging sustainability, as well as on the events surrounding my enforced idling.

Vaught was next, and Marty and I left the courtroom to go over my final testimony, as well as to spare my having to listen to Vaught. The court record showed Vaught testified that I was a bad IDT leader because I was a poor communicator. Then he explained that there really was no such thing as unit expansion. Moreover, Rittenhouse's tirade at the management team meeting was only 'strident,' and that it was all my fault anyhow, and I shouldn't have taken it personally.

Vaught also asserted that my team's logging plan hadn't been comprehensive, but just looked at areas that could be logged uncontroversially. According to Vaught, my responsibilities were never diminished, and if they were, it was because I was a bad IDT leader. And there were no instances that Rittenhouse took retaliatory actions against me because of my alleged disclosures.

Corrie cross-examined and referred Vaught to his deposition where he had stated that he wasn't aware of any deficiencies in my performance. She led back through the other issues, but he held the company line as glibly to Corrie as he had previously. The man was incorrigible. If I hadn't directly been a party to the events on the Tongass which he described, he might have convinced even me his answers were true.

Marty called me to the stand as the final witness, which meant I had to get within 8 feet of the window. I called upon the gods to hide my fear. To dispel the notion that I was a bad communicator, Marty had me testify about the cash award and engraved plaque I received in D.C for outstanding teamwork. He led me through testimony on the dysfunctional nature of my position under Eide.

Marty asked if there were a single endemic issue among all my disclosures. There was, and it was over-logging. The forest plan rationalized an unsustainable level of logging that would meet the commitments to the long-term contracts. The older EISs tried to implement this forest plan, and found that it didn't work on the ground, which created falldown. To compensate for the falldown, the agency resorted to unit expansion. Because the unit expansions were not analyzed, they led to illegal proportionality, or high-grading. The unit expansion also gobbled up units needed for CPOW, and when the notice of intent was modified to remove 240,000 acres from CPOW, the units got squeezed too close together, resulting in oversized clearcuts. And when I brought this information forward, the managers decided to slam-dunk me, instead of admitting their malfeasance.

Chris took over cross-examination and handed me a copy of the buyout information packet, clipped open to a single page and highlighted. She had me read a single sentence, which she hoped would prove her premise that I could have revoked my resignation after Rittenhouse announced he was leaving. The sentence was "... the law clearly says that agencies may offer incentive payments to individuals who <u>voluntarily</u> resign or retire." Chris whisked the document away from me.

Tough darts, Chrissie! We had expected this line of questioning, and I had brought my own copy of the buyout packet to the stand. With Marty's help of shouting down her objections, I read, "I encourage you to be certain about your decision before you apply for this buyout. Barring dramatic changes in your personal circumstances, there should be no need for withdrawal of an application after it has been submitted." Chris lay her forehead on the desk.

There were a few final questions for me from both sides, but that was about it, and I was dismissed from the witness stand and away from the hateful window. A few final issues were discussed between counsels and the judge. Seemingly, plaintiff's motion to disqualify the judge had been removed from the record and needed to be replaced. Lastly, a preliminary decision by the judge was due March 2. Because of the complexities of the hearings and, it was already Feb. 13, it was agreed to defer filing of closing arguments until March 17.

We wrapped things up and got back on street level again. Marty and Corrie took me over to Marty's office, where Marty gave me a book, <u>Shackleton's Incredible Journey</u>, and Corrie gave me a copy of <u>The Last Curlew</u>. We hugged, and I caught the bus out to the airport and flew back to Ketchikan.

On March 17, 1997, Corrie filed closing arguments. To this date, I have never again seen Corrie or Marty, and we have never heard from Judge Freet. His decision is over a year overdue.

22

Ding Dong, the Mill Is Dead

(March 1997 - May 1997)

"Now Main Street's whitewashed windows and vacant stores.
Seems like ain't nobody wants to come down here no more.
They're closing down the textile mill across the RR tracks.
The foreman said these jobs are going, boys, and they ain't coming back."
   -- Bruce Springsteen, "My Hometown"

"The British guns were aimed, and the shells were coming fast.
The first shell hit the Bismarck, they knew she couldn't last.
That mighty German battleship is just a memory.
'Sink the Bismarck' was the battlecry that shook the seven seas."
   -- Johnny Horton, "Sink the Bismarck"

A lot was going on while we were busy with the depositions and the trial. The area just north of the CPOW project was the site of the Lab Bay timber sale, a project that was being led by Larry Lunde. This area had been as heavily clearcut as any industrial forest lands I had ever seen, including International Paper Corporation lands in coastal Oregon. Nonetheless, the Forest Service was determined that their mission, "Caring for the Land and Serving the People," required them to log another 85 mmbf in this area. I was ashamed to have ever been a part of this agency.

In the extreme northwest corner of this area, at the tip of Prince of Wales island, lay two sleepy fishing villages, Port Protection and Point Baker. Baker, the larger of the two, had a school, mercantile store, and a fuel dock, but there was no road access to the rest of the island. These were quaint, peaceful villages, whose residents were almost wholly dependent upon fishing income to supplement their subsistence-based lifestyles. Only a thin stringer of trees isolated their paradise from the clearcut desolation of National Forest System land.

The residents wanted to preserve this stringer of trees, as well as to limit further logging abuse to the few remaining stands of trees on their end of the island. But the Forest Service wanted to feed these trees to KPC, even to the point of clearcutting the villages' public water supply area, as well as the headland that provided shelter to their bay. The townsfolk had been pushed until their backs literally were against the sea, and they were prepared to make a final stand. There was a definite 'lock and load' mindset.

The residents of Port Protection and Point Baker were largely fishermen with callouses on their hands and a distrust of bureaucrats in their hearts. Most of the old-timers, who had watched the decimation of their Eden, harbored an abject hatred of the pulp mill and the Forest Service. They had vehemently opposed the Lab Bay sale from its inception, and now when it seemed it would be rammed down their throats, they called on another fisherman living over in Ketchikan to help them out.

While Corrie and Marty were battling the bad guys in the courtroom, the Forest Service issued the record of decision to proceed with the Lab Bay sale. One night I got a phone call from Joe Sebastian, a Point Baker fisherman who went back a long way with me. Joe first came to see me many years ago when my planning team was working on our comprehensive logging plan, which at that time still included the Lab Bay area. I remember he had set down a backpack on my office floor, while we looked at some maps. Suddenly I saw the pack move and was startled to see the world's most beautiful child snuggled in the pack, papoose style.

Later that same week I had run into Joe and his wife, Joan, in the grocery store. They had run their commercial troller to Ketchikan to pick up their yearly cache of groceries and other supplies. They had a mountain of stuff and were going to have to move it from the store to the dock, box by box. Naturally, it was pouring outside. I asked Joe if he wanted to load the stuff in my truck and save himself some work. Just as Joe started to nod, Joan screamed at me that, "We don't need any help from the Forest Service." Joe was pretty embarrassed, so he just kinda shrugged. The rest of the story is that the next Christmas, after I had written my infamous public comment letter, I got a card from Joe and Joan, in which she called me one of her heroes. I teased her about the change in her attitude toward me.

The night Joe called, he asked me to file an appeal for the locals against the Lab Bay sale. I initially balked at his request, because I knew he was a member of the SEACC board of directors. He told me that I'd gotten screwed by SEACC and understood my current resolve to act strictly solo, but would I consent to help some fellow fishermen? I thought for a minute and said OK, but that the appeal was between them, me, and the Forest Service. I didn't want the appeal forwarded to SEACC, who as yet hadn't decided whether they were going to appeal the Lab Bay sale.

In between trips to Seattle and courtroom battles, I hung gillnets in the daytime and worked on the Lab Bay appeal at night. When I completed it, I had a final phone conversation with Joe, and something in his tone convinced me there was a possibility that he might forward my appeal to SEACC, even though he had given me his solemn oath that he wouldn't. It is hard to refuse to accept a man's word when he has given you no previous reason to doubt him, yet there was simply no trust left in my soul. Much to Joe's consternation, I refused to send him a preliminary review copy of our joint appeal and sent it directly to the Forest Service.

Of course, this pissed off everyone in the communities of Port Protection and Point Baker. As time passed, sentiments mellowed, and I received a couple notes of thanks from the people who had asked for my help. Lance Howell, who ran a small sawmill at Point Baker, sent me a gorgeous Shaker box he and his wife had personally handcrafted from a monster Sitka spruce log they found floating in nearby Sumner Strait. I was touched and considered it exceptional payment for my work.

In his declaration of harm against the Lab Bay sale, Lance wrote:

> "There is no separating Point Baker and Port Protection from the forest and sea that encompass the whole of the community. The same raven watches the child playing on the same rocks, on the same beach that children have played on for thousands of years. The child and the raven live the years together. I know my daughter is that child, and now she is that woman anticipating bringing her own children to those same rocks. On the limestone ridge above Port Protection grow ancient trees. Each crown is an individual, each ragged top is different from the next, each is a living memory and expression of centuries of living in a community. When I read commentary on the rootlessness and alienation in modern society, I realize that this is a precious thing to have, this home, this bond with community and landscape."

Eventually SEACC filed their own appeal of the Lab Bay timber sale, and it was compelling. Of course, the "Ketchikan Daily News" ran the story of the appeals on page one, trying to stir up the Ketchikan residents against radical environmentalists trying to lock up the forest.

Just as Lance Howell had spoken so poignantly about the value of community, the Ketchikan community had taken an alarming, decided downturn in the last year. Despite their assurances that there was plenty of wood out there, the Forest Service was finding it increasingly difficult to find enough of this alleged plentitude to keep KPC operating full bore. To make matters worse, the bottom had fallen out of the global pulp market, as the new mill in South Africa could easily undercut anyone else's price.

The final straw was increased focus on the carcinogenic poisons pumped into the air and water by the KPC pulp mill, dubbed "Mordor." EPA had done studies and had hundreds of pages of mill violations, but had to back off when Senator Ted Stevens, who chaired the Senate appropriations committee, threatened the continued viability of the EPA budget. The Alaska Department of Environmental Coordination similarly backed off giving the mill anything other than a handslap. Interestingly, DEC had hassled me about the fresh shrimp I was selling off my boat, concerned I wasn't putting enough bleach in the final rinse water. I thought it was ironic that they had sent someone down to my boat to investigate the sale of the most delectable, fresh seafood on the planet, while they ignored the shenanigans of one of the largest point-source polluters in the U.S.

Although mill supporters liked to say it was "just steam" coming from the smoke stacks, it was more than bad-smelling vapor. A group of local doctors sent a request for the state of Alaska to do an investigation into the unusually high rate of cancer within a 5-mile radius of the mill site. What was pumped into the ocean was even more deadly, as divers could find no sign of marine life in the cove surrounding the mill, as well as in the adjacent channel. Greenie groups seized the opportunity to focus on public health concerns in lieu of the more inflammatory attacks on the timber operations.

It was apparent to all that KPC was under attack from many sides ... the Tongass was running out of timber, the pulp market was abysmal, the mill would require huge cash infusions to be upgraded to meet current pollution control standards, and the whole Tongass issue was becoming a significant black-eye to the beleaguered parent company, Louisiana-Pacific.

Just as a buzzard spots dying prey, just as a con artist spots a mark, a "wise use" group spotted Ketchikan and saw it was fertile ground for their particular seeds of hatred. The "wise use" movement held that the gods gave man dominion over all the resources of the planet to use as he saw fit, and if the resources get screwed over, well, too bad. And if anyone spoke up about it, well, that person just might need hanging.

One of the national leaders of the "wise use" movement, Chuck Cushman, visited Ketchikan to incite the locals and to sprinkle his own unholy water on a newly formed local group, C.A.R.E., or "Concerned Alaskans for Responsible Environment." CARE placards appeared all over town, as well as a campaign to tie yellow ribbons on vehicles' radio antennae to indicate support for the timber industry.

I made it a practice to tie non-yellow ribbons on my antenna and was amazed that people would throw me the finger or would block me in so I couldn't pull into traffic from a parking lot. When I first moved to Ketchikan, there was only one stoplight on the entirety of the island, and it was a widely practiced local tradition to stop and let waiting rigs enter traffic flow. Not anymore. My ribbon would never last more than a day or so before some CARE-ing citizen would tear it off. Oh well, I had lots of forester's flagging, but it was this kind of factionalism that turned Ketchikan into a virtual war town. I'm certain that, if it weren't for the tourists' flocking in on the cruise ships, they would have installed barbed wire and machine gun turrets on the roof tops.

Delighted to have such a show of solidarity among Ketchikan residents (voters!), the Alaska congressional delegation made a grandstand show of introducing mindless timber bills into Congress that had absolutely no chance of passing. There was one to extend KPC's contract another 15 years. Another one was to declare the Habitat Conservation Areas (wildlife reserves for the goshawk and wolf) illegal. One was to cede thousands more acres to the Native corporations, knowing full well they'd show their reverence for the land by immediately clearcutting it as soon as the ink was dry. More land was proposed for the University of Alaska, for the same purpose. There were bills to take the Tongass from U.S. Forest Service and give it to the state, and another proposal to mandate that Tongass logging levels continue as they had in the past.

The Tongass Timber Reform Act (TTRA) contained language which modified and inserted new language into the Alaska National Interest Lands Conservation Act (ANILCA). The new language stated:

> "... to the extent consistent with providing for the multiple use and sustained yield of all renewable resources, seek to provide a supply of timber from the Tongass National Forest which (1) meets the annual demand for timber from each forest ..."

The Alaska congressional delegation kept repeating a PORTION of this phrase over and over like a mantra, insisting that the Forest Service seek the hell out of enough timber to meet market demand, whatever that demand might be. They totally ignored the fact that the law required the Forest Service to make sure that the logging of this mightily sought supply of timber FIRST had to provide for the multiple use and sustained yield of all other resources like, fish, wildlife, water quality, and recreation. And of course, logging old-growth, ancient forests and converting them to worthless second-growth pulp farms resulted in the decimation of all other renewable resources. But our congressmen didn't want to hear this, so they selectively ignored it. It was like taking the sentence, "It is wholly false that Clint Eastwood is homosexual," deleting the first five words, and concluding that Dirty Harry is gay.

On and on came these insane proposals and all would get major play in the "Ketchikan Daily News," keeping the townsfolk in a constant state of agitation. SEACC would then have a reason to flounce around D.C., jousting Quixote-like at these phony windmills. Of course, this accomplished exactly what Stevens, Young, and Murkowski apparently wanted ... stir up a lot of fuss, gain some votes back home, and make sure no one was guarding the hen house. They actually convinced people the Forest Service was against logging!

Finally, despite all the hype, KPC threw in the towel and announced they were going to close their pulp mill March 24, 1997 ... seven years, three months, and six days before the anticipated end of their 50- year-contract. KPC made a big hoopla that they really didn't want to close, but they simply couldn't afford to invest more money in the pulp mill to bring the pollution-control devices up to snuff, unless they were given a 15-year contract extension over which time they could amortize their investments. The truth was that they had reached the point when they could make more money through litigation against the government than they could selling pulp. The lumber market was booming, so they opted to continue running their sawmill.

KPC had a huge lawsuit against the Forest Service for unilaterally modifying their long-term contract, as was required by the Tongass Timber Reform Act. It was a can't-lose lawsuit for KPC. However, they weren't necessarily a squeaky clean company. There were the allegations that they had stolen billions of feet of Tongass timber, their pollution convictions, their anti-trust conviction, their breaking the labor union at the mill, and the overall decimation of the largest temperate rain forest on Earth. So rather than allow a judge to rule on the matter, KPC and the Forest Service cut a quiet little deal. KPC dropped their lawsuit, and the Forest Service gave them 300 mmbf of timber to run their sawmill for three more years and $840 million. That's right, eight-hundred-forty million dollars of taxpayer money got forked over to KPC!

In dealing with the loss of Ketchikan's primary employer, the town exhibited the classic grief reactions ... denial, anger, and blame displacement. The fact of the matter was that 43 years before, Ketchikan's economy had been given a jump-start when the U.S. government seemingly gave the Tongass National Forest to Japan. Ketchikan had since developed the infrastructure to take off on its own, and it was long past time to remove the jumper cables, but the local elected officials were so used to federal subsidy that they had no backup plan. It was amazing that these alleged leaders had been so devoid of foresight and in such a complete state of denial that they hadn't even considered the possibility of the mill's closure.

Mayor Allerie Stanton made an impassioned statement that, "Ketchikan is still a timber town!" Stevens siphoned umpty-ump million dollars of taxpayer money to assist SE Alaska communities, which had been declared economic disaster areas. The local leaders, who were largely the yellow-ribbon set, spent most of it on an advertising campaign to improve the image of the timber industry.

Around this time, National Public Radio ran a story on the three U.S. cities with the fastest growing economies. I can't remember all three, but do recall that Boise, Idaho, was one of them. Anyhow, these cites all boasted cheap labor, transportation, and access to resources, as well as low taxes and cost of living. Ketchikan had the highest cost of living of any city in the U.S. Gas was a buck-seventy, and people needed to mortgage their house to go to the dentist. Everything had to be barged up or flown in. This was what the local leaders had to find a solution for, but instead they squandered their money on an advertising campaign trying to convince people that it was terrific to clearcut rainforests. My god, they only convinced the masses Down South that there were a bunch of backward whackos living up here!

A sunny day in mid-March found me out in the yard at the cabin, stretching my gillnets out on a tarp, mending holes. My lawsuit on CPOW was bubbling quietly on the back burner, and the Lab Bay appeal had just been filed. My whistleblower case was pending, and the pulp mill was shutting down. For once, all seemed right with the world. When I went in for lunch, there was a call on the message machine from some unidentified woman asking about the "Bill Shoaf Legal Defense Fund." I figured it was a crank call and erased it.

Later that afternoon I came in to change into my running gear. Just as I was stretching, I got a call from Nikki Murray Jones, a reporter for the local paper. Nikki told me that she had received a FAX at the "Daily News" that said I was planning a big party out at the North Tongass community center to celebrate the mill's closure. Moreover, I was charging admission for the party, with all proceeds going to the "Bill Shoaf Legal Defense Fund." However, the FAX stated that I agreed to waive the admission fee for any soon-to-be-unemployed mill worker if they'd wear green.

I didn't have a clue what she was talking about. She insisted it had been FAXed all over town ... to the chamber of commerce, to the pulp mill, and had been posted on the bulletin boards of all the grocery stores. I told Nikki that it was utter BS and that I'd never even heard about it until she called. She asked if I wanted to make a statement of response. I asked what for, certainly you're not going to print a story about that obvious hoax? Well, why not, hee hee, it's news. I hung up.

A while later, Nikki called back and suggested reconsidering making a statement. The "Daily News" was going to run the story the next day on page one and there was ... ahem, concern for my personal safety. Maybe I should call the state police. I couldn't believe this was actually happening, so I gave Nikki a statement denying the whole thing. I told her I sympathized with anyone losing their job, as I had lost mine and was trying to struggle along on sub-poverty wages. Then I asked her to print an invitation to the cowardly liar who had published the hoax to come out to my cabin, knock on the door, and ask for Bill.

The next day, Forest Service law enforcement called to get a statement from me. They were going to conduct an investigation, because it was acknowledged that the letter might have been drafted by someone within the Forest Service. I agreed, but said it could just as easily have come from the yellow-ribbon crowd. Nothing came of the Forest Service investigation. Imagine my surprise!

A few weeks later, I was talking to my diesel mechanic. He told me that he heard 30 guys from the pulp mill set out after me the day the hoax was posted, only to get stopped by 15 guys who thought they ought to leave me alone. At any rate, the cowardly plan to get me killed fizzled, as I never even received a harassing phone call, much less any physical violence or damage to my property.

I thought about the full circle I had come in 10 years. In Oregon I had chased a GreenPeace canvasser down the street and had attended a rally to hang in effigy someone who had brought a halt to the local timber industry. Now I was vilified in my adopted home town for having contributed to the demise of the local pulp mill. Had I changed? Had the people around me changed? Or was it just a different situation?

I was hated by many, admired by some, but genuinely liked by few. There was no doubt that the events of the past few years had changed me, and seemingly not for the better. Gone was any faith in my fellow man or belief in the existence of any form of justice.

The taking of the Tongass saddened me, but it was a wound that might ultimately heal. What numbed my very soul was the taking of the United States by the industrial-military complex, under the guise of the United States government. I had observed all three branches of our government ... executive, judicial, and legislative ... with stoic impunity, break laws, lie, and cover up to protect the interests of the powerful. Anyone who still believed our founding fathers' precept of "a nation of the people, by the people, for the people," had better take a serious reality check. It recalled a quote from the wonderful, old movie "Billy Jack:"

> "When the government breaks the law, there is no law, only a struggle for survival."

Depression covered me like a sticky goo, and I gradually became a complete recluse, avoiding all public contact. Self-esteem vanished, as the wolf and my workouts became my only consolations.

Soon the Forest Service sent a letter denying my appeal of the Lab Bay sale. I glanced at it and noted that the 10 points I had appealed were all overturned. It occurred to me that the Forest Service had never admitted I was right on a single issue in any of this. Not only had I never won a battle in the war, seemingly I had never even landed a single solid punch. How could anyone, especially an allegedly bright, thoroughly experienced professional forester armed with insider information, be so profoundly wrong on every single issue?

Wouldn't the law of averages say that I would be right at least once? Or maybe just kinda get lucky one time?

But, nope, through all my whistleblower disclosures and complaints, all my timber sale comments, appeals, and lawsuits, I was never, ever right, even once. How could that be? Was I really that wrongheaded, stupid, or unlucky? I dunno, but the fight was out of me. I didn't want to even hear about Tongass timber sales or the Forest Service. I didn't want to fight with other fishermen. I just wanted to be left alone, because the next person to push me into an unescapable corner was likely to face a true berserker. And I didn't want that to happen.

23

Spirit of the Wolf

(April 1997 - March 1998)

"Think I'll pack it in and buy a pick-up.
Take it down to L.A.
Find a place to call my own and try to fix-up,
Start a brand new day."
    -- Neil Young

"In the clearing stands a boxer and a fighter by his trade.
And he carries the reminders
Of every glove that laid him down or cut him, til he cried out
In his anger and his shame, 'I am leaving, I am leaving.'
But the fighter still remains."
    -- Paul Simon, "The Boxer"

There's a continuity to the seasons in SE Alaska. A greening of the Earth, and a time for leaves to fall. A raging of the sea, and a time for calm waters. So with the fishermen, especially this one.

Late March and early April found me in the boat yard once more, getting ready for the upcoming season. Because I was now partnerless, it was necessary to set up the *Blind Faith* for solo fishing. I installed a new autopilot, and went round the boat focusing on fixing small glitches in the operation of the fishing gear, which had required two sets of hands previously. I did my best to alter things so one guy could handle it alone.

Halibut can't be fished solo, as the fish are too big and there is simply too much going on. In fact, there's more than enough to keep two people fully occupied. I hired a young guy, Jim Foster, to deckhand for me and, although Jim didn't know a halibut from a salmon, he was bright, honest, hard-working, and had a good attitude. My kinda guy, and we hit it off from day one. I violated all the rules of captain/deckhand working relationships by personally setting the gear on the back deck, while Jim ran the boat. I felt he was too inexperienced to be exposed to that much danger.

At one point while we were hauling a set, Jim watched in amazement as I steered the boat, slipped in and out of gear, synchronized the power block with the hydraulic reel, unsnapped the hooks, ripped off the old bait, racked the hooks, shook free the trash fish, and gaffed the halibut ... essentially two unbroken hours of running in place. He said it was the most awesome display of raw energy he had ever seen. And we slammed the halibut, almost finishing up the season's quota on the second trip. The final trip was a light-hearted affair, floating in Clarence Strait and playing cribbage, while the gear soaked some hundred fathoms beneath us.

One of my friends in town, Carolyn Stallings, had another vision of my halibut fishing:

> "Wait, out on that gray landscape, ocean scene, a boat solo strides across the face of nothing. Skipper clipping on the bait, sheets of paper, 8 1/2 x 14 inches, triple spaced, formal type.
> clip...EVIDENCE...ARTICLE a-1091 ab12
> clip...USDA v Shoaf
> clip...Shoaf v USDA
> clip..."God, do you see the man in question here in this courtroom?"
> clip...God: "No. I've seen him before. I've seen his face among those that walk through the trees, among those that give voice to my loyal creatures, whose voices rise in prayer during the nights of longing. I've seen this man sit above a cliff and view the destruction of my gift, and I've seen him ache with regret. I've never seen that of you."
> clip...blank page
> clip...amen"

After the last halibut had been gaffed over the side. but before the first gillnet set, I passed a personal milestone by running my 20,000th mile. It had been a long time since I had started running so I could keep up with my presale crew while laying out timber sales on the Mapleton District. The miles had become intertwined with the years, and both passed beneath my feet and through my soul. I wrote a feel-good editorial to the "Ketchikan Daily News" extolling the benefits of a healthy lifestyle.

I started out the 1997 gillnet season with the best of attitudes, even though the docks buzzed with rumors of abysmal prices. The first opening was absolutely bleak, with almost zero fish. I'd set my net in my favorite spot, make a perfect hour and a half drift, and catch nothing, a "water haul," as we say. Some of my buddies had already unloaded their fish at the tender and were doing some major grumbling about the price. I refused to let them tell me the price over the marine radio, wanting to find out the bad news for myself when I unloaded.

I pitched my fish to my tender at 6:00 p.m. on Monday night, looked at my check, and pointed *Blind Faith* toward Ketchikan. I called my buddies, and they left with me. We got in around midnight, and the next morning we found half the fleet had run in. No fish and no price. Those words were to haunt us the rest of the season. A fisherman can make it through periods of few-fish-good-price and through periods of lotsa-fish-and-no-price, but no-fish-no-price was equivalent of multiplying zero by zero.

The fish wars started with Canada. I used to like to talk to Canadian skippers at night, when the radio wave "skip" allowed enhanced reception. They were generally very cordial and pleased to talk to a 'Yank' boat. But the failure of our respective nations to reach agreement on the Pacific salmon treaty led to a major falling-out, culminating when a flotilla of Canadian fishermen blockaded the Alaska state ferry, *M/V Malaspina*, in the harbor at Prince Rupert, British Columbia. The B.C. fishermen staged the blockade to protest Alaska fishermen's intercepting southbound sockeye salmon heading for B.C. rivers. They considered these to be their fish, as their natal streams were in B.C.

The state of Alaska denied their fishermen were intercepting Canadian sockeye, which was ludicrous, as I was sitting there in

Blind Faith about a net-length from the international border. In my hold were sockeye salmon that the whole gillnet fleet knew were bound for B.C.'s Skeena River system. The next week we would probably be catching fish from B.C.'s Nass River. It was a fairly predictable cycle. Then the radio carried the story that Alaska Department of Fish & Game had curtailed the Tree Point gillnet opening that week to protect Skeena River fish. That was a lie ... not only wasn't the opening curtailed, it was actually extended an additional day beyond what was scheduled. I ought to know, as I was there with my net in the water.

This was not to say I agreed with Canadian arguments or methods. I was loyal to Alaska and to my own fishing fleet and would fight on their side, if it came to that. But was a little honesty really that dangerous to our cause? Personally, I thought both nations had abandoned any form of scientific reasoning in their salmon treaty negotiations. The ultimate loser was the fish, as both nations vied for the right to catch the last salmon.

The gillnet season dragged on and became a financial disaster. El Nino had so screwed up the currents and warmed the waters that salmon had all but disappeared. Then the last week in July, a catastrophic nightmare occurred when I caught a Dall's porpoise in my net. It was dead! The poor thing was so tangled in the net that I had to drum it aboard to free it. Then there was the back-breaking job of wrestling the 200+-pound body, which didn't feel like any fish I'd ever handled, over the side, where it sank like a rock. I was devastated. If I had caught a wolf in my net, it wouldn't have upset me more. It was one thing to be out here killing everything in the sea from shrimp to octopus to salmon to halibut to rockfish to sharks to rays, but what was I doing killing dolphin? I wept. Then, being a fisherman, I reset my net.

I wondered how it could have happened. It was the middle of the day, and my net was caked with algae slime, which made it as visible as a cyclone fence. Dolphin have incredible sonar. What went wrong? The next morning, I got up at 2 a.m. as usual, and I was making my morning set in the dark. Suddenly I could hear dolphin blowing all around the boat. I didn't know whether to continue setting my net or to try to stop it and reverse drum it back aboard and risk getting the gillnet web tangled in the boat's wheel. I finished setting the net, then patrolled it for the next hour, trying to head off the dolphin. But I didn't see them again that day, and when I hauled my net, it had only salmon, and few of those.

When I got back to town, James stopped by. I told him about the dolphin, and he said he had intuited it. He said he had already discussed it with the elders and they said to carve a dolphin figure out of cedar, and the next time a pod came to play around the boat, to throw my carving in the water. They said to tell the dolphin that I felt bad about their friend, but from now on to stay away from my boat when I'm fishing, because I'm a big predator, just like they are. The elders said to make sure that I did NOT apologize, because then the dolphin would need to exact revenge. I did as they said.

I could tell that my time as a fisherman was drawing to a close. I was tortured with dreams of drowning at sea, specifically of getting tangled in the gear and getting pulled overboard. A diver friend of mine had perished the winter before when he was coming back from a sea cucumber trip in the *F/V Cape Chacon,* and the old wooden boat sank without a trace near where I fished halibut. In a dream, my friend came to me and told me I would see him on his boat real soon. I woke up from the dream, with the '*Faith* floating in our little gillnetter's anchorage. It was 2:00 a.m. and time to set my net in the dark. How eerie!

I muddled through the remainder of the gillnet season, then spun my net off early and blew off fishing for fall coho. Instead I used my cold storage plant's crane and forklift to offload my reel, so that I would have more deck space for shrimp. Then I bought new large shrimp pots, which I felt could be fished singly, eliminating the more dangerous setup required by my old small pots, which had been fished 10 per set on a longline. It worked beautifully.

James came by and said he had talked to the elders again and had learned a chant for the blue heron, who was also a fisherman and who would watch out for me as I was going to sea alone. My part of the bargain was to leave food whenever I could, and to know that it was well received, even if the blue heron didn't eat it. It felt good to have something watching over me.

I tried to keep my head down and just let events on the Tongass pass. The new Tongass Forest Plan was released, and logging levels were calculated at about half of what was previously proposed. This sounded amazingly like what I had said five years before, but there was no-one around to whom I could say, I told you so. Thirty-five organizations and individuals filed appeals, but truthfully, I had no inclination to even look at the new forest plan, much less file an appeal.

Liam Sherlock, my pro bono attorney on the CPOW lawsuit, called. He said the case was irrevocably stalled in Alaska District Court, where the conservative Republican judge would sit on it until all the trees were cut. Moreover KPC had finally joined the case as intervenors and had indicated a desire to file a slap suit against me, which I could not afford to fight. Realizing that Liam had never gotten paid a dime for all his hard work, I asked him if he wanted to drop the case. He did.

And that was the end of CPOW. KPC logged it all, every bit.

A little while later, I got a note from Andy Stahl. Apparently AFSEEE had sent out their annual brochure to beat the bushes for contributions. In it, they had claimed to have stopped the CPOW sale and included a quote attributed to me.

> "FSEEE [they recently dropped the 'A'] stopped the nation's largest timber sale by helping the sale's planning team leader prove that proposed logging levels violated sustained yield rules.
>
> 'Without FSEEE's support, I never would have tackled my whistleblowing action to stop illegal logging. Thanks to FSEEE's help at every turn, we were given a real chance to save millions of trees on the Tongass National Forest -- and the wildlife they support, the water they purify, and the recreation they provide.'
>
> -- Bill Shoaf, Forest Planner (retired), Tongass NF"

My friend Robert, sick of seeing the last of the CPOW logs driven past his home in Thorne Bay, wrote the following note to Andy:

> "Why, oh why, must you resort to distortions of the truth, just

as my employer does? I worked with Bill Shoaf on the CPOW project, which neither you nor anyone else stopped. In fact, it is still being cut. I applaud your efforts in making FSEEE what it is, and it serves a critical watchdog role. But stop prostituting Bill's name and his situation. It has been nearly five years since he filed his whistleblower disclosure, and it ruined his career and his life. He is now leaving Alaska, where he found a home he said he would never leave. I used to give money to you, but I can't when I see distortions of the truth. Bill couldn't work for the Forest Service for the same reason. Sometimes the truth is ugly, and you don't win. But at all costs, tell the truth."

-- Robert Wetherell

Andy, unaware of my close friendship with Robert, asked me to talk to him, as he was concerned about Robert's misunderstanding the situation. The three of us engaged in some e-mail dialogue, and Andy conscionably agreed to remove the statement from future fund-drive banners. He said that the reason he did it was because, if he told the truth, people wouldn't contribute to AFSEEE because they'd know the battle was hopeless.

I thought about this a long time. It brought me back to that question Corrie asked me the previous year in the bar, after the trial in Ketchikan. "Bill, why'd you do it?" I think I have an answer for her now. The real answer.

I didn't object to cutting trees. Hell, I liked to cut them myself and had even begged for the privilege of felling the symbolic first tree on the CPOW timber sale. What I objected to was dishonesty. CPOW, the Tongass, and the Forest Service had shown themselves to be cesspools of untruths, half-truths, and misleading information, and I simply refused to roll myself in that squalor.

It doesn't matter whether it is the Forest Service's blatantly lying to let them sell more timber, the Alaska Department of Fish and Game's lying to make themselves look like the good guys in the fish wars with Canada, the state of Oregon's falsifying information to get increased child support for a constituent, or my chief benefactor, AFSEEE's, stretching the truth a bit to sell more memberships. Although it's nonsensical to equate the malevolence factors, it's still the same issue.

We're simply not a society who places high regard on honesty. Indeed honesty makes many people feel ... well, uncomfortable. We seem to believe we can roll-our-own reality or rewrite history to fit the situation and to rationalize the conclusion we're trying to re-verse-engineer. I maintain that when honesty is relegated to the background, there is no common denominator, only ideology. Without the rigor to simply present the facts and let the chips fall where they may, all that is left is to argue about which ideology is right. And to me, that has no more merit than arguing which is the prettiest color in the rainbow.

But perhaps that's what we're all about. Apparently my greatest mistake was assigning the highest value to something most people think is worth spit. Honesty.

And so I return to my boxes, sorting out the stuff that gets moved Down South with me, the stuff that gets sold at the garage sale, the stuff that goes to the dump, and the stuff that gets sold with the boat. Pretty black and white, but that's the kind of task at which we whistleblowers excel.

But at least my search down memory lane gave me an idea what really happened up here and why. The government entered into long-term timber contracts to provide some economic stability for the Alaska frontier. But the contracts went on too long and ran afoul of changing environmental laws and a renaissance in forest science. Because the contracts had become caught up in our cold war policy, and later with balancing our trade with Japan, they were permitted to continue in an outlaw refugia, a policy which was wildly embraced by Alaska's congressional delegation.

Finally, things got so out of hand that it became apparent that the whole house of cards was going to crash. Dinosaur Forest Service managers ran for the tar pits, while those with some time left tried to balance the need to carry out their orders to continue the contracts with covering their butts. Quite simply, they were looking for a fall guy. Enter a small-time forester, with a stubborn streak and an honest nature. Coinciding with his entrance was a cessation of the cold war, a change in U.S. fiscal policy with Japan, and a newly elected presidential administration with an environmental agenda.

When I fired my big cannon and submitted my whistleblower disclosure, it was only a teeny pop, because the high rollers in the Clinton administration had already decided to take down the contracts. But to appease Alaska's congressional delegation, the dismantling needed to be done piecemeal. Also the administration wanted to make sure that the feather for straightening out the Tongass mess was placed in their own bonnet. So they used my disclosure briefly for a bargaining chip, then buried it deeply because they didn't want a scandal turning up on their watch. The greenies were plugged into the big picture and whole-heartedly approved.

OSC might have balked at the cover-up, had there been a single party or administration on whom they could have pinned the blame, thereby ingratiating themselves to the opposing party. But the Tongass fiasco spanned many presidential regimes, and in fact was backed by the big boys themselves ... the U.S. military. There was simply no way they, a governmental agency, were going to admit with Pogo's simplicity, "We have met the enemy, and he is us!"

And everything turned out well. The Alaska economy got jump-started, Japan was rebuilt with Tongass logs, corporations made profits, congressmen were re-elected, agencies perpetuated themselves, and a presidential administration got to claim being a broker between environmental and commodity interests.

I guess in a way I got what I wanted too ... responsible management on the Tongass. Oh, it's not here yet, but it's on its way through incremental reductions in logging levels, which have fallen from 450 mmbf in 1979 to 418 mmbf in 1991 to 267 mmbf in 1997. I imagine the next Tongass forest plan in 2007 will place the logging level under 100 mmbf, and maybe that's simply as fast as the Forest Service can reduce it without admitting their hand in the travesty that occurred here.

I know I can't stay here. The Tongass surrounds me ... I breathe it, see it, smell it, hear it, take joy in it, and mourn for it. Its abuse and torment rent my soul. There will be never be peace for me here. James told me that my task here was done, that my mission was to plant seeds. To plant them deep and well in fertile soil. To water them, and say a prayer for them, and then turn and go.

Like all well-intentioned stewards, I feel a sadness at my departure, from loss as well as concern for the welfare of my former charge. But it's beyond me now, and time to let go.

Dave Person, the wolf researcher, told of two separate instances involving young, radio-collared wolves. For some unknown reason, these wolves split from their pack and made a beeline down the length of Prince of Wales island. In each case, the wolves blipped off the radar screen near Cape Muzon, the southernmost tip of the island. Dr. Person speculated they simply couldn't accept their established place within the pack, and struck off for something new, far away. Apparently they threw themselves in the sea and swam to their deaths.

Chacon paces in his kennel, sensing it's time to leave this place and move on. May the gods have mercy on our souls, grant us peace, and accept our thanks that we don't have to swim.

Afterward

On Sept. 11, 1998, 18 months after his decision was due, Judge James H. Freet dismissed our whistleblower complaint case. He said none of it happened.

On Dec. 18, 1998, Corrie appealed Judge Freet's decision to the full Merit Systems Appeal Board. We have never heard from them.

Acronyms and Abbreviations

AFSEEE...Association of Forest Service Employees for Environmental Ethics

ANCSA...Alaska Native Claims Settlement Act

ANILCA...Alaska National Interest Lands Conservation Act

APC...Alaska Pulp Corporation

ASQ...allowable sale quantity

CPOW...central Prince of Wales

DEC...[Alaska] Department of Environmental Coordination

DOJ...U.S. Department of Justice

EIS...environmental impact statement

FEMAT...Forest Environmental Management and Assessment Team

FOIA...Freedom of Information Act

FORPLAN...forest planning model

GAO...U.S. General Accounting Office

GAP...Government Accountability Project

GIS...geographic information system

GPS...global positioning system

IDT...interdisciplinary team

LSTA...logging system transportation analysis

KPC...Ketchikan Pulp Company

mbf...thousand board feet

MELP...multi-entry logging plan

mmbf...million board feet

mmmbf...billion board feet

MSPB...Merit Systems Protection Board

MUSY...Multiple Use Sustained Yield Act of 1960

NEPA...National Environmental Policy Act of 1969

NF...National Forest

NFMA...National Forest Management Act
NRDC...National Resouces Defense Council
NRC...Natural Resources Conservation
NWF...National Wildlife Federation
OIG...U.S. Office of Inspector General
OSC...U.S. Office of Special Counsel
PIG...personal immersion gadget
PNW...Pacific northwest
ROD...record of decision
RPA...Resources Program and Assessment
SCLDF...Sierra Club Legal Defense Fund (not affiliated with the
　　　　Sierra Club)
SE...southeast (Alaska)
SEACC...Southeast Alaska Conservation Council
TLMP...Tongass Land Management Plan
TTRA...Tongass Timber Reform Act of 1990
USC...U.S. Code [of law]
USDA...U.S. Department of Agriculture
VRP...virtual reality timber planner
WPA...Whistleblower Protection Act

List of Characters

There is no intention to define individuals' previous or subsequent achievements, but rather to merely identify their role within this text.

Archie, Anne ... ranger (replacing Johnson) for the Thorne Bay District of the Tongass NF

Arrasmith, Dave ... planning staff officer (replacing Dortch) for the Ketchikan Area of the Tongass NF; my supervisor from 1992-93

Beasley, Lamar ... Washington office employee who said the "missing" whistleblower retaliation report didn't exist

Baichtal, Jim ... geologist and cave expert for the Ketchikan Area of the Tongass NF

Barton, Mike ... regional forester for the Tongass NF

Canterbury, Jackie..member of the board of directors for TCS, SEACC, and AFSEEE

Carnell, Joyce......employee at OSC

Carr, Mary..........writer/editor and member of the CPOW IDT for the Ketchikan Area of the Tongass NF

Cavallo, Michael....philanthropist, founder of the Cavallo Foundation

Chacon..............timber wolf who lives with me

Chelstad, Gene......director of timber management for the regional office of the Tongass NF

Click, John.........check-scaler (replacing Clothier) for the Thorne Bay District of the Tongass NF

Clothier, Tom.......check-scaler for the Thorne Bay District of the Tongass NF

Cushman, Chuck......an organizer for the "wise use" movement

Debi...............my girl friend at Ketchikan

DeMasters, Dave.....forest technician for the Emmett District of the Boise NF; my "pardner"

Diablo ... my first dog, St. Bernard x German Shepard

Diane ... my first wife

Dortch, Walt ... planning staff officer for the Ketchikan Area of the Tongass NF; my supervisor 1990-92

Edwards, Larry ... GreenPeace activist and member of the board of directors for SEACC

Eide, Gene ... timber staff officer for the Ketchikan Area of the Tongass NF; my supervisor 1993-95

Estes, Dick ... ranger for the Emmett District of the Boise NF

Foster, Jim ... halibut deckhand

Freet, James ... presiding judge on the whistleblower retaliation lawsuit

Funk, Dan ... shrimping deckhand

Garfinkel, Marty ... lawyer on whistleblower retaliation lawsuit

Geraghty, Sylvia ... environmentalist and member of the board of directors for the SEACC; personal friend

Glodowski, Rich ... law enforcement officer for the Ketchikan Area of the Tongass NF

Goldman, Linda ... personnel specialist for the California Region of the Forest Service

Grabinsky, Leonard ... employee for OSC who closed my whistleblower disclosure case

Graham, Owen ... timber manager for KPC

Gore, Al ... U.S. Vice President

Griffin, Pete ... environmental coordinator (replacing Voight) for the Ketchikan Area of the Tongass NF; chief author of the CPOW supplement

Grousebane, Camilleri ... my springer spaniel

Haalck, Henry ... University of Connecticut forestry professor

Haught, Adrian ... my supervisor at the Washington Office

Heiken, Doug ... legal advisor for AFSEEE

Holbrook, Sumner ... rancher near High Valley, Idaho

Howell, Lance ... resident of Point Baker, Alaska

Hunt, Brian ... organizer for AFSEEE

Janik, Phil ... regional forester (replacing Barton) for the Tongass NF

Johnson, Norm ... renowned forester from private and academic sector, who wrote professional letter of support

Johnson, Pete ... ranger for the Thorne Bay District of the Tongass NF

Jones, Nikki Murray ... reporter for the "Ketchikan Daily News"

Katz, Dave ... environmentalist for SEACC

Kessel, Mick ... ranger for the Mapleton District of the Siuslaw NF

Kilanowski, Jerry ... forester for KPC

Kittams, Jay ... forester for the Emmett District of the Boise NF

Knight, Becky ... member of the board of directors for SEACC

Klee, Chuck ... forester for the Thorne Bay District of theTongass NF; layout partner

LeMasters, Chris ... personnel clerk for the Ketchikan Area of the Tongass NF; "lawyer" for government in the whistleblower retaliation lawsuit

Llanos, James ... Tlingit, computer analyst, member of the CPOW IDT for the Ketchikan Area of the Tongass NF; personal friend

Larsen, Doug........wildlife biologist for the ADF&G

Leonard, George ... associate chief of the Forest Service

Levitt, Sarah ... lawyer for GAP

Lindekugel, Buck ... lawyer for SEACC

Lunde, Larry ... planning team leader for the Ketchikan Area of the Tongass NF

Lunn, Michael ... forest supervisor for the Ketchikan Area of the Tongass NF

Marsch, Alecia ... employee for OSC

Matson, Norm ... wildlife biologist, member of the CPOW IDT; IDT leader (relacing Shoaf) of subsequent timber projects for the Ketchikan Area of the Tongass NF

Max ... my dog, Rhodesian ridgeback x Newfoundland

McCleese, William ... Washington office employee responsible for the decision to continue the CPOW timber sale

McMullen, Catherine ... employee for OSC

Minor, Carolyn ... news reporter for Ketchikan radio station

Miller, George ... California congressman; chairman of the House committee on natural resources

Mills, Tom ... RPA staff director for the Washington office

Murkowski, Frank ... Alaska senator; chairman of the Senate committee on energy and natural resources

Nightingale, Bill ... member of CPOW IDT; IDT leader for subsequent timber projects for the Ketchikan Area of the Tongass NF

Norbury, Fred ... director of planning for the regional office of the Tongass NF

Oien, Jack ... engineer technician for the Ketchikan Area of the Tongass NF

Person, Dave ... wolf researcher

Powell, Brad ... forest supervisor (replacing Rittenhouse) for the Ketchikan Area of the Tongass NF

Reinhart, Troy ... executive director for the Alaska Loggers Association and spokesperson for KPC

Reno, Jane ... U.S. Attorney General

Rittenhouse, Dave ... forest supervisor (replacing Lunn) for the Ketchikan Area of the Tongass NF

Robertson, Dale ... chief of the Forest Service

Rose, Charlie ... North Carolina congressman who requested copy of my whistleblower disclosure

Rossotto, Mike ... lawyer for GAP; co-author of my whistleblower disclosure

Sebastian, Joe ... fisherman and member of the board of directors for SEACC

Sheehy, Tom ... environmental coordinator for the regional office of the Tongass NF

Sherlock, Liam ... lawyer on CPOW litigation

Shipley, Linn ... assistant ranger for the Thorne Bay District of the Tongass NF

Shoaf, Bill ... author, forester, whistleblower, fisherman, recluse

Sloan, Milton ... Washington office employee who said the "missing" whistleblower retaliation report was with another agency

Somrak, Tom ... forester for the Ketchikan Area of the Tongass NF

Sprague, Kim ... New England logger and sawmill operator

Stahl, Andy ... NWF forester who successfully sued the Mapleton District of the Siuslaw NF; executive director (replacing Williams) for AFSEEE

Stallings, Carolyn ... personal friend from Ketchikan

Stanton, Allerie ... mayor of Ketchikan

Stevens, Ted ... Alaska senator; chairman of the Senate appropriations committee

Stine, Steven ... Washington Office employee and author of investigative report in response to my whistleblower disclosure

Streuli, Charley ... forester for the Thorne Bay Ranger District of the Tongass NF and "co-leader" of the CPOW IDT

Terrill, Bill ... forester for Emmett District of the Boise NF

Terzich, Michael ... member of the CPOW IDT for the Ketchikan Area of the Tongass NF

Thomas, Jack Ward ... chief (replacing Robertson) of the Forest Service

Vaught, Bob ... deputy forest supervisor for the Ketchikan Area of the Tongass NF

Vein, Ruth ... budget analyst for the regional office of the Tongass NF and author of "missing"report on whistleblower retaliation

Victoria ... my commercial fishing partner

Voight, Mark ... environmental coordinator for the Ketchikan Area of the Tongass NF

Welles, John ... forester for the Washington Office

Wetherell, Robert ... landscape architect for the Thorne Bay District of the Tongass NF; member of CPOW IDT; personal friend

Williams, Buzz ... acting executive director for AFSEEE

Williams, Gwen ... personnel officer for the Ketchikan Area of the Tongass NF

Williams, Lew ... owner/publisher of the "Ketchikan Daily News"

Woods, Cat ... recreation forester for the Thorne Bay District of the Tongass NF; Robert's girl friend

Yackulic, Corrie ... lawyer on whistleblower retaliation case

Young, Don ... Alaska congressman; chairman (replacing Miller) of the House committee on natural resources

Yvonne ... my second wife

Order Information

Additional copies of :

The Taking of the Tongass: Alaska's Rainforest

are available for $17.95 per copy, plus $2.00 shipping for the first copy and $1.00 for each additional.

Washington state residents should include 7.9% sales tax.

Checks should be made to **Running Wolf Press**. Sorry, no COD or credit cards. Please allow two weeks for delivery.

Running Wolf Press
P.O. Box 3011
Sequim, WA 98382

ORDER FORM

Please send _____ copies of:

The Taking of the Tongass: Alaska's Rainforest

at $17.95 per copy, plus $2.00 shipping for the first book and $1.00 for each additional. Please allow two weeks for delivery.

Washington state residents include 7.9% sales tax.

Please make checks payable to **Running Wolf Press.** Sorry, no credit cards or C.O.D.

Name: _____

Address:_____

_____

City: _____

State: _____ ZIP: _____

Phone: _____

e-mail: _____

Send to: Running Wolf Press
              P.O. Box 3011
              Sequim, WA 98382

ORDER FORM

Please send _____ copies of:

The Taking of the Tongass: Alaska's Rainforest

at $17.95 per copy, plus $2.00 shipping for the first book and $1.00 for each additional. Please allow two weeks for delivery.

Washington state residents include 7.9% sales tax.

Please make checks payable to **Running Wolf Press.** Sorry no credit cards or C.O.D.

Name: _____

Address: _____

_____

City: _____

State: _____ Zip: _____

Phone: _____

e-mail: _____

Send to: Running Wolf Press
P.O. Box 3011
Sequim, WA 98382